KT-212-829

The Future for Palliative Care

Issues of policy and practice

EDITED BY

David Clark

OPEN UNIVERSITY PRESS

Buckingham · Philadelphia

KING ALFRED'S COLLEGE
WINCHESTER

362.19
CLA

0143850b

Open University Press
Celtic Court
22 Ballmoor
Buckingham
MK18 1XW

and

1900 Frost Road, Suite 101
Bristol, PA 19007, USA

First published 1993

Copyright © David Clark and the Contributors 1993

All rights reserved. Except for the quotation of short
passages for the purposes of criticism and review, no part of
this publication may be reproduced, stored in a retrieval
system, or transmitted, in any form or by any means,
electronic, mechanical, photocopying, recording or
otherwise, without the prior written permission of the
publisher or a licence from the Copyright Licensing Agency
Limited. Details of such licences (for reprographic
reproduction) may be obtained from the Copyright Licensing
Agency Ltd of 90 Tottenham Court Road, London,
W1P 9HE.

A catalogue record of this book is available from the British
Library

ISBN 0 335 15764 5 (pb) 0 335 15765 3 (hb)

Library of Congress Cataloging-in-Publication Data
The future for palliative care: issues of policy and practice/
edited by David Clark.
  p.   cm.
Includes bibliographical references and index.
ISBN 0–335–15765–3. – ISBN 0–335–15764–5
1. Palliative treatment. 2. Hospice care. I. Clark,
David, 1953–   .
  [DNLM: 1. Palliative Treatment – trends – Great Britain.
  2. Public Policy – Great Britain. WB 310 F996]
R726.8.F88   1993
362.1′75′0941–dc20
DNLM/DLC
for Library of Congress   92–49440
                                              CIP

Typeset by Colset Private Ltd, Singapore
Printed in Great Britain by
Biddles Ltd, Guildford and King's Lynn

£12.99

The Future for
Palliative Care

KING ALFRED'S COLLEGE
WINCHESTER

To be returned on or before the day marked
below:-

24 MAR 95

27. NOV

1 6 FEB 2010

KA 0143850 6

WITHDRAWN FROM
THE LIBRARY
UNIVERSITY OF
WINCHESTER

Contents

Contributors

Sam Ahmedzai is the medical director of the Leicestershire Hospice, honorary consultant physician in palliative medicine to Leicestershire Health Authority, and associate director at the Trent Palliative Care Centre. He has wide ranging research interests in palliative care, including: the evaluation of quality of life, palliation of respiratory distress in advanced disease, and computer assisted decision making.

Richard Atkinson is consultant in charge of a pain management clinic at Chesterfield and North Derbyshire Regional Hospital, medical director of the Ashgate Hospice, and consultant in pain management at the Trent Palliative Care Centre. He has been with North Derbyshire District Health Authority for 15 years and is also joint co-ordinator of regional pain policy in Trent.

Bronwen Biswas has been employed as matron of the Leicestershire Hospice since it opened in 1985 and served for a year as honorary nurse advisor to the Trent Palliative Care Centre. A qualified health visitor, she is a graduate of the Open University, secretary of the Hospice Matrons Association and a member of the National Council for Hospice and Specialist Palliative Care Services.

David Clark is co-director of the Health Research Centre at Sheffield

Hallam University and senior research fellow (Sociology) at the Trent Palliative Care Centre. He has written and edited numerous works on sociological
aspects of family life, health and illness. His current interests are in the development and evaluation of palliative care services and the sociology of death.

Tony Crowther has been medical director of St Luke's Hospice, Sheffield,
since 1986. He has a background of 28 years as a principal and trainer in
general practice and is an honorary clinical lecturer in the Department of
General Practice, University of Sheffield Medical School. Having left general
practice in 1991, he now works from the hospice with the Macmillan
Support Teams in Sheffield and Barnsley and is an associate director of the
Trent Palliative Care Centre. He is local representative on the Education
Sub-committee of the Association for Palliative Medicine of Great Britain
and a member of the National Council for Hospice and Specialist Palliative
Care Services.

Graham Davies is a consultant cardiothoracic anaesthetist at the the Northern
General Hospital, Sheffield, and consultant in pain management at the Trent
Palliative Care Centre. He became interested in the management of pain
during his time as a visiting assistant professor in the United States in the
late 1970s. He established a pain clinic in Sheffield in 1982 and more recently
has pursued an interest in palliative care.

Ann Faulkner is developing research and teaching initiatives in Trent region
in the areas of communication, counselling and bereavement work, with
an emphasis on a multidisciplinary approach. A nurse/psychologist with
a background of experience in cancer and terminal care, she is deputy
director of the Trent Palliative Care Centre and holds the chair of communication studies in the Medical School at Sheffield University. She is involved
in national multidisciplinary workshops aimed to improve care of patients
and families who are trying to deal with the impact of terminal illness. Her
committee work includes the Education and Executive Committees of Help
the Hospices, CRUSE and the Sheffield Bereavement Forum. She is editor
of the *Journal of Cancer Care*.

David Field is a senior lecturer in the Department of Epidemiology and
Public Health at the University of Leicester. He has considerable experience
in teaching about terminal care to medical students and nurses. His main
research work in the area concerns nursing the dying, which has resulted
in a number of papers and a book of that title. He has also been involved
in research into hospice care and has written an analysis of the development
of the hospice movement with Nicky James.

Shirley Firth has been a part-time tutor for the Open University since 1978
and also teaches in the Extra-mural Department of Southampton University.

She was born and educated in South India and studied social science as a postgraduate at the London School of Economics. She is currently completing an inter-disciplinary PhD on Hindu approaches to death and bereavement, with reference to British Hindus, for the School of Oriental and African Studies. She is a counsellor and bereavement visitor and writes and runs workshops on multicultural aspects of death and bereavement.

Irene Higginson is a senior lecturer/consultant in public health medicine at the Health Services Research Unit, London School of Hygiene and Tropical Medicine and at Parkside Health Authority. She has worked in oncology and radiotherapy as well as in a hospice and was consultant to the Bloomsbury Support Team, London. Her research has led to the development of measures of outcome and quality for palliative care for people with cancer, HIV/AIDS and dementia. She founded and edited the poetry magazine *Zenos* and has published a collection of her own poetry, *Fairground of Madness*.

Nicky James is a senior lecturer in the Department of Nursing and Midwifery Studies, University of Nottingham. Having completed SRN training at Middlesex Hospital, London, she went to Aberdeen University to read sociology and completed a PhD there, 'Care and Work in Nursing the Dying', in 1986. She worked as a researcher with Ty Olwen Macmillan Unit in Swansea before taking up her current post.

Brenda Neale is a research sociologist, working at the Trent Palliative Care Centre. Her doctoral research, completed in 1985, was on the sociology of marriage. She has contributed to health and social policy research on services for elderly people, adult learning needs, unemployment, and the management of child abuse. Her current interests are in the evaluation of palliative care services, inter-agency collaboration and communication, informal care and community care.

Neil Small is a senior research fellow in the Social Policy Research Unit, University of York, where he is currently working on aspects of the implementation of the NHS and Community Care Act. Prior to his current post he was a lecturer in social work at Bradford University, with special interests in health policy and HIV/AIDS.

Eric Wilkes is emeritus professor of Community Care and General Practice, University of Sheffield, a co-chairman of Help the Hospices and honorary vice-president of the National Hospice Council. He served as a hospice medical director for many years, was honorary consultant advisor to the Trent Palliative Care Centre and is a fellow of the Royal Colleges of Physicians, of General Practice and of Psychiatrists.

Foreword

April 1991 heralded in what are arguably the most major changes ever to have occurred in the National Health Service; palliative care services, as with all other aspects of health care, are now being provided and purchased against the background of defined service specifications and agreed contracts. Such terminology would just a few years ago have been unheard of, or even thought heretical, by carers in this often emotive and public spirited field. It is therefore with great pleasure that I introduce this innnovative book, in which acknowledged experts in the field contribute chapters on all aspects of palliative care: historical details, contemporary practice and future trends.

Many of the authors are members of the Trent Palliative Care Centre, where they are concerned with the promotion and development of education, training, research, evaluation and audit. These aims are exemplified in the chapters they have written. In addition, a more cosmopolitan flavour is introduced by distinguished invited contributors.

In the chapters that follow, we see different perspectives through the whole spectrum of palliative care. There are erudite reviews of the processes of care, starting with the most important member of the team – the dying patient – and moving on to the often troubled situation faced by non-professional carers. Bereavement, in danger of becoming a 'bandwagon' topic, is given a very balanced overview, as is the often misunderstood topic of euthanasia. Cultural issues are explained and recent experience with AIDS has lessons for us all. We have the personal views of a hospice matron and medical director on the problems and benefits of the now increasing role of specialist consultants in palliative care in the hospice movement. One area in which that involvement is proving highly effective is in pain control and this deservedly has a chapter of its own. As hospices become more integrated within the National Health Service, issues of quality, audit and cost come to the fore; this difficult-to-assess field is given factual yet sympathetic coverage. The introduction asks pertinent questions about the future of 'hospice' care and the final chapter addresses these issues in a thought-provoking but positive style.

Palliative care is above all a multidisciplinary subject, so it is entirely appropriate that doctors, nurses and social scientists have all contributed to this cohesively edited, excellent book. I enjoyed reading it and learned a lot – I hope you will too!

Professor Barry Hancock
Department of Clinical Oncology
University of Sheffield, and
Trent Palliative Care Centre

Acknowledgements

This book is a direct product of my involvement over the last few years in the work of the Trent Palliative Care Centre and I am grateful to members of the 'small lively team' there for their encouragement and support with this project. Special thanks are due to all of the contributors, who, despite many other clinical, teaching, research and management commitments, have found the time to write for this volume. They have endured my cajoling and pestering with great good humour. Thanks also go to Richard Baggaley and Joan Malherbe at Open University Press for their efficient handling of editorial matters. The literature on palliative care stresses that it is a multidisciplinary endeavour, yet most writing on the subject totally ignores the importance of secretarial and administrative support within the enterprise as a whole. I therefore want to thank in particular Pauline Hutchinson and Barbara Grimbley for their unstinting supply of assistance, skills, wit and friendship throughout this and numerous other pieces of work. Lastly, I am grateful to Pauline Heather for help with the index.

David Clark

Introduction

ERIC WILKES

Now that the hospice movement has grown to be an acknowledged component of our health care system, it is timely to look at that strange amalgam of idealism, commitment, compromise and paradox characteristic of many human activities and to which the world of palliative care is no exception.

Just as there is a natural sequence from infancy on to senescence, so there is with organizations an equivalent progress. There are many exceptions, but in general the era of creative expansion yields slowly to a rigid preservation of roles, the bureaucracy expands, flexibility shrinks, and there is a genuine difficulty in sloughing off enthusiasms or policies that have outlived their usefulness. Some of these problems are discussed later in this book, but the whole situation is further complicated by the position of the hospice movement at first outside, but more recently closer to, the mainstream of conventional care.

In the USA, one has seen the considerable difficulties experienced by hospices when their involvement with patients posed a direct threat to the power and income of the physician. This, combined with restrictive funding arrangements, led American hospices in the main to be community-orientated with the emphasis on volunteers, psychotherapy and self-help activities. When this worked well and gained increasing acceptance, the physicians tended to become interested and their influence grew. What was stimulating and profitable for the physician began to be more frequently encountered by hospice patients. The increased incidence of the intravenous feeding of dying patients was a fairly typical and costly manifestation of this involvement.

Such procedures would hopefully raise eyebrows in the UK, yet we have had to compromise in order to achieve acceptance and reliable standards. The privilege of care is now associated with training posts, diplomas, the recognition of palliative medicine as a sub-speciality of the Royal College of Physicians, all making the old amateur enthusiasms less appropriate. The hospice atmosphere, at any rate in the larger units, now more closely resembles the hospital culture, with the medical director ordering more investigations and teaching and research inching up the agenda against patient care. This contrasts with the more care-free and seditious atmosphere of yesterday. Yet we need to weigh the occasionally excessive medical involvement against the sustained neglect or the unsuitably aggressive therapy that may, in the real world, be the alternative. Since multi-professional teamwork and colleagueship is more genuine in palliative care than in most other fields of health care, these problems of course are not exclusive to medicine.

One must not criticize today's nurse, who may be highly trained in dialysis or defribillation, for looking towards Project 2000 and higher degrees and salaries. Although tremendous disadvantages persist in the separation of nurse education from practice, most of these nurses are not academics who want to distance themselves from the distress at the bedside. But, all the same, there have been changes in the climate of nursing. They may affect hospitals more than hospices but they are becoming generalized: the temptations towards a senior management post, a fierce reaction to any threat to the status of the nurse, combined with the acceptance of an incidence of pressure sores horrifying to the nurses of 40 years ago, all require understanding but not necessarily acceptance.

Even the well-qualified and senior nurse is not highly paid; yet the advances made here have tended to price the nurse away from the bedside. The dilution of nursing establishments by nursing auxiliaries is therefore inevitable on cost grounds. This causes some anxiety in the centres of excellence that the hospices purport to be. The more affluent units exclude them, whereas others may be excessively dependent.

The unqualified nurse can represent the extremes in quality, from the ageing and unteachable auxiliary deeply embedded in bad habits, proudly hostile to change and expertly evading all in-service training opportunities, to the superb natural nurse whose skill and charm make her (or him) above all others the one to cherish and console.

The auxiliary will be especially popular with those who wrestle with financial problems and who talk of quality control when they are practising cost control. This means that tomorrow's hospice will face the same stringencies as the private nursing homes. These may be taking on a greater share of the burden of caring for the elderly frail yet their profitability is more secure the lower the proportion of qualified staff on their payroll. One remembers with wry amusement the rather different reasons that led Florence Nightingale so bitterly to oppose any certification of nurses after attending approved courses of training.

So far, the hospices have maintained their high nursing establishments and their quota of registered nurses. This must be preserved or we shall fail to maintain, in Cecily Saunders' phrase, competence with compassion.

Volunteers were originally introduced into hospices not as a cost-cutting exercise but as part of the intentional deprofessionalization of the care of the dying. One had seen the great advances in medicine inevitably associated with a loss of confidence and deskilling of the community. The recruitment of volunteers helped to avoid the institutional atmosphere, added a whole range of life experience, and helped us to be less intimidating in achieving bonds of affection and respect with the relatives. One has had to prepare and train units to integrate with the volunteer workforce and wryly to accept the aspiration of the volunteers and their co-ordinators towards greater professionalism!

The crucial role of relatives and volunteers is now more widely acknowledged and their needs more researched. Senior officers of hospice units who have tended to ignore these needs in the past must now deploy more effectively basic and personnel management skills to colleagues as well as to volunteers and relatives. This training has been neglected for too long.

These two important groups – volunteers and relatives – come closest together in the bereavement support services now characteristic of the hospice movement; for volunteers, after training, play a conspicuous part in many of these services. These vary in quality and are overdue for assessment but are clearly helping to correct the neglect of the bereaved typical of yesterday. They may be of enormous value, yet one suspects on occasion exhibit a dangerous combination of being over-professionalized and under-trained, when realistic objectives may be in shorter supply than unrealistic expectations.

An element of unrealistic expectations may also have been partly responsible for the great proliferation of hospice units over the last 20 years, although a more potent cause will have been the lamentable quality of care for the dying locally on offer. There have been genuine and widespread improvements in care and this uncontrolled hospice proliferation cannot go on. Hospices are expensive and money spent on the dying cannot be retrieved to be spent again on the living.

It now looks as if the contract culture and the purchaser–provider relationship, for all its crudities, will at last control the enthusiasm of those who wish to provide hospice facilities in the face of reasoned official opposition. Since hospice services should be provided in some form of locally co-ordinated plan, this control will be helpful in the long term even if traumatic and discouraging in the shorter term.

Such control makes it more essential than ever before that newer hospice units are geared to respond to genuine local needs. It is disquieting to note in David Clark's chapter that too many of the new projects are based on yesterday's ideas, and although still sometimes valid, some of these may be old before their time. The necessary yet rather more novel pursuit of cost-effectiveness also carries subtle dangers. If the improved community services allow the postponement of many admissions until shortly before death, this allows no time to develop trusting relationships in the hospices. This is a strain on patients, upsetting for relatives, greatly increases pressure on nursing staff, and threatens to reduce their vitally important job satisfaction. All this can be further exacerbated if the expensive Macmillan community nurses are required to be a consultant resource to the health professionals more than a friend to the family. So if we carry this search for efficiency too far, we may save a few pounds while we lose the hospice soul. There is a tightrope here, waiting to be walked.

What, then, should characterize tomorrow's hospice? First, one must accept that a hospice is more of an attitude, accepting death, sharpening skills, and not a building: yet very often one needs a building or part of one. This will provide the headquarters, the meeting place for patients, carers and professionals, a place of information and support, encouraging self-help activities and day-care. Day hospices now outnumber in-patient units for they can service smaller centres of population. Beds there must be, but they could be at home or in hospital and encountered more rarely in the newer hospices because the smaller the number of beds, the more expensive they are to run.

Since one anticipates a slowing of growth in hospice numbers, close co-operation with the statutory services in general and the oncology services in particular must be improved and maintained. For the foreseeable future, cancer will be the main target but we must be ready and willing to accept other challenges and especially the growing problems of AIDS, including mothers and babies. Access for ethnic minorities to hospice care must be improved by the provision of cancer support nurses who must be well trained both professionally and in the bridging of cultural gaps, and acceptable to the local community. Nothing else will do.

No longer can the Christian foundation for hospice work be taken for granted. It is already attenuated in a society not embarrassed by sex or death now, but immediately ill at ease at any mention of God or spiritual distress. Yet the spiritual needs of the irreligious must be skilfully addressed and the Christian contribution to hospice work remains more real perhaps than apparent.

The new hospices will exploit the more valuable and relevant of the complementary therapies and of the creative arts in an attempt to combine high-quality conventional and holistic care. They will respect the autonomy of the patient, encourage patient-held record cards for day- or out-patients, both to improve interprofessional communication and to give suitable patients a more central role. One hopes devoutly that all this will make the demands for euthanasia less appealing even to the most enthusiastic of legislators.

The health services of the UK, despite massive denigration, remain very good. Standards are maintained because often doctors and nurses work far harder than their hours or their contracts require. Morale may be lowered and this commitment eroded in a greedy, litigious and delinquent society. We who work in hospices should remain undismayed not because we are superior beings but because we are continually inspired by the trust, courage and humour of our patients. For all we accept that the patient is the teacher and the family, with all its problems, still the unit of care, and that management is ever more dominant, the final paradox is that in a difficult and changing world, the health professional involved in the care of the dying will still have more responsibility than ever.

We can look back and see that the hospice movement has irreversibly improved the standards of care for the dying. Because of this, our easy great days may be behind us, but we still have much to offer. These are the thoughts about the past and the future that bubble untidily to the surface on reading this varied and fascinating book.

1

Where and How People Die

DAVID FIELD and NICKY JAMES

In the UK, as in any society, where death takes place and how it is handled reflect societal values and priorities. Changes in the typical place of death this century reflect broader social changes, such as changing family and occupational structures, increased geographical and social mobility, secularization, and the decline in the importance of communal relationships. Today the care of dying people occurs in a range of settings, consideration of which is the focus of this chapter. We start by reviewing major changes which have affected the pattern of dying and the care of terminally ill people in our society.

The UK, in common with other advanced industrial societies, is characterized by an ageing population. A decline in death rates has been continuing for over a century, with the reduction in infant mortality rates being particularly marked. Life expectancy has increased, standing at 73.2 years for males and 78.2 years for females in 1991, and the survival of the very old has continued to improve, with 2.1 million people over the age of 80 in 1991 (Central Statistical Office 1992). The major source of these changes has been improvements in standards of living, primarily through nutrition and hygiene. Running alongside these changes, and strongly related to them, has been a shift in the nature and pattern of disease. Acute diseases now rarely have fatal outcomes, and the primary causes of death are chronic, degenerative diseases of the circulatory and respiratory systems and cancers.

The net effect has been that the age at which people normally die has been pushed back to beyond retirement age, with a high proportion of terminally ill people over the age of 75. As Blauner (1966: 379) puts it: 'as death . . . becomes increasingly a phenomenon of the old, who are usually retired from work and finished with their parental responsibilities, mortality in modern society rarely interrupts the business of life'.

The 40 years since the establishment of the National Health Service (NHS) have seen significant changes in the organization and delivery of health care. Organizationally, there has been a progressive move away from the original 'tripartite' division of care between local authority, general practitioner (GP) and hospital services, towards a more integrated structure that emphasizes and facilitates the interconnection between hospital- and community-based services. The shift towards community care has meant that hospitals are increasingly becoming places where acute, intensive, short-stay treatment is given, whereas the community (including residential and nursing homes) is now the preferred place for long-term care. This in part reflects the changing nature of disease. Concurrently there has been a move towards a managerially organized and operated service driven by considerations of resource management and cost containment, seen in the 1989 White Paper *Working for Patients* (Department of Health 1989a), which also articulates a shift towards an increasing emphasis upon individual and private sector responsibility. Such changes in the philosophy, organization and functioning of the NHS have consequences for the changing patterns of care offered to dying people and for the expectations which people hold about such care.

Economic factors significantly influence health provision. Since the 1960s, approximately 6 per cent of gross domestic product (GDP) has been spent on health services (Flynn 1990). The expansion of health services during the 1960s in response to demographic need, consumer demand and techno-logical developments took place in a period of economic growth and affluence. Subsequently, although these factors continued to be influential, a less buoyant British economy has restricted increases in 'real' expendi-ture on health, with inevitable consequences for health services. This has particular relevance for new labour-intensive systems of terminal care, pioneered by the hospice movement.

Modern families continue to fulfil their familial responsibilities of care, but smaller families and changing household structures mean that there are fewer people available to provide such care. The current pattern of deferral of child-bearing is likely to continue. Combined with the fragmentation and complexity of modern family and household structures, and the increasing involvement of women in the labour market, it is likely to lead to a pro-gressive reduction in the availability of unpaid lay carers. This will inevitably have consequences for the care of the chronically sick and terminally ill (see Chapter 3).

Associated with these changes has been an increase in the number and proportion of people dying in institutions caring for the sick and a decline in home deaths. Well into the twentieth century the majority of deaths occurred in domestic homes, but this practice has changed over the life of the NHS. By the mid-1960s, two-thirds of all deaths in the UK occurred in hospitals or other places caring for the sick, and by 1989 this had risen to 71 per cent with only 23 per cent of 'home deaths' (Table 1.1). These figures disguise the extensive movement of patients between settings (Fig. 1.1), and the more recent shift of institutional deaths away from NHS hospitals. The summary in Table 1.1 provides a systematic comparison of the main settings where death occurs: NHS hospitals, domestic homes, hospices, residential and nursing homes. Selected features of terminal care in these settings will be considered in the rest of this chapter.

Hospitals

The most common place for people to die is in NHS hospitals, and death occurs in a wide range of settings within them. Approximately 22 per cent of NHS hospital beds were occupied by terminally ill patients in 1986, a reduction from the 25–30 per cent occupancy ratio in 1969 (Cartwright 1991a). While dying is unique and highly personal to each person and those close to them, looking after dying patients is part of the routine work of hospital staff, and the ways in which staff define and perform this work has an important effect on the experience of dying for patients and their relatives. Such definitions and performance are themselves shaped in various ways by the organizational demands and routines of hospital life (Field 1989). In general, more resources of all kinds are allocated to the 'acute' services than to 'chronic' services.

The management of death and dying

Staff working in general hospitals have widely different experiences of dying people. A death in a maternity unit, an acute surgical ward, an intensive-care unit (ITU), a young disabled unit or a psycho-geriatric ward will involve patients whose lives are more or less highly valued in our society, and whose deaths will be experienced very differently by the staff caring for them (e.g. as tragic, an unexpected shock, failure, release, or the peaceful end to a full life). An important factor is the age of the patient. In British society, people find it is easier to accept the death of old than of young people. In particular, staff may find it psychologically difficult to nurse infants and young children who are terminally ill.

Relatively few people in our society die unexpectedly. With the control of infectious diseases, sudden deaths affecting young people are caused by accidents on the road, at work or in the home, while in older people sudden

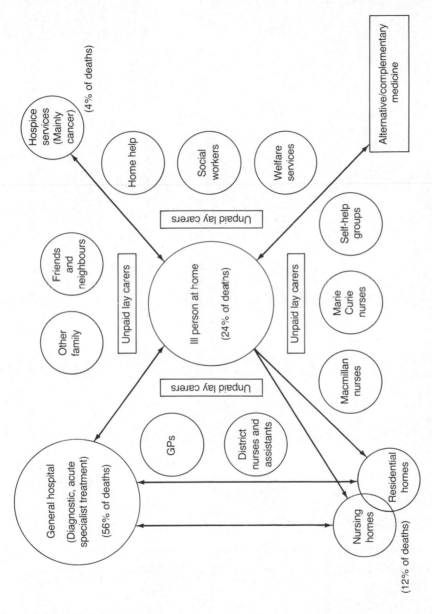

Fig. 1.1. The main sources of help for terminally ill people.

Table 1.1. Where and how people die: Variations in the experience of dying according to setting

Aspect	Hospital	Hospice	Own home	Nursing or residential home
1. Medical aspects of death				
Estimated % deaths[a]	54	4	23	13
Age of ill people	All ages; young people very stressful for staff	Two-thirds over 70; specialist services for children	All ages; professional community support patchy	More severely restricted and older than in own home
Type of patient/client	Increasingly restricted to acute/crisis cases	Usually highly selective and restricted to cancer patients	Most long-term care here, but death may be elsewhere	Long-term and restricted
Symptoms and their control	Acute; control variable, can be excellent or poor	Often severe but over a limited period; specialists in symptom control	Long-term control may be problematic; can be alleviated by visiting health professionals	Symptoms chronic; control variable; acute illness may need transfer to hospital
Locus of control	The organization tends to take over	Ethos of community commitment but with individual choice	Individual and family primarily	Running of homes the key organizing feature
2. Patient experience				
Experience of dying	Subject to rules and routines; social death	Supported and inclusive; increasingly professionalized?	Very variable but home is familiar and thought best	Subject to rules, routines and staff availability; social death
Disclosure of prognosis	Avoidance and mutual pretence common; affected by staff divisions	Openess about prognosis in a supportive setting	Depends on family wishes and prior relationships	Disclosure not usual
Patients' rights	Minimal; relatives often informed when patient is not	Patient and family encouraged to take part in decisions	Depends on family relationships, response to crisis and attitudes of main unpaid carers	Varied but likely to be minimal

3. *Unpaid lay carers*

Relation to patient	Staff tend to respond to presumed relationship stereotypically	Staff try to respond to actual relationships	Patient and 'family' primary in defining this	Very variable; a significant number of residents have no lay carers
Information received	Diagnosis and prognosis given but often minimal discussion	Planned access to information and discussion	Commonly first recipient of information; informal discussion	Variable; may depend on the number of visits
Role of unpaid carer	Excluded or minimal	Theoretically encouraged to participate; not all choose to do so	Major; can be difficulties for carers with additional responsibilities	Absent or minimal except to negotiate care; may feel powerless
Help to bereaved	Generally not seen as part of remit; patchy and weak, but improving	Planned help and follow-up, but vulnerable to workplace pressures	Depends largely on cause of death and staff involved; miscarriage often neglected	Minimal and denied to other residents

4. *Impact on health care staff*

Staff relations	Mainly hierarchical and based on strong professional ideologies	Rhetoric of teamwork, but signs of re-emerging hierarchy	Often fragmented among many professional and non-professional carers	Hierarchical and subject to disputes between Home and NHS staff
Stress	Can be high and amplified by working conditions and staff divisions	Buffered by team support and agreed goals	Can be minimal, but late call-in and staff divisions may lead to stress	Arises from the general working conditions
Emotional involvement	Subject to working methods and care; often discouraged	Expected; often with specific support	Depends on length and nature of relationship with family	Variable, and may be discouraged

[a] Based on a variety of sources, including OPCS *Mortality Statistics, 1990* (OPCS 1991).
Totals do not add to 100 per cent as some deaths occur elsewhere.

deaths are primarily caused by heart attacks and strokes. Only a minority
of these reach the hospital, and few progress beyond the accident and
emergency departments or specialist units. Thus, the deaths which most
hospital staff have to deal with are those which take place over a period
of time as a result of a chronic condition, and which can be anticipated by
the staff. Further, the terminally ill people involved will typically be adults
beyond middle life. Although staff may be able to avoid those areas characterized by high levels of death, in most acute settings staff will on occasion
have to manage relatively rapid, and sometimes unexpected, deaths.

One of the main causes of admission of terminally ill people to a hospital
is the control of their symptoms, especially pain. The physical care of
terminally ill patients seems to vary widely not only between hospitals but
also within them. Symptom control is generally better in hospitals than in
the dying person's own home, with hospice care providing the best symptom
control (Parkes 1985; Twycross 1986; Seale 1991a). Pain relief in hospitals
has improved over the last two decades as the knowledge of effective pain
control developed by hospices is being disseminated to the hospital sector
(e.g. Parkes 1985), but deficiencies remain (Lunt and Neale 1987; see also
Chapter 9, this volume). Iatrogenic distress also persists as a problem.

Staff relations

Hospitals are traditionally characterized by the dominance of doctors.
Within the medical sphere, the continuing development of medical, surgical
and pharmacological technology has led to more powerful and sophisticated
interventions into matters of life and death, especially within hospitals. At
the same time that medical intervention has become more powerful, it has
also become more complicated and difficult to co-ordinate the various
elements of the hospital treatment of chronic and terminal conditions
(Strauss *et al.* 1985). One of the consequences of the predominant influence
of medicine for the care of dying people has been to limit attention to the
personal needs of those who are dying by focusing on intervention for the
treatment and control of disease processes. Physical needs may assume a
primary position while other, less easily identifiable social and psychological
needs are ignored. However, all forms of attention to the needs of those
who are dying – physical, psychological and social – presuppose that a
prognosis of 'terminal illness' has been reached.

The quality of care and the transition from curative to palliative care
depend upon a complex process of clinical and social assessment negotiated
between doctors, nurses and sometimes lay carers and patients. It is often
difficult for doctors to switch from the active management of disease
towards a pattern of care in which the concerns and quality of life of the
patient become paramount. Medical definitions of terminal care may be
challenged by nurses or other carers, but in most cases nurses go along with

medical definitions of appropriate patient care. Even where they do not agree with the actions and orders of doctors, they have little power to change them. One of the main areas of conflict between ward sisters and doctors is the care of terminally ill patients, and especially their unnecessary resuscitation (Field 1989). The dependence of patients upon health care staff makes it difficult for them to challenge staff, as to challenge medical definitions of need may be felt to jeopardize care of their basic needs.

Communication and disclosure

One critical dimension to the care of those who are dying is the knowledge which staff, the patient and relatives have about the terminal prognosis. The control of information and communication is an important way in which people control others, for sharing knowledge is equivalent to sharing power. Withholding information from patients denies them autonomy, and makes it impossible for them to break down the hierarchical relations which are the normal pattern within hospitals, and so contributes to the depersonalization of patient care. Imparting information about terminal conditions is not necessarily straightforward, for the clarity and certainty of both the fact and the time of death have become blurred with the predominance of chronic disease and the capacity of modern medicine to intervene in disease processes to avert and retard the dying process. Certainty of death may develop slowly over a long period of time, and even when the fact of death is certain its timing may remain in doubt. In NHS hospitals, 'social death' and a process of 'social dying' as staff and others withdraw from social interaction with terminally ill patients may often precede 'biological' death (Sudnow 1967).

Some hospital consultants still forbid nurses to disclose a terminal prognosis, although 'open awareness', where a terminal prognosis is known by all persons involved, is an increasingly common situation in our hospitals, and one which many staff see as desirable. Where before the needs of the dying patient as a person were ignored, now more active efforts to respond to patients' unspoken apprehensions and questions and to their more direct queries can be found. However, while doctors will tell most dying patients about their condition, they are less likely to inform them about their terminal prognosis, especially for diseases other than cancer (Seale 1991b). One of the most compelling reasons for such disclosure is the evidence that most terminally ill patients eventually become aware that they are dying. Hinton (1980) found that 66 per cent of his sample of dying patients told him they were dying although they had not necessarily revealed this knowledge to anyone else.

This move towards greater openness and responsiveness has brought with it many challenges. Most nurses and doctors find the task of conveying a terminal prognosis very difficult and stressful, and few health workers have received adequate training in appropriate communication skills (Stedeford 1984; Buckman 1988). When they are uncomfortable talking openly with patients about their likely death – even when they believe that this is the right thing to do – it is likely that they will to a greater or lesser extent avoid and limit their contact with terminally ill patients. Studies have shown that evasion and non-disclosure, poor communication between doctors and nurses, and impersonal treatment of dying patients can still be found in NHS hospitals, and according to Seale (1991b) closed awareness 'may still be quite common, even though open awareness is the most common situation'.

Emotional involvement and workplace stress

The care of dying patients is a major source of stress for nurses and doctors (Payne and Firth-Cozens 1987; Vachon 1987). Vachon claims that it is not so much the dying person who causes problems, but aspects of the environment within which care takes place. A number of factors have been identified as being linked to high levels of stress. Hierarchical and impersonal structures, lack of control over one's own work, high levels of staff turnover, the lack of clear and agreed ways of dealing with dying patients, and conflict between staff are all associated with higher levels of stress. The most important mechanisms for buffering the impact of stress are good communication and mutual support within a team of carers working together to achieve agreed goals. Within NHS hospitals, little attention is paid to alleviating work-induced stress or to helping staff who are experiencing difficulties in coping with the stresses of their work. Whether it be provided informally by colleagues or formally by the provision of counselling and support services, such help is crucial. With shorter lengths of stay, higher patient throughput and more complex disease conditions to deal with, the general levels of workplace pressure upon staff seem to have increased over the lifetime of the NHS.

   Staff may experience particular emotional difficulties with infants, children and young people who are dying. This seems to be in part related to the general emphasis on and positive evaluation of youth in our ageing society. Also, changes in the philosophy and practice of in-patient hospital care for children have generated closer and more emotionally laden contact between nurses, dying children and their parents (Alderson 1990). More fundamental may be the problem of closely identifying with such patients and/or their parents: young patients raise the possibility of one's own death and bereavement in a directly personal way that dying elderly patients do not. For young doctors and nurses who have still to develop their own personal views about death and dying, this may be very disturbing.

   There is some debate about whether staff can entirely avoid emotional involvement with the patients for whom they care, and whether such involvement is desirable. There are positive and negative sides to both involvement and detachment. Over-involvement with patients is identified by Vachon (1987) as one source of stress. On the other hand, there is also evidence that lack of involvement has negative consequences for nurses (Gow 1982; Field 1989). What does seem clear is that changes in the functioning of NHS hospitals are affecting the nature and forms of emotional involvement that develop between staff and patients, perhaps making these more transitory and less intense.

It may well be true that the standards and quality of care of people dying in NHS hospitals has improved over the last 25 years, but great areas of deficit still remain, as conversation with staff in virtually any hospital will confirm. Despite improvements in the control of pain and physical symptoms, it is hard to be optimistic about the attention given to the psychological and spiritual needs of people dying in our hospitals as inadequate information-giving and communication deficiencies persist. There is still ample scope for improvement, especially in terms of interdisciplinary staff communication and relations, holistic care, the provision of appropriate information and communication with patients, the respect for patient's rights, and their involvement in decisions and choices about treatment.

Domestic care in the community

The main alternative to hospital care is care in the sick person's own domestic home. Most people who die at home will do so as the result of a long-term illness, often marked by persistent and distressing symptoms which may be inadequately controlled (Cartwright 1991b). It is not so much the type or cause of death which distinguishes the care of people dying at home from that found in other settings, but the basis and duration of care. Although less than a quarter of all deaths in the UK occur in the domestic home, there is considerable movement between the home and health care institutions (Cartwright 1991a). During the course of their terminal illness, it is highly likely that dying people will spend some time in a hospital or hospice for treatment of their condition, but that most of their terminal care will take place in their own homes provided mainly by unpaid lay carers.

Management of death and dying

Dying comfortably in one's own bed in the familiar surroundings of home with family and friends in attendance is deemed by many people to be an ideal way to die. There are a number of possible benefits to domestic care for both the dying person and their intimates. Being in a familiar environment can, of itself, provide psychological comfort, reassurance and support to the dying person, and may enable them to come to terms with their apprehensions and anxieties about terminal illness. It is also likely that they will be able to influence the quality of life more easily and retain greater control over it in their own home than in an institution. There are also advantages to domestic care for intimates and families. Caring for the dying person may assuage feelings of guilt and enable the maintenance of family ties, even while it is demanding and stressful. It has been suggested that intimates cope better with their bereavement if they have taken an active part in care, and this is easier for them to do in the domestic home than in a formal institution.

The situation is more complex than this, however. The experience of dying in one's own home appears to vary widely, partly because homes and families vary widely in their material, social, psychological and spiritual make-up. It also depends upon the nature of the condition and the availability and support given to unpaid lay carers. Symptoms are less well controlled in the domestic home than in either hospitals or hospices, and the main cause of hospital admission from home is symptom control. It may be that people are prepared to trade-off less than ideal control of physical symptoms for the social and psychological benefits of remaining in their own home (Parkes 1985). Even if symptom control is satisfactory, there may still be serious difficulties. The desirability, and even the possibility, of a 'home death' depends primarily on the human resources available to help not merely with the control of symptoms, but also with all the accompanying constant attendance (often through broken or sleepless nights) and extra domestic work. Although many families wish to look after their relative at home, some are unable to fulfil this hope or promise to the moment of death, and feel guilty as a consequence. The lack of support for the main care-givers from family or friends may be crucial – the other main reason for hospital admission from home is the inability of lay carers to cope.

Lay and professional carers

The experience of dying at home will be affected by the degree and quality of involvement of support services for terminal care in the home. Most of the professional health care received by terminally ill people in the community is delivered by community nurses. These often have heavy caseloads and receive variable support from GPs. Cartwright (1991c) reports that a third of dying people were visited in their own homes by a community nurse in 1987, the same proportion as in 1969, although their nursing care was provided over a longer period of time. In addition, 24 per cent of her sample, mainly those aged more than 65 years who were living alone, were visited by home helps. Home visits from GPs declined from 88 per cent in 1969 to 77 per cent in 1987. Since 1980, a national network of 800 Macmillan nurses, specializing in cancer care, has been developed. Their primary role is to advise and support community nurses and GPs, and their relationships with primary care teams vary from close collaboration to strained and difficult contacts. In some areas, Marie Curie nurses provide night cover in the dying person's own home.

Professional support and backup to unpaid lay carers (usually the partner or adult daughters) is a vital element in the capacity of unpaid domestic carers to cope with the care of people who are dying. The physical help given by such staff and their access to other resources is crucial, as is the social and psychological support provided. In addition to symptom management, such things as the provision of practical aids (e.g. a commode or laundry services), opportunities for respite care, financial aid, home help services and the support which is offered from the primary health care team, may make all the difference between care at home or admission to a hospital. Having an outsider to talk to, or to ask advice outside the patient's hearing, can help unpaid carers keep a sense of perspective. Community or Macmillan nurses are also important in negotiating in-patient care when it is necessary, and in facilitating the realization that unpaid carers can no longer manage on their own (see Chapter 3, this volume). Nevertheless, the day-to-day practical care of people dying at home can still be improved by better co-ordination and liaison (as recommended by Cartwright *et al.* 1973), and a greater willingness from health and welfare staff and voluntary sector workers to negotiate with patients and their families about the nature of such care. Major improvements in domestic care will only be possible if 'community' care comes to mean collective and institutionally supported care, and not just care provided by the 'nuclear family'.

Care of people dying in residential and nursing homes

Given the ever-present background of death, the management of death and dying in residential and nursing homes and the degree to which they are explicitly addressed assume different dimensions to elsewhere. Currently, 12–15 per cent of all deaths occur in residential and nursing homes, a figure which is likely to rise. Seventy per cent of nursing homes cater for long-stay elderly clients, and approximately half of all old people over the age of 85 live in residential or nursing homes (Bury and Holme 1990; Cartwright 1991d). Research information is sparse and sometimes contradictory, and rapid changes in community care provision add to the difficulty of presenting a factually well-grounded discussion.

Changes in the levels of state support and the implementation of changes in community care mean that alterations in care provision in these institutions are likely to continue, and that both types of institutional home will play an increasingly significant role in the care of elderly dying people during the 1990s (Audit Commission 1986; Department of Health 1989b).

In some areas, nursing homes have already largely replaced long-stay geriatric wards. Private residential homes have become increasingly prominent, with a dramatic increase in their numbers (from around 19 300 in 1974 to 159 000 in 1990), while the number of local authority homes has remained constant during a period of rising numbers of old people in the population. There is financial pressure on local authorities to close their own homes and to subcontract their responsibilities for residential care to private homes, although such homes are themselves subject to financial pressures (Wright 1992). Thus, cost-savings and profit-making will become increasingly salient and will directly affect the range and quality of care, potentially reducing already limited opportunities for staff training.

Nursing and residential homes require a different kind of licence, although a dual licence may be issued. Nursing homes must have a trained nurse on the premises, whereas residential homes do not because their residents are supposed to be largely self-sufficient and free from illness. However, the division of clients between the two categories of home into 'well' and 'requiring nursing care' is in practice very blurred, and residential homes may contain many residents who are physically unwell, confused or demented (Willcocks *et al.* 1987). Overall, nursing homes for the elderly will be characterized by higher levels of dependency among their residents than will residential homes. Fitter (and more wealthy) populations are found in private than in publicly funded homes.

A symbolic mark of the difference between institutional homes and other forms of care is that the people being cared for are referred to as 'residents' or 'clients' rather than as 'patients'. This indicates the primacy of factors other than health status, for instance the ability to pay for the care received. Two factors differentiate these settings from the hospice, hospital and domestic home. The first is that the cost of the care is discussed and planned for each resident or client, and that the client's own finances are taken directly into consideration and may dictate the type of care available to them. For some residents and their families, there may be severe difficulties in paying for their long-term residential care, which may necessitate the sale of the home which they had hoped to pass on to their children. This may be distressing for the old person and their family, although it is required for legal and practical reasons. Fees for homes which specialize in terminal illness are at the top end of the board and lodging allowances made to nursing homes, but most people will not die in such specialist units, but in a residential home that provides 'care until death'.

The second factor is that the matron or person in charge of the home, acting either on their own or as a representative for the proprietors, exerts enormous power within the home in a way which is not regulated by statutory obligation (e.g. Hockey 1990). Most people who are in institutional homes are there either because there were no unpaid carers available to support them when they lived in the community, or because such carers are unable to continue to do so. For example, Cartwright (1991d) reports that unmarried old people are much more likely than married people to be resident in such institutions. Those with no relatives to act as go-betweens or advocates for the old person are especially vulnerable to the powers invested in those running institutional homes. For others, relatives are the link between the institutional home and the outside world. Sometimes visitors are viewed as an unwarranted and irritating intrusion by paid staff as they question ideas and practices, whereas in the best of homes they are welcomed and their views are actively sought.

The care of dying clients

Old people in institutional homes are more likely to be suffering from chronic and long-term conditions than those living in their own or relatives' homes, and to have significantly greater restriction of their activities with a lower capacity to do things unaided than those living elsewhere (Bury and Holme 1990; Cartwright 1991d). They also have a different pattern of symptoms from those dying elsewhere. Cartwright reports higher levels of mental confusion, greater loss of continence, more constipation, more bad temper, and greater difficulty in seeing and hearing among residents of communal homes. Indeed, these conditions, especially mental confusion or incontinence, may have contributed to their admission to the home. They are less likely to die from cancer and more likely to die from respiratory diseases (nursing homes) or strokes (residential homes). The use of GPs and community nurses by home residents, especially in private homes, is much greater than by those old people in their own homes (Cartwright 1991d), despite the reluctance of some homes to pay for these services and the apparent reluctance of some health practitioners to provide them. In nursing homes, symptom control will depend primarily upon the quality and training of the nurses employed by the home, whereas in residential homes, symptom control will depend on the involvement of GP and other community services. In both settings, the everyday care for those who are dying is primarily provided by low-paid, largely part-time staff as part of their general care work.

The quality of symptom control is variable in both nursing and residential homes. Even in those homes which have the support of domiciliary hospice services, symptom control regimes seem to be haphazard so that, for example, the significance of strict regimes of analgesia for pain control is not always recognized. Particular problems are posed by the often high levels of confused or senile residents, as it may be difficult for staff – particularly untrained staff – to assess the severity of their symptoms. As with terminally ill people being cared for in the domestic home, admission to hospital is likely when acute episodes or problems arise. However, it may be difficult for homes to negotiate admission to hospitals for their residents because of the pressure of demand for hospital beds, and Cartwright (1991d) reports that home residents are less likely to be admitted to hospital than those living elsewhere. When a resident is transferred (at a time of life when adapting to new circumstances is difficult), they may lose contact with what has been their home and companions for many years.

In many homes, death is 'marginalized' and seen primarily in terms of the practical problems which it causes for staff, e.g. body disposal, arranging the funeral. Most homes seem to operate with a policy of 'closed awareness', keeping those who are dying in ignorance of their prognosis, even if residents are alert, conscious of their deteriorating condition and able to cope with such news. As in hospitals and hospices, the good intentions of individual staff may help clients to know that someone cares for them and understands them. However, the normal practice of the institution may overwhelm such individual efforts to provide personal care and attention, and the staff themselves may succumb to the pressure to conform to the standards of other staff. Most elderly residents in institutional homes have entered the homes for the rest of their lives, and such attitudes and practices run counter to the stated policy of many homes to provide 'life until death'. There are, of course, exceptions to this generalization, but as many of those resident in institutional homes do not have close relatives who can monitor their care, the quality of dying depends on the tone set by the staff. While briefly stating that the dying resident should be comfortable in 'mind and body', the 'Code of practice for residential care' also notes that 'appropriate terminal care should be provided wherever practical' (quoted in Challis and Bartlett 1988). The acknowledgement that it may not be practical to give such care is an indication of how standards have yet to be improved in institutional homes, since this proviso would not be acceptable in any of the other settings we have considered.

If the care of dying people is generally poor in residential and nursing homes, even minimal bereavement care is practically non-existent, and does not even rate a mention in the code of practice for residential care. Bereavement will only be acknowledged where death itself is significant, and in most homes the routinization and denial of death denies also the likelihood of sorrow or loss. Those most likely to suffer from this poor quality of bereavement care are not so much the relatives (if there are any), but fellow residents who obviously need to be informed of a death with care and compassion, since it is likely to touch closely on their own situation.

Disclosure and communication

It seems that the bad practices and communications inadequacies found in post-war hospitals are still to be found in contemporary nursing and residential homes. Despite not being legal guardians, institutional home staff may assume proprietary rights for their clients. They may, quite rightly, need to act to protect their clients, for instance in excluding a particular visitor, in which case they are supposed to give written explanation that will satisfy licensing authorities. However, this same 'protective' right can also be used for the benefit of the staff rather than the client. Avoidance of dying people and 'social death' are common in these institutions. The practice of maintaining residents in ignorance of their own terminal condition is not necessarily a well thought-out and reasoned policy decision. Often it is a practice which has developed over time and become part of the unquestioned 'staff culture' of the institution. Blanket statements that clients 'would not be able to cope', or that it 'would only depress them' are used, as they were used in hospitals, to set a uniform standard for communication to all patients, not merely the ones for whom they are true. Despite the increasing likelihood of death for elderly residents, dying often becomes something which cannot be contemplated or discussed in conversations between staff and residents because there is little active recognition and no developed policy for the care of residents who are dying.

Emotional involvement and stress for staff

Strong bonds of affection can develop over time between home staff and residents, and undoubtedly residents have favourite staff and staff their favourite residents. Overall, the emotional involvement of staff with clients in homes is highly variable, and is likely to depend more on the conditions of work and staffing levels than it does on the characteristics of individual staff and residents. The 'us' and 'them' divide between staff and clients bodes poorly for emotional involvement, and under these circumstances the types of relationship reminiscent of old-style psycho-geriatric wards occur, where a few clients are 'favourites', most go unremarked, and some groups of clients are categorized as 'difficult' (Hockey 1990).

If the significance of caring for dying residents goes largely unrecognized, so do staff needs. The 170 000 trained and untrained staff, many working part-time, may recognize the inadequacies of their care of dying people without being able either to discuss or improve it. This may be in itself stressful. Vachon (1987) has shown that the key stressors in the care of people who are dying lie in workplace problems, so stress could be partially alleviated by improvements in workplace conditions and arrangements. Having said that, it is the case that confused, demented and incontinent residents require great patience and tact, and are likely to cause high levels of physical labour and stress for staff.

Residents' rights

Residential and nursing homes may be the settings where people have least respect paid to their basic rights as citizens and adults, let alone their rights to information about their condition. Informal as well as formal rules limit their actions, as do the large number of duties staff are expected to perform. In theory, the rights of individual residents in institutional homes should be an improvement on those in hospital, for three reasons. First, in most instances there has been a choice of homes, and it might be expected that the client and relatives would choose the home that best suits their needs. Secondly, since in many cases residents are paying for their care, it might be expected that they would feel at liberty to state their demands clearly. Thirdly, the scale of the institutions is much smaller and therefore it might be expected that the service would be more personal. In practice, the resident's choice will be limited by the services available, and choice is only at the point of entry. Many residents are in homes because they can no longer manage by themselves, and once in a home are therefore especially vulnerable to the regime of the home in which they live. According to Challis and Bartlett's (1988) survey, few private nursing homes offer facilities which promote independence and outside contact, even for clients who are well (e.g. half the homes they surveyed did not have a telephone for residents' use). A more positive picture is presented by Bury and Holme (1990) and Cartwright (1991d). Anxieties over finance may make residents vulnerable to the joint pressures of family (if there are any) and staff, even in local government provided homes. Without greater awareness of, and provision for, the needs of the living, there are unlikely to be improvements for clients who are dying.

Although death is an inevitable, indeed planned for, outcome of long-term entry to a nursing or residential home, death and dying are routinely minimized and denied. This is possible because clients are particularly vulnerable, relatives are frequently not present or able to exert pressure on staff to ensure that adequate attention is paid to these issues, and greatly overworked policing authorities have neither the time nor the statutory powers to investigate the adequacy of care. Until licensing, authorities have a responsibility and statutory means through which to enforce minimum standards and the capacity to make regular visits and investigations, care of people dying in our institutional homes is likely to remain poor, although with honourable exceptions to this generalization.

Hospice care

The modern hospice movement developed out of dissatisfaction with the care of dying people in Britain after the Second World War. Its very existence

Table 1.2. Hospice services in the UK

In-patient hospices (2820 beds)	175
Day-care hospices	186
Home care teams	360
Support nurse/teams in hospitals	160

Source: Directory of Hospice Services, St Christopher's Hospice Information Service 1992.

is an implicit criticism of the quality of other forms of terminal care. Recognizing that dying is a social, psychological and spiritual experience as well as a physical process, hospices pioneered non-authoritarian teamwork and incorporated a wide range of carers within the team. Originally focused around in-patient centres of excellence promoting holistic care of dying people in a homely environment, hospice care now takes a variety of forms (Table 1.2). Unlike hospitals, nursing homes or residential homes, which serve multiple functions, hospice services are united by their commitment to the dying person and their family and by their aim to improve the quality of 'the life that is left'. Hospice organizations are funded through both the voluntary and statutory sectors and cater mainly for cancer patients. Relative to other forms of terminal care, they are highly specific in their development, their aims and their organization.

Management, communication and disclosure of dying and death

Over the last 20 years, hospices have helped transform the quality of pain control not only among hospice patients, but among many other sufferers too. Much has also been learned about the control of other symptoms. They have led the way in the disclosure of diagnosis and prognosis to terminally ill patients, demonstrating that this can be done to the benefit of all parties concerned, although hospital doctors and GPs are now the main sources of such information (Seale 1991a). Hospices should be, and usually are, places where a good quality of life during the process of dying is actively sought. Despite the absence of clear research evidence, it is thought that the management of physical symptoms in combination with attention to the person's emotional needs is rarely implemented as well in other settings. In practice, the lofty aims are sometimes circumscribed by a number of practicalities like length of referral, waiting lists and even burned-out or 'battle-fatigued' staff. Also, staff turnover may cause problems of continuity in some hospices, particularly those which share staff with the 'home' NHS hospital. Pressure upon beds from patients waiting to enter has led to pressures for 'revolving door care' in a number of institutions, which may erode the highest quality of care. These difficulties are likely to be exacerbated by current changes in the health service, and increasing difficulties in funding hospice care (James and Field 1992; see also Chapter 10, this volume).

Referral to a hospice is an important stage in a terminal illness conveying a number of messages to those concerned. A few in-patient hospice services will only accept referrals if patients have already been informed of their diagnosis and prognosis, so that an 'open awareness' is assumed. However, it is not that uncommon for hospice in-patients to be unaware that they are dying at the time of their first admission (Seale 1991a). For relatives and hospice staff, admission is a clear signal that death is imminent, and indicates to staff that this is now an appropriate time to talk about their prognosis to the person who is dying. Talking about the person's death and dying is expected to be one of the strengths of hospice staff. Through the teamwork which breaks down the inter- and intra-professional hierarchies, the channels for disclosure are left open, removing the proscriptions against disclosure found in so many hospital settings. It is a moot point whether hospice staff actively encourage patients and their informal carers to discuss their concerns and to seek the information they want, but they do provide more reassurance and support than domiciliary care nurses (Seale 1991a; Field *et al.* 1992).

Emotional involvement and staff stress

The notion of 'total pain' means taking account of psychological, social and spiritual factors, in addition to physical symptoms. The hospice approach to dealing with this is to encourage the expression of all forms of pain, so that they may be attended to. The staff's role in supporting a patient in the expression of pain must come from an acceptance of the patient's loneliness, anger, anxiety, misery, joy, sorrow and elation, as well as listening to the patient's expression of physical pain. Staff are given permission, or even actively encouraged, to express their own feelings, rather than to hide behind their professional role. Emotional involvement usually develops over a period of time, and shared feeling often brings with it bonds of affection and a sense of loss when the patient dies. In practice, the implied intensity of emotional involvement is not as dramatic as it may first appear. Though staff involvement is encouraged, it is also subject to individual and group regulation, so that while attachments may occur, the depth of relationship is not the same with each patient. Staff develop their own defence mechanisms, and looking after hospice patients is not the emotional equivalent of looking after a dying member of one's own family. When 'over-involvement' occurs – and it does – the hospice environment helps both to mitigate its impact upon the staff member and to cope. An important component within this is to give the carer 'permission to grieve', which may be denied in other settings. Aware of the pressures of such involvement, some hospices have pioneered staff support systems, or 'care for the carers' schemes. In terms of stress and 'battle fatigue', hospice staff encounter many of the same problems as those working in other institutional settings, yet the supportive environment of the hospices and their focus on agreed goals of care should mean that there are fewer major difficulties of workplace stress and may make such stress easier to handle.

The role of unpaid carers

As the patient and family are, together, the unit of care in hospices, so families and friends are encouraged to take part in decision-making processes to a degree not common in most other health care institutions. At in-patient units a room is usually provided for the overnight stay of relatives, and in domiciliary teams it is recognized that it is the unpaid carers who do the key work, so respite and holiday care are planned where appropriate. Early hospice ideals integrated bereavement as part of the 'total care' they offered, and most services offer some form of bereavement follow-up. However, while the significance of bereavement is recognized and acted on by hospice services in a way that is almost absent from hospitals and nursing homes, it is also the aspect of the service which is most commonly felt by staff to be inadequate, and it appears that bereavement work is vulnerable to pressures of time and caseload (Field *et al.* 1992; see also Chapter 4, this volume). There may be difficulties when a patient dies shortly after they are admitted, or shortly after the first domiciliary visit. In these circumstances, staff may not have built up the trusting relationships which allow them to offer bereavement support.

All hospice services use unpaid volunteers to help them to provide their services, but the ways in which they are co-ordinated and used varies greatly. In some in-patient or day-care hospices, volunteers have very little contact with patients and relatives, and are confined to 'safe' areas such as reception, catering and fund-raising. Elsewhere, volunteers play more active roles in care, and may be used as 'active listeners' or counsellors for patients and their relatives. They are widely used in the vital role of transporting patients. Volunteers can and do make invaluable contributions to patient care and to the maintenance of the hospice ethos (Field and Johnson 1993; Hoad 1990).

Patients' rights

Hospice philosophy embraces the idea of a dying person's right to choose, since there can be no dignity without choice. Some hospice literature puts forward the idea that the patient is the leader of the inter-disciplinary team, which is made up of professional and lay people. Theoretically, then, patients' rights are not only recognized but built into the system of organizing care, and therefore part of the structure of hospice care. Having said that, hospices do not propose an individualistic philosophy but a participative one, in which decisions are negotiated rather than total responsibility being left with any one person – patient or professional. It is thereby hoped to achieve optimum satisfaction for all those involved, especially the patients and their family. In practice, some hospice services support ill people in their choices to a greater degree than others, especially where there is conflict between the patient and their family. Family members may exert a very powerful influence over whether diagnosis and prognosis are disclosed or not, so that patients' rights should be understood in conjunction with the hospice idea that the patient and his or her family are the unit of care. Another restraint which may affect individual rights is that the good of the community must be taken into consideration, as exemplified by the restrictions on smoking and drinking in many hospices.

The hospice movement has provided an important and welcome contrast to the care of terminally ill people in hospitals and other institutions, and demonstrates quite clearly that a sharp decline in the quality of life is neither an inevitable nor necessary consequence of becoming terminally ill. Its importance lies not so much in the number of patients treated, but in the wider impact in raising the issues of how we deal with dying and death, and how best to help patients and their relatives. Its extensive educational network has brought knowledge of the principles and practice of symptom control, as well as the broader issues of 'good' care of dying people to an international audience of health care professionals and lay people. While generating national interest in terminal care, current changes in financing and management have brought elements of uniformity between the hospice and other health authority services – something the original hospices sought to escape (James and Field 1992). Concerns have been expressed from within the hospice movement about the proliferation of hospice units and its focus upon cancer patients. Concerns about the appropriate boundaries for hospice care are thrown into sharp relief by the emotive questions of providing hospice care for children and for people with HIV/AIDS (see Chapters 5 and 10, this volume).

Concluding comments

The settings where the care of dying people takes place vary and there is considerable movement of people between them. There is also a wide range of health and social services staff involved in the delivery of terminal care. For example, up to 25 different paid carers may visit a person's home during the course of a terminal illness. Not surprisingly, communication of information about the terminally ill person and their needs, and the co-ordination of services between carers and settings, is frequently imperfect. This may lead to the fragmentation of care between the various experts (such as doctors and nurses) and paid 'lay' workers (such as home helps, bathing assistants) who are involved in the care of a dying person. It may also lead to the marginalization or exclusion of both the dying person and their intimates from decisions about care. One implication of the movement of people who are dying between settings and this array of paid helpers is that optimum 'care teams' need to be identified for different circumstances (see Chapter 3, this volume). Although important, improved co-ordination and communication are insufficient in themselves to effect major improvements in the care of dying people. The paradox for terminal care is that at a time when doctors, nurses and support staff are being encouraged to widen their focus beyond physical symptoms to provide 'total' care of the 'whole person', current trends in the health services may limit their opportunities to do so. Yet the care of dying people is of such central importance to all members of our society that the manifold inadequacies are something which must be re-addressed, re-discussed and improved.

References

Alderson, P. (1990) *Choosing for Children: Parents' Consent to Surgery*. Oxford: Oxford University Press.

Audit Commission (1986) *Making a Reality of Community Care*. London: HMSO.

Blauner, R. (1966) Death and social structure, *Psychiatry*, 29, 378–94.

Buckman, R. (1988) *I Don't Know What to Say: How to Help and Support Someone Who is Dying*. London: Papermac.

Bury, M. and Holme, A. (1990) *Life After Ninety*. London: Routledge.

Cartwright, A. (1991a) The role of hospitals in the last year of people's lives, *Age and Ageing*, 20, 271–4.

Cartwright, A. (1991b) Balance of care for the dying between hospitals and the community: perceptions of general practitioners, hospital consultants, community nurses and relatives, *British Journal of General Practice*, 41, 271–4.

Cartwright, A. (1991c) Changes in life and care in the year before death, *Journal of Public Health Medicine*, 13, 81–7.

Cartwright, A. (1991d) The role of residential and nursing homes in the last year of people's lives, *British Journal of Social Work*, 21, 627–45.

Cartwright, A., Hockey, L. and Anderson, J.C. (1973) *Life Before Death*. London: Routledge and Kegan Paul.

Central Statistical Office (1992) *Social Trends 92*. London: HMSO.

Challis, L. and Bartlett, H. (1988) *Old and Ill, Private Nursing Homes for Elderly*

People. Institute of Gerontology, Research Paper No. 1. Mitcham: Age Concern.

Department of Health (1989a) *Working for Patients: Caring for the 1990s.* Cmd 555. London: HMSO.

Department of Health (1989b) *Caring for People: Community Care in the Next Decade and Beyond.* Cmd 849. London: HMSO.

Field, D. (1989) *Nursing the Dying*. London: Routledge/Tavistock.

Field, D. and Johnson, I. (1993) Satisfaction and change: a survey of volunteers in a hospice organisation, *Social Science and Medicine*, forthcoming.

Field, D., and, P., Ahmedzai, S. and Biswas, B. (1992) Care and information received by lay carers of terminally ill patients at the Leicestershire Hospice, *Palliative Medicine*, 6, 237–45.

Flynn, N. (1990) *Public Sector Management*. New York: Harvester Wheatsheaf.

Gow, K.M. (1982) *How Nurses' Emotions Affect Patient Care*. New York: Springer.

Hinton, J. (1980) Whom do dying patients tell? *British Medical Journal*, 281, 1328–30.

Hoad, P. (1990) Volunteers in the independent hospice movement, *Sociology of Health and Illness*, 13, 231–48.

Hockey, J.L. (1990) *Experiences of Death*. Edinburgh: Edinburgh University Press.

James, N. and Field, D. (1992) The routinization of hospice: bureaucracy and charisma, *Social Science and Medicine*, 34, 1363–75.

Lunt, B. and Neale, C. (1987) A comparison of hospice and hospital: care goals set by staff, *Palliative Medicine*, 1, 136–48.

Office of Population Censuses and Surveys (1991) *Mortality Statistics: General. Review of the Registrar General on Deaths in England and Wales, 1991.* London: HMSO.

Parkes, C.M. (1985) Terminal care: home, hospital, or hospice? *Lancet*, 1, 155–7.

Payne, R. and Firth-Cozens, J. (eds) (1987) *Stress in Health Professionals*. Chichester: John Wiley.

Seale, C. (1991a). A comparison of hospice and conventional care, *Social Science and Medicine*, 32, 147–52.

Seale, C. (1991b) Communication and awareness about death: a study of a random sample of dying people, *Social Science and Medicine*, 32, 943–52.

Stedeford, A. (1984). *Facing Death: Patients, Families and Professionals*. London: Heinemann Medical.

Strauss, A.L., Fagerhaugh, S., Suczek, B. and Weiner, C. (1985). *Social Organization of Medical Work*. Chicago, Ill.: University of Chicago Press.

Sudnow, D. (1967) *Passing On: The Social Organization of Dying*. Englewood Cliffs, NJ: Prentice-Hall.

Twycross, R.G. (1986) Hospice care. In R. Spilling (ed.) *Terminal Care at Home*, pp. 96–112. Oxford: Oxford University Press.

Vachon, M.C.S. (1987) *Occupational Stress in Caring for the Chronically Ill, the Dying, and the Bereaved*. Washington DC: Hemisphere.

Willcocks, D., Peace, S. and Kellaher, L. (1987) *Private Lives in Public Places:*

A Research-based Critique of Residential Life in Local Authority Old People's Homes. London: Tavistock.

Wright, F. (1992) *Fee Shortfalls in Residential and Nursing Homes: The Impact on the Voluntary Sector*. London: Age Concern Institute of Gerontology, Kings College, London.

2

Quality, Costs and Contracts of Care

IRENE HIGGINSON

When death is imminent, there is no second chance to improve the quality of care for the patient and family. Patients are usually unable to complain about poor care, because of ill-health or because they die before a complaint can be considered. Therefore, perhaps more than in any other aspect of health or social care, quality of care for people who are dying must be a priority. Quality has to be achieved within a limited budget, however. During this century, health and social care costs have escalated, resulting in an emphasis on value for money and efficiency. The National Health Service (NHS) and Community Care Act 1989 introduced a new system of funding for the NHS, where health authorities or budget-holding general practices and provider units (e.g. hospitals or community services) agree, using NHS contracts, the required quality, quantity and costs of services to be secured for their populations. This chapter considers the quality of care of dying people, the costs and efficiency of care and how these facets can be integrated into the contracting process.

What is quality?

The *Oxford Dictionary of Current English* (1984) defines quality as a 'degree of excellence; general excellence'. Such a general statement is of no use in assessing health or social care, where the specific dimensions of quality need to be considered. Readers of the North American literature may find that quality is limited to the scientific–technical ability of health workers and the humanity with which care is delivered (Black 1990). Although both of these are important, such a definition could lead to superbly technical and humane services which were also ineffective, inequitable and inefficient. A better and broader definition of quality, now widely accepted in the UK, states that quality of health care should include (Shaw 1989; Black 1990):

- effectiveness (achieving the intended benefits in the population);
- acceptability and humanity (to the consumer and to the provider);
- equity and accessibility (the provision and availability of services to everyone); and
- efficiency (the avoidance of waste).

There is also growing concern to consider the appropriateness of the care offered and to empower patients and their families – so that they may increase control over the services received.

The quality of care for dying people: the evidence to date and future priorities

During the 1970s and 1980s, many studies demonstrated deficiencies in conventional care of dying people both in hospitals and in the community. Dying patients suffered severe, unrelieved symptoms, particularly pain; they had unmet practical, social and emotional needs, and suffered as a result poor co-ordination of services with health professionals appearing unwilling to share information (Wilkes 1965, 1984; Cartwright *et al.* 1973). Their families also had suffered because of poor communication by health professionals, and needed emotional, practical and bereavement support (Cartwright *et al.* 1973; Parkes 1978; Bowling and Cartwright 1982). Cancer patients were found to have high psychiatric morbidity, while their families often developed social and psychiatric problems (Maguire 1980). Attention shifted to home care when further work emphasized the increased severity of many problems while patients were at home, where they spent most of their time (Ward 1974). Also, care at home could be provided more cheaply and may be preferred by many patients (Working Group on Terminal Care 1980; Creek 1982). In response to concern over this evidence of ineffective, inhumane and unacceptable care, the modern hospice movement and palliative care developed. The voluntary sector was largely responsible for initiating many of the studies and outlining standards of good practice (Saunders 1978; Lunt and Hillier 1981).

Table 2.1. The quality of care of the dying: Current evidence

---

Effectiveness
Conventional care shown to fail in several circumstances. Specialist hospices or palliative care as good as or better than conventional care in terms of symptom control and care of the family. In-patient hospices have been more widely researched than home care teams, although there is evidence for both

Acceptability and humanity
Conventional care shown to fail in several circumstances. Specialist hospices or palliative care as good as or better than conventional care. Some evidence that most patients prefer to be cared for in their own homes

Equity and accessibility
Least research done in this area. Being middle-class appears to give better quality of life and access to services than being working-class

Efficiency
Specialist palliative care may be more efficient than conventional care, but cost of different units varies greatly. Small in-patient hospices cost more per patient than large units. Home care support is proportionally cheaper than in-patient hospice care

---

Evaluation of palliative and hospice care

The evaluations of palliative care have tended to concentrate on the effectiveness, humanity and acceptability of care, with a few studies considering efficiency. Table 2.1 summarizes the main evidence, for each aspect of quality, for the care of people who are dying and of their families. The following sections review the studies in more detail.

British evaluations

Evaluations of individual services

The first formal evaluative studies of in-patient hospices appeared in the 1970s. Three research groups (Hinton 1979; Parkes 1979a, b; Lunt and Neale 1985) independently showed in-patient hospice care to be more effective than hospital care. Parkes (1979a, b) showed that bereaved spouses retrospectively reported better patient pain control, lower patient and family anxiety and distress, and increased satisfaction than matched hospital care controls. Hospice care also cost less. However, in a follow-up study 10 years later, Parkes and Parkes (1984) failed to show better pain control in the hospice: pain control in hospital appeared to have become as effective. Using his own interviews with patients and spouses and the reports of a senior nurse, Hinton (1979) found 20 hospice in-patients to be less depressed and anxious than 20 in an acute hospital ward or 20 in a Foundation Home.

In a comparative study of in-patient hospital and hospice care in Southampton, Lunt and Neale (1985) observed that hospice doctors set more goals for dying patients than did hospital doctors. They believed goal setting was an integral part of good practice, and so, as process evaluation, indicated hospice care to be more effective. However, there were no differences between the two settings in the goals set by nurses, and no outcome measures were used.

The results of evaluations of hospice services for out-patients or home care were less positive. Hinton's (1979) comparative study included 20 hospice out-patients who showed less anger than patients in hospital or the Foundation Home but no less depression or anxiety. Although Parkes (1980) initially showed a domiciliary service increased the amount of time patients spent at home and cost less than hospital or hospice care, in 1985 he found that bereaved spouses reported that patients had more pain and anxiety when at home than in a hospice or hospital (Parkes 1985).

However, these studies considered only individual hospices. They cannot indicate the effectiveness of palliative care more widely, because of variations in hospice services. The studies of Parkes and Hinton were based on patients at St Christopher's Hospice, Sydenham, London. This is the pioneer centre for the hospice movement and 'a centre of excellence'. It therefore demonstrates the potential of palliative care rather than its effect.

Multi-centre evaluations
Comparing the costs of 40 in-patient hospices, Hill and Oliver (1988) showed that the cost of in-patient care per bed per week ranged between £300 and £750. The smallest hospices had the highest costs. The cost of home care teams ranged between £12 300 and £23 000 (including medical support, overheads, etc.) per full-time nurse per year, but cost per patient per week was not calculated. However, in London, the cost per patient per week in the care of a home care team was calculated as being £80 (Higginson, 1989, unpublished observations).

Interviewing patients in the care of two support teams about their hospital and home care experiences, Higginson *et al.* (1990) showed that support teams received the most praise and were rated by 89 per cent of patients and 91 per cent of family members (defined as the nearest family member or friend) as good or excellent. General practitioners and district nurses were rated good or excellent by 71 per cent of patients and 71 per cent of family members, but 9 per cent in each group rated the service as poor or very bad, and ratings in the inner-London district were significantly worse than those in outer London. Hospital doctors and nurses achieved the lowest ratings, and were rated good or excellent by 43 per cent of patients and 54 per cent of family members, but poor or very bad by 22 per cent of patients and 23 per cent of family members. The study identified continuing problems with communication, co-ordination of services, the doctor's attitude, delays in diagnosis and difficulties in getting doctors to visit at home.

To consider the effectiveness of support team care, Higginson *et al.* (1992) used the Support Team Assessment Schedule (STAS), a 17-item instrument, previously developed and validated to audit palliative care. Of the 17 items, 15 showed significant improvements during support team care; family anxiety and spiritual needs did not. Patient anxiety and symptom control, although improved, remained relatively severe at death. One support team was shown to be ineffective in controlling dyspnoea (Higginson and McCarthy 1989a).

When considering access to care, the referral rate to five support teams in the south-east of England was between 23 and 31 people per 100 district cancer deaths (Higginson 1992). Barnett and McCarthy (1987) attempted to describe the needs of patients not referred to a London support team. Data from national and local cancer registries proved very unreliable but did identify some patients who were in severe difficulties and not yet receiving care. Cases identified by local GPs tended to be in much better circumstances and not in need of extra support team care. Poor access to palliative care services for dying patients who do not have cancer was highlighted as a cause for concern in a recent audit of general practitioners (Finlay *et al.* 1992).

A national random sample of deaths in England
Cartwright and Seale's (1990) study of life before death, gives insight into the effect of hospices (and support teams) and into the equity of care for people who are dying – a feature hitherto largely ignored. This national survey was based on a random sample of 639 adult (aged 15 years or more) deaths registered in England. Interviewers tried to contact the person who could tell them most about the last 12 months of the life of the deceased. Only a small proportion, 7 per cent, received some form of hospice care (25 per cent of cancer deaths), whether in-patient or support team or both (Seale 1991a). These patients were reported to have had better pain relief, greater awareness of their diagnosis and prognosis, and were more satisfied with the services they received (Seale 1991a, b).

However, the characteristics of patients receiving hospice care may have been different. There were social class differences: more middle-class people had been in private hospitals and hospices than working-class people (7 *vs* 1 per cent: Cartwright 1992); middle-class people died at an older age and were reported to have a better quality of life before death. Cartwright (1992) concluded that: 'Money and class contribute to the quality of life before death, as well as postponing death'.

Patients who did not have cancer often suffered severe symptoms, although these were not as common as in cancer patients (statistically significant) for 10 out of 23 symptoms, including pain. Despite the lower prevalence of pain, it was reported in 67 per cent of non-cancer deaths in the last year of life. Symptoms of bad temper, and difficulty seeing and hearing were more common in the non-cancer than the cancer deaths.

North American evaluations

The differences between North American and British health services may mean that the findings of North American studies are not directly transferable (Editorial 1986). The North American provision of home hospice care was either through home health agencies or independent home care units. The latter, especially, are primarily a nursing initiative with variable access to doctors (Mor 1988a). In the UK, medical services, even if there are no doctors in the home care team, can be provided by GPs. However, the American literature is useful because it includes the only two randomized trials of hospice care, and a major comparative study.

Randomized trials of hospice care
One difficulty of all the studies discussed so far is the problem of self-selection by patients into either the hospice or control group. Any apparent effect of palliative care may be due to existing differences between hospice and control groups. In response, Kane *et al.* (1984, 1985) carried out the only randomized trial of in-patient hospice care. Patients admitted to the Veteran's Medical Center were randomly allocated to either hospice or conventional care. Altogether, 137 hospice and 110 conventional care cancer patients were compared. The results were equivocal. Apart from improved patient and family satisfaction, there was no significant advantage of hospice care over conventional care in the control of pain or symptoms, activities of daily living, affect, use of therapeutic procedures, number of in-patient days or cost. Equally, hospice care showed no disadvantages over conventional care.

However, during the study, 'hospice' patients received both hospice care and conventional care. When the hospice unit was full, 'hospice' patients were admitted to general medical wards. Only 60 per cent of the 'hospice' patients died in the hospice, 3 per cent died at home and the rest died elsewhere in the hospital. During the trial, 'hospice' patients spent an average of 13.2 days on general medical wards, not much less than the average of 20.7 days of the control group. Further, the hospice and general wards were close to each other, so we cannot exclude the possibility that staff treating the 'control' patients changed their management after observing the therapy and practices used in the care of 'hospice' patients. These contaminations would reduce the likelihood of finding differences between control and hospice groups. However, if this contamination theory is true, then improvements in the care for dying people could be achieved relatively easily and cheaply through education and training. An educational effect of hospices has not been found in other work (e.g. Cartwright and Seale 1990).

A positive benefit for home care was reported in a randomized trial in 1984. In Rochester, New York, Zimmer *et al.* evaluated one model of home care using a randomized controlled trial. The home care team consisted of a physician, a nurse practitioner and a social worker, who provided 24-hour on-call medical care and nursing and home care services. Elderly patients with either terminal or severe chronic illness were referred and then allocated to either team care or to the usual home health agencies services. Team patients spent less time in hospital, had lower overall costs and died at home more frequently. Satisfaction with care was higher for team patients and their carers than for the control group. There were no significant differences between team and control patients in health status, functional status or survival. Other positive results of home care were reported, although randomized designs were not used (Creek 1982; McCusker and Stoddard 1987).

The National Hospice Study of in-patient hospice, home hospice and conventional care

The National Hospice Study, USA, was devised to demonstrate whether hospice care was effective, so as to consider whether it should receive Medicare funding. The 3 million dollar project collected prospective data from 40 hospice and 14 conventional care centres. A total of 833 hospice home care, 624 hospice in-patient and 297 conventional care patients and their nearest carers were interviewed (Greer *et al.* 1986). The hospice patients were less likely to receive therapies such as chemotherapy, surgery, radiation therapy, transfusions and intravenous therapy and significantly more likely to receive social services (Mor *et al.* 1988a). Home care hospice patients spent more time at home (Mor *et al.* 1988b).

There were few differences in quality of life outcomes measured between conventional care and hospice care. Some small but significant differences in pain, symptoms and satisfaction of family members were found to the benefit of hospice in-patients but none for home care patients. However, there were no consistently observable differences between hospice and non-hospice patients in performance status, quality of life, or satisfaction with care as reported by patients' families (Greer *et al.* 1986; Morris *et al.* 1988).

The results of cost savings were mixed. Home care hospices saved money over conventional care by substituting care at home for hospital care. The savings occurred mainly in the last months of life, and for both in-patient and home care patients the longer the stay in a hospice, the more likely that the costs incurred would exceed those of conventional care patients in the last year of life (Kidder 1988a, b).

Sampling inconsistencies limit the conclusions of this study, however [see Mor (1988a, b) and Greer *et al.* (1983) for details of the study design, and Higginson and McCarthy (1989b) for a detailed review]. First, the main sites of the conventional care group were not representative, since the criteria for inclusion in the conventional care group and the hospice group differed. Conventional care units were probably better than average due to their four extra selection criteria of good records, follow-up, willing doctors and nurses and proximity to regional centres. Secondly, the criteria for selection of patients differed in conventional care and hospice care settings. In conventional care settings, patients with a low mobility were actively selected (Karnofsky score of 50 or less), there was a much higher refusal rate (20.6 per cent compared to 3.3 and 3.5 per cent in the hospice settings) and patients were selected in conjunction with the oncology nurse clinician. In addition, the physician was asked for permission to contact the patient. The authors do not state the number of cases in which the oncology nurse or physician objected to the contact. Thirdly, we cannot say whether patients were selected fairly or not, since no details are given of the full conventional care denominator populations. In the hospice group, from an initial denominator of 13 374 patients, only 1457 (11 per cent) were interviewed. It is not clear what proportion of patients died before they could be interviewed, were too ill for interview, or were selected out by the staff or by random selection.

Future needs for study

The evaluations to date show that hospice care is viable and, in some studies, is an improvement on and cheaper than conventional care. It has been argued that in a pluralistic society such choice is justified on its own merits (Greer *et al.* 1986). The research evidence suggests that evaluations in the future must look at ways of improving palliative care, at its effectiveness in all patients and at the equity and access to care. Studies to date have highlighted failings for certain conditions.

Clinical audit would give any service which cares for dying patients the opportunity to develop ways of looking at and measuring its work, and the quick feedback of results is likely to improve co-operation. Audit would allow comparisons of working, and show differences in need between patients with different characteristics (e.g. diagnoses or ethnic groups). It could identify patients who benefit least from the services and could lead to changes and improvements in practice. In a climate of increasing interest in care for people who are dying, whatever their disease, this is even more important. Audit can be used to consider any of the aspects of quality. It is not, as sometimes wrongly confused, concerned only with the scientific or technical aspects of effectiveness. The access to a service or the equity of care given to patients can be audited equally well.

Role for audit in the quality assessment of care for people who are dying

Audit: definition and measures

The Department of Health (1989) publication *Medical Audit* defines medical audit as: 'the systematic, critical analysis of the quality of medical care, including the procedures used for diagnosis and treatment, the use of resources, and the resulting outcome and quality of life for the patient'. All doctors in the NHS are now required to undertake medical audit, as part of the NHS review (Department of Health 1989), and audits of hospital and general practice are regularly published. Shaw (1980) provides a variety of other terms for audit:

Medical	Care	Evaluation
Health	Standards	Assessment
Clinical	Activity	Assurance
Professional	Quality	Audit
		Review
		Monitoring

The concept of audit is not new. In 1518, the Charter of the Royal College of Physicians included: 'to uphold the standards of medicine both for their own honour and public benefit' (Shaw 1989). Ward rounds, postgraduate lectures and clinical presentations are existing activities which contribute to the review of medical performance. However, these tend to concentrate on individual and often unusual cases and are not based on explicit criteria for good practice. The following are the criteria necessary to change review into formal audit (Shaw 1989):

- explicit criteria for good practice;
- objective measurement of performance;
- random case selection;
- comparison of results among peers;
- identification of corrective action;
- documentation of review procedure and results.

Quality assurance and audit are sometimes confused, but most practitioners (e.g. Shaw 1989; Black 1990) consider audit to be one component of quality assurance. Quality assurance is defined by Shaw (1989) as the 'definition of standards, the measurement of their achievement and the mechanisms to improve performance'.

Audit is a cycle. At the outset standards are set. The practice is observed and compared with the standards, following which changes are made to reach those standards (Royal College of Physicians 1989; Shaw 1989). The cycle is then repeated with the same standards or with new standards developed from the practice. Variations of the original cycle have been proposed, e.g. including a preliminary stage of observing practice before standards are set (Coles 1990).

Medical audit has developed in general practice and hospital settings where doctors usually lead the decision making (Sheldon 1982). In palliative care, doctors often work in teams, sharing the tasks of assessment and decision making with other professionals. Clinical audit is more appropriate to review this type of work. Although defined in similar terms, clinical audit is the systematic, critical analysis of the quality of clinical care, rather than of only medical care (Shaw 1980).

Audit requires clear standards or goals of care, a way of measuring these, a mechanism to review practice and a process of feedback so that standards can be re-set and measured. Developing measures which reflect the goals of care and are relevant is perhaps the most difficult stage. For example, it is not appropriate to use mortality rates to assess palliative care which aims to reduce pain, discomfort and anxiety (Donabedian and Arbor 1982). Also, when monitoring the effects of an intervention, instruments should be able to measure those aspects of health and disability that are susceptible to change within the time-span of the audit.

Measures of structure, process or outcome

The model of structure, process and outcome has been used over the last 40 years to measure the quality of health care. It is adapted from manufacturing industry: raw materials (structure or input) are handled in a certain manner (process) to produce a finished article (outcome) (Shaw 1980). Audit can measure any of these aspects. An audit of structure would be based on organizational criteria, whereas an audit of process or especially outcome would use clinical criteria.

Structure represents the relatively stable characteristics of the providers of care, of the tools and resources they have at their disposal, and the physical and organizational settings in which they work (Donabedian 1980). Structure includes the human, physical and financial resources needed to provide care. *Process* represents the activities that go on with and between the practitioners and patients. In simpler terms, Shaw (1980) described it as the use of resources. It includes measures of throughput and whether patients are assessed and treated according to agreed quality guidelines (Donabedian 1980), such as treatment protocols. Guidelines are based on the values or ethics of the health profession or society (Donabedian 1980). *Outcome* represents the change in a patient's current and future health status that can be attributed to antecedent health care. If a broad definition of health is used, such as the World Health Organization (WHO 1947) definition of total physical, mental and social well-being, then improvements in social and psychological functioning are included. Donabedian (1980) included patient attitudes (including satisfaction), health-related knowledge and health-related behaviour within the definition of outcome.

The structural characteristics of care influence the process of care so that its quality can be either diminished or enhanced. Similarly, changes in the process of care, including variations in its quality, will influence the effect of care on health status and outcomes. Thus, there is a functional relationship as follows: structure → process → outcome.

Structure is easiest to measure because its elements are the most stable and identifiable. However, it is an indirect measure of the quality of care and its value depends on the nature of its influence on care (Donabedian 1980). Structure is relevant to quality in that it increases or decreases the probability of a good performance. Although structure is important in designing health services, as a measure of quality it can only indicate general tendencies.

Process is one step closer to changes in the health status of individuals. The advantage of process is that it measures the most immediately discernible attributes of care activities. However, it is only valuable as a measure once the elements of process are known to have a clear relationship with the desired changes in health status (Donabedian 1980). For example, services often have to count the number of patients they see (throughput). But seeing a large number of patients may not mean that the service is any better than one which sees fewer patients but whose patients are more satisfied with their care.

Outcome reflects the true change in health status, and thus is the most relevant for patients and society. However, Donabedian (1980) argued that changes in health status are useful as a measure of quality of care only if other causes for change have been eliminated. For example, prior care or other factors may be equally important. A useful approach is to focus on the difference between the desired outcome and the actual outcome (Shaw 1980). Services can then identify whether or not their goals are being achieved and investigate any failings.

Relevant outcome measures are much more difficult to develop than process measures, especially if these are to include the total definition of health. Over the last 40 years, it has become increasingly important to develop relevant outcomes for health care. Mortality rates have reduced during this century and, as a consequence, health care has aimed increasingly to improve health status and quality of life (Katz 1987). This is especially true in the context of chronic illness and disability. The development of palliative care is a move even further in this direction – to improve quality of life while a person is dying, and to improve the quality of death.

Measures for palliative care

Palliative care outcomes have been slow to develop, because they require a measure which includes the specific objectives of quality of life while dying, and the quality of dying. Working with five support teams, Higginson *et al.* (1992) developed the Support Team Assessment Schedule, a 17-item measure that reflects the goals of home care teams in caring for dying patients and their families and which can be used to audit care. Ten items are concerned with the patient and family and seven with the services (see Table 2.2). These items can be seen as intermediate outcomes, for without these quality of life while dying cannot be achieved. Each item is defined on a scale of 0 (best) to 4 (worst) with agreed definitions for each point.

The STAS was tested and used in five support teams, and has since been used more widely. The median time to complete a patient rating was 2 minutes (Higginson 1992). The schedule proved useful in determining the condition of patients and their families on referral to the teams, and could be used to determine in which instances teams were most and least effective. The STAS was shown to be reliable and was validated against independent assessments from patients and families, and by comparison with quality of life measures (Higginson 1992).

A report from a Working Group of the Research Unit, Royal College of Physicians (1991) suggests guidelines for good practice and audit measures for palliative care. In addition to STAS, the unit proposed other aspects which should be measured, covering effectiveness, acceptability, equity and humanity, although these measures have yet to be tested in practice. Other services have developed audits and measures of palliative and hospice care across a wide range of topics including individual symptoms, procedures, treatments, bereavements and education (for examples, see Higginson 1993). More recently, audits have been evaluated to determine staff's views of their effectiveness.

Who should assess quality?

Measures of quality may rely on assessments made by patients, their families, external researchers or by health professionals. All of these approaches have their drawbacks and there is no ideal choice. Each study must choose the most appropriate assessor(s) depending upon the aims of the study. Any form of assessment must be validated and the likely biases considered when interpreting the results. Some important biases are discussed below.

Patients

Taking assessments directly from the person who is dying would seem to give the most valid information. However, this has been criticized mainly for two reasons. First, in some instances it is considered an intrusion. No detailed evidence is available, but, in one study, the relatives reported that they believed dying patients were willing to help in research, often in the hope that this would help others (Mor *et al.* 1988b). Fallowfield *et al.* (1987) found that most breast cancer patients reported that taking part in a psychological study was a helpful extension to their treatment. Thus, intrusion may not be the problem thought by professionals.

Second, the reliability and completeness of assessments from severely ill people has been questioned. Ward (1985) and Lunt and Neale (1985) found that of patients in hospice and home care settings, only one-half to one-third survived and were well enough to be interviewed. Maguire (1980) warned that self-rating scales may be subject to error, due to a wish to give socially desirable answers, a favouring of extreme or central positions on the scale (position bias), or because a far greater proportion of cancer patients than is usually realized may have impaired attention, concentration or memory. The National Hospice Study, USA, the largest comparison of hospice and conventional care, included a small proportion of patients receiving care. If the most ill patients cannot be assessed by interview, this is a potential source of bias.

Table 2.2. Definitions of the 17 items in the Support Team Assessment Schedule (STAS)

Item	Definition	Range (best–worst)
Pain control	Effect of pain(s) on the patient	None – severe and continuous, unable to concentrate, eat, sleep or describe
Symptom control	Effect of symptom(s) on the patient	None – severe and continuous, unable to concentrate, eat, sleep or describe
Patient anxiety	Effect of anxiety on the patient	None – severe and continuous, unable to concentrate, sleep or describe
Patient insight	Patient's knowledge of his or her prognosis	Full knowledge of prognosis – not knowing he or she has cancer
Family anxiety	Effect of anxiety on the family [a]	None – severe and continuous, unable to concentrate, sleep or describe
Family insight	Family's [a] knowledge of prognosis	Full knowledge of prognosis – expecting to become completely well
Predictability	Patient and family's [a] need to know likely future events and time-scale related to the team's ability to provide this information	Future events clearly predicted or stable – no idea of likely disease progression and future arrangements
Planning	Further need for the patient, as desired, to organize his or her affairs and special meetings	Completed or unnecessary – major decisions outstanding, patient at a loss where to begin
Spiritual	Effect of any crises in beliefs, faith or religious practices on the patient	Content in own beliefs – distraught with uncertainty or guilt, and in chaos how to resolve this
Communication between patient and family	Depth and openness of communication between patient and family [a]	Communicating openly and honestly – both pretending
Practical aid	Further need for practical aid at home reflecting the difficulty for patient and family [a] without aids	None needed – patient incapacitated without basic aids

Table 2.2. Contd.

Item	Definition	Range (best–worst)
Financial	Further need for benefits reflecting the difficulty for patient and family[a] without benefits	No benefits due – many entitled, patient and family with no money and in chaos
Wasted time	Amount of patient's time lost for tests which could have been avoided, the patient not wishing to attend	No time lost – several days wasted
Communication: professionals to patient and family	Depth of information given to patient and family[a], when they require this, from other professionals[b]	Full information with any changes explained – avoiding answering all questions and visiting
Communication between professionals	Speed, accuracy and depth of information communicated between other professionals[b] reflecting any difficulties for patient and family[a]	Correct messages to all involved on the same day – no communication or idea of who else is involved
Professional anxiety	Effect of anxiety on other professionals[b] reflecting any difficulties for patient and family[a]	None – overwhelming anxiety with inappropriate action
Advising professionals	Amount and speed of advice needed for other professionals[b]	No advice needed or previous advice implemented – major difficulties unrecognized by key workers

[a] Family = the patient's nearest carer; [b] other professionals = the other involved professionals including GP, district nurse, social worker, hospital staff.
Source: Higginson *et al.* (1992).

Relatives, friends or family members

Assessments taken from family members are necessarily limited to cases where a close relative or friend exists, and will be affected by the family members' own process of grief (Parkes 1985), by the relationship between the family member and the patient and by whether the patient is at home or in a hospital or hospice (see Chapter 3, this volume). Parkes (1985) suggested that relatives may over-report symptoms when patients are at home.

Only a few very recent studies have compared patient and family member's assessments. Epstein *et al.* (1989) tested for correlations between the ratings of 60 subjects and their closest relatives or proxies on scales measuring social activity, emotional status, overall health, functional status and satisfaction. A correlation coefficient of 1 would have indicated that the two raters' scores exactly reflected each other, 0 would have indicated that there was no relationship. Pearson's correlation coefficients for all 60 pairs were of medium strength, and ranged from 0.43 (satisfaction) to 0.73 (functional status). However, if the subjects had below median health, or there was below median subject–proxy contact, or the subjects and proxies lived apart, the subject and proxy ratings showed no or very weak correlations, suggesting that the proxy did not reflect the subject's view (e.g. coefficients of 0.12, 0.02 and 0.12, respectively for satisfaction). A study of 65 support team patients in London found that family members' ratings of pain control, symptom control and patient anxiety were significantly worse than the patients' ratings, and yet family members expressed more satisfaction with the services than did the patients. Variations between patients' and family members' ratings in this study were not related to any particular category of family member (e.g. husband, daughter, etc.), although the numbers in some categories were small (Higginson *et al.* 1990).

Assessments made in the bereavement period by family members have also been shown to reflect only moderately the patient's view or in some cases not at all. A study comparing the assessments of family members in the bereavement period showed that these did not correlate with the assessments of patients made during their lives (Ahmedzai *et al.* 1988). Cartwright and Seale (1990) compared patient and bereaved family members' (or close friends') assessments of symptoms and services: mean squared contingency, a measure of agreement based on the chi-squared statistic, ranged from 0.00 (bad temper) to 0.67 (constipation) – a rating of 1 indicated the best agreement and 0 indicated no agreement. The relatives tended to be more critical of services and to report more symptoms. The evidence suggests that, at the moment, we can tell only a little about what a person thinks (or thought) from their family member's assessment. When a family member's assessment is used, it should be considered as measuring that family member's 'pain', 'anxiety', etc., more than that of the patient's. However, palliative care also aims to support family members and in this context their assessments are relevant (see Chapter 3, this volume).

External assessors

External assessors can provide an independent view of the patient's circumstances, free from many of the biases of professionals or family members. However, these may cause intrusion and may interfere with the practice of team members. If the interviewer asks searching questions concerning the patient's insight and future plans, they could be replicating or altering the support team's work. The assessments cannot be made 'blind' to the service received, for the patient is likely to refer to their services during interview. When assessing psychological circumstances during an interview, an external assessor sees only a very limited sample of a person's behaviour (Miller and Morley 1986).

Professionals

Slevin *et al.* (1988), Mercier *et al.* (1987) and Wilkes (1984) found that hospital and community staff gave different assessments of quality of life compared with dying patients themselves. These results may be biased by the professionals' own expectations and hopes of a positive outcome. Professionals may be disposed to recall successful treatments rather than failures (Miller and Morley 1986). However, professionals have the advantage of being able to provide data on all of the patients in their care.

Setting contracts

Under the new funding arrangements of the NHS, the purchasing and providing functions of health care have been divided. Health authorities or budget-holding general practices may purchase services from a variety of providers. The quantity, quality and delivery of a service is agreed between purchaser and provider through a contract. There are three types of contract:

- *Block contracts*: these specify the inputs in terms of facilities to be provided (e.g. staff, clinics, etc.) and are most similar to the pre-1990 arrangements in the NHS. These are the least demanding in terms of activity data, but will increasingly include workload agreements.
- *Cost and volume contracts*: these are the most common form of contract and specify the output in terms of patients treated. These place the obligation of providing a fixed level of service on the provider.
- *Cost per case contract*: these cover the cost of treatment for individuals. Because of the high costs involved in administering such contracts, purchasers tend not to like them.

In all contracts, but particularly cost and volume contracts, the provider and purchaser have to agree levels of quality and price of service. Contracts initially concentrated on the 'housekeeping' aspects of quality, such as the waiting time between referral and an appointment, or the waiting times in clinics. These have evolved to include aspects such as being met by a named nurse or the unit taking part in audit. However, as the contracting process develops, quality will be measured in more sophisticated ways and may be subject to inspection visits and special surveys of the patients and families receiving care. Contracts must consider all aspects of quality, not just the scientific–technical. Attention to quality is needed at all points in health care, from before referral and into bereavement. Through the contracting process, it is possible to improve the quality of care for dying patients, but there are four clear dangers which must be avoided:

1. The overuse of the structure and process aspects because they are easy to measure when it is not known that they truly improve outcome.
2. Concentration on the quality of care of dying among patients in

hospices or specialist palliative teams, rather than in all settings.
3. Concentration on the technical aspects of quality at the expense of other aspects, e.g. acceptability, humanity, equity and access.
4. Concentration on the costs of the service at the expense of other aspects of quality.

Cost–benefit, cost-effectiveness and cost–utility analysis

Why bother about costs?

The interest in the costs, benefits and efficiency of health services is based on the premise that resources for health care provision are scarce and will never be sufficient to meet human wants completely. Therefore, when choosing to use resources for any programme, or to change their level of provision, the community forgoes the opportunity to use the resources for another activity. New medical technologies and the increasing number of elderly people in the UK cause health care costs to increase at a faster rate than inflation. Unless the amount of money devoted to health care is increased in line with these changes, purchasers will have to ask providers for efficiency savings and will strive to purchase services which give the greatest health gain (improvement in health and/or quality of life of the population). Purchasers will need to compare services in terms of the outcomes achieved for a given input (in terms of costs).

Comparing different programmes in terms of cost and outcome

The input costs of the service should ideally include not only the direct costs of providing it, but also the indirect costs (e.g. the cost of withdrawing an individual from work to receive therapy) and the intangible costs associated with therapy, such as pain and suffering. The outcomes (called outputs in some texts) can be considered in terms of money (the value of a life) or in terms of health:

1. *Cost–benefit analysis* measures outputs in monetary units, e.g. the medical savings resulting from improved health, or the production gains from an earlier return to work. How much money a person is prepared to pay for the service is sometimes used.
2. *Cost-effectiveness analysis* measures outputs in health terms, e.g. years of life, absence of symptoms, quality of life.
3. *Cost–utility analysis* is usually considered as a form of cost-effectiveness analysis, but any extension of life gained is adjusted for its value by 'utility' weights reflecting the relative value of one health state *vs* another. The most common outcome used in cost–utility analysis is Quality

Adjusted Life Years (QALYs), where the number of years of remaining life are adjusted by an estimate of the quality of those years based on the expected amount of distress and disability a person will experience. A year of high quality will count as 1 QALY; a year with moderate distress and disability might count as 0.7 QALY.

All these techniques are complicated, and have numerous pitfalls (for a critique and guidance, see Drummond 1987; Sisk 1987; Smith 1987; Cohen and Henderson 1988; McGuire *et al*. 1988; the above definitions were extracted from these texts). Cost-effectiveness, the technique most commonly employed by health professionals, is probably the most straightforward. It is of most value in comparing programmes that are expected to have similar health outcomes, for example palliative care at home or in a hospice. However, it cannot compare different health outcomes, for example palliative care, diabetic care and liver transplants. Cost–utility and cost–benefit analyses are used for this. QALYs are becoming increasingly popular and league tables of different procedures and the cost per QALY gained are now published (see Williams 1985).

Although QALYs, or similar measures, can contribute to the debate about choices for health care, they should be used with caution and only alongside ethical and humane considerations and other information on the quality and effectiveness of care. The validity of QALYs is not yet established; they were developed using assessments from 70 subjects (including doctors, psychiatric patients, members of the public) who differed in their views. The scale considers only distress and disability, and misses a multitude of important aspects of palliative care. QALYs are unusual in that some states of severe distress and disability are rated as worse than death. Therefore, although palliative care probably does reasonably well in the QALY league tables, when people are very disabled and in pain so does euthanasia. If only QALYs are considered, euthanasia – with its lower costs – might appear preferable to palliative care.

Cost considerations will influence the development of palliative care, but the debate will be complex whatever technique is used to analyse costs. Much progress could be made to improve the cost-effectiveness of care for people who are dying and of their families. Given the variations in cost and quality, this would seem an appropriate place to begin.

Conclusions

This chapter demonstrates that improvements in the quality of care for dying people and their families were often brought about by hospices and palliative care support teams. However, although the effectiveness, humanity, acceptability and efficiency of such care is demonstrated, the quality debate must consider the equity of and access to high-quality care. There is continuing evidence of difficulties as regards access to services, and too few studies consider access or equity, especially for people from disadvantaged or minority ethnic groups. Further research to understand the differences and similarities between assessments from family members, patients and professionals would help purchasers and professionals to understand the meaning of existing studies.

Valid and appropriate outcome measures of palliative care are becoming available, Support Team Assessment Schedule being one example. These should be used to audit the care of dying people and their families in all settings, not just of cancer patients receiving specialist palliative care. People who do not have cancer, and those who are receiving general practice, oncology, district nursing and geriatric care need to be included. Through the contracting process in the NHS, there is a mechanism to improve the quality of care of dying people, by proposing standards of the quality of care and insisting on the measurement of care outcomes. However, purchasers must ensure that they do not simply concentrate on those aspects which are easy to measure, or use over simplified analyses of costs.

References

Ahmedzai, S., Morton, A., Reid, J.T., and Stevenson, R.D. (1988) Quality of death from lung cancer: patients' reports and relatives' retrospective opinions. In M. Watson, S. Greer and C. Thomas (eds) *Psychosocial Oncology*. Oxford: Pergamon Press.

Barnett, M. and McCarthy, M. (1987) Identification of terminally-ill patients in the community. In D. Doyle (ed.) *1986 International Symposium on Pain Control*, pp. 78–80. International Symposium Series No. 123. London: Royal Society of Medicine.

Black, N. (1990) Quality assurance of medical care, *Journal of Public Health Medicine*, 12(2), 97–104.

Bowling, A. and Cartwright, A. (1982) *Life After Death: A Study of the Elderly Widowed*. London: Tavistock.

Cartwright, A. (1992) Social class differences in health and care in the year before death, *Journal of Epidemiology and Community Health*, 46, 81–7.

Cartwright, A. and Seale, C. (1990) *The Natural History of a Survey: An Account of Life Before Death*. London: King Edwards Hospital Fund.

Cartwright, A., Hockey, L. and Anderson, J.L. (1973) *Life Before Death*. London: Routledge and Kegan Paul.

Cohen, D.R. and Henderson, J.B. (1988) *Health, Prevention and Economics*. Oxford: Oxford University Press.

Coles, C. (1990) Making audit truly educational, *Postgraduate Medical Journal*, 66, S32–S36 (suppl. 3).

Creek, L.V. (1982) A homecare hospice profile: description, evaluation, and cost analysis, *Journal of Family Practice*, 14(1), 53–8.

Department of Health (1989b) *Working for Patients Medical Audit.* Working Paper No. 6. London: HMSO.

Donabedian, A. (1980) *Explorations in Quality Assessment and Monitoring, Vol. 1: The Definition of Quality and Approaches to its Assessment.* Michigan: Health Administration Press.

Donabedian, A. and Arbor, A. (1982) An exploration of structure, process and outcome as approaches to quality assessment. In H.K. Selbman and K.K. Uberla (eds) *Quality Assessment of Medical Care,* pp. 69–92. Gerlingen: Bleicher Verlag.

Drummond, M.F. (1987) Resource allocation decisions in health care: a role for quality of life assessments? *Journal of Chronic Disease,* 40(6), 605–616.

Editorial (1986) Hospice comes of age, *Lancet,* i, 1013–14.

Epstein, A.M., Hall, J.A., Tognetti, J. *et al.* (1989) Using proxies to evaluate quality of life: can they provide valid information about patients' health status and satisfaction with medical care? *Medical Care,* 27(3), S91–S98.

Fallowfield, L.J., Baum, M. and Maguire, G.P. (1987) Do psychological studies upset patients? *Journal of the Royal Society of Medicine,* 80, 59.

Finlay, I., Wilkinson, C. and Gibbs, C. (1992) Planning palliative care services, *Health Trends,* 24(4), 139–141.

Greer, D.S., Mor, V., Sherwood, S. *et al.* (1983) National Hospice Study analysis plan, *Journal of Chronic Disease,* 36(11), 737–80.

Greer, D.S., Mor, V., Morris, J.N. *et al.* (1986) An alternative in terminal care: results of the National Hospice Study, *Journal of Chronic Disease,* 39, 9–26.

Higginson, I. (1992) The development, validation, reliability and practicality of a new measure of palliative care: The Support Team Assessment Schedule. PhD thesis, University of London.

Higginson, I. (ed.) (1993) *Clinical Audit in Palliative Care.* Oxford: Radcliffe Medical Press.

Higginson, I. and McCarthy, M. (1989a) Measuring symptoms in terminal cancer: are pain and dyspnoea controlled? *Journal of the Royal Society of Medicine,* 82, 1716–4.

Higginson, I. and McCarthy, M. (1989b) Evaluation of palliative care: steps to quality assurance? *Palliative Medicine,* 3, 267–74.

Higginson, I., Wade, A. and McCarthy, M. (1990) Palliative care: views of patients and their families, *British Medical Journal,* 301, 277–81.

Higginson, I., Wade, A. and McCarthy, M. (1992) Effectiveness of two palliative support teams, *Journal of Public Health Medicine,* 14(1), 50–56.

Hill, F. and Oliver, C. (1988) Hospice – an update on the cost of patient care, *Health Trends,* 20, 83–7.

Hinton, J. (1979) A comparison of places and policies for terminal care, *Lancet,* i, 29–32.

Kane, R.L., Wales, J., Bernstein, L. *et al.* (1984) A randomised trial of hospice care, *Lancet,* i, 890–94.

Kane, R.L., Klein, S.J., Bernstein, L. *et al.* (1985) Hospice role in alleviating the emotional stress of terminal patients and their families, *Medical Care,* 23(3), 189–97.

Katz, S. (1987) The science of quality of life, *Journal of Chronic Disease,* 40(6), 449–63.

Kidder, D. (1988a) The impact of hospice on the health-care costs of terminal cancer patients. In V. Mor, D.S. Greer and R. Kastenbaum (eds) *The Hospice Experiment*, pp. 48–68. Baltimore, MD: Johns Hopkins University Press.

Kidder, D. (1988b) Hospice services and cost savings in the last weeks of life. In V. Mor, D.S. Greer and R. Kastenbaum (eds) *The Hospice Experiment*, pp. 69–87. Baltimore, MD: Johns Hopkins University Press.

Lunt, B. and Hillier, R. (1981) Terminal care: present services and future priorities, *British Medical Journal*, 283, 595–8.

Lunt, B. and Neale, C. (1985) *A Comparison of Hospice and Hospital Care for Terminally Ill Cancer Patients and Their Families: A Comparison of Care Goals Set by Staff*. Paper D. Southampton: Department of Community Medicine, University of Southampton.

McCusker, J. and Stoddard, A.M. (1987) Effects of expanding home care programs for the terminally ill, *Medical Care*, 25(5), 373–84.

McGuire, A., Henderson, J. and Mooney, G. (1988) *The Economics of Health Care: An Introductory Text*. London: Routledge and Kegan Paul.

Maguire, P. (1980) Monitoring the quality of life in cancer patients and their relatives. In T. Symington, A.E. Williams and J.G. McVie (eds) *Cancer: Assessment and Monitoring*, pp. 40–52. London: Churchill Livingstone.

Mercier, M., Schraub, S. and Bourgeois, P. (1987) Quality of life (letter), *Lancet*, ii, 161–2.

Miller, E. and Morley, S. (1986) *Investigating Abnormal Behaviour*, pp. 210–2. London: Weidenfeld and Nicolson.

Mor, V. (1988a) Participating hospices and the patients they serve. In V. Mor, D.S. Greer and R. Kastenbaum (eds) *The Hospice Experiment*, pp. 16–27. Baltimore, MD: Johns Hopkins University Press.

Mor, V. (1988b) The research design of the National Hospice Study. In V. Mor, D.S. Greer and R. Kastenbaum (eds) *The Hospice Experiment*, pp. 28–47. Baltimore, MD: Johns Hopkins University Press.

Mor, V., Greer, D.S. and Goldberg, R. (1988a) The medical and social service interventions of hospice and non-hospice patients. In V. Mor, D.S. Greer and R. Kastenbaum (eds) *The Hospice Experiment*, pp. 88–108. Baltimore, MD: Johns Hopkins University Press.

Mor, V., Greer, D.S. and Kastenbaum, R. (eds) (1988b) *The Hospice Experiment*. Baltimore, MD: Johns Hopkins University Press.

Morris, J.N., Sherwood, S., Wright, S.M. and Gutkin, C.E. (1988) The last weeks of life: Does hospice make a difference? In V. Mor, D.S. Greer and R. Kastenbaum (eds) *The Hospice Experiment*, pp. 109–132. Baltimore, MD: Johns Hopkins University Press.

Parkes, C.M. (1978) Home or hospital? Terminal care as seen by surviving spouses, *Journal of the Royal College of General Practitioners*, 28, 19–30.

Parkes, C.M. (1979a) Terminal care: evaluation of in-patient service at St Christopher's Hospice. Part 1. Views of surviving spouse on effects of the service on the patient, *Postgraduate Medical Journal*, 55, 517–22.

Parkes, C.M. (1979b) Terminal care: evaluation of in-patient service at St Christopher's Hospice. Part II. Self-assessments of effects of the service on surviving spouses, *Postgraduate Medical Journal*, 55, 523–7.

Parkes, C.M. (1980) Terminal care: evaluation of an advisory domiciliary service at St. Christopher's Hospice, *Postgraduate Medical Journal*, 56, 685–9.

Parkes, C.M. (1985) Terminal care: home, hospital or hospice? *Lancet*, i, 155–7.

Parkes, C.M. and Parkes, J. (1984) Hospice versus hospital care – re-evaluation after 10 years as seen by surviving spouses, *Postgraduate Medical Journal*, 60, 120–24.

Royal College of Physicians (1989) *Medical Audit: A First Report. What, Why and How?* London: Royal College of Physicians of London.

Saunders, C.M. (1978) *The Management of Terminal Disease.* London: Edward Arnold.

Seale, C. (1991a) Death from cancer and death from other causes: the relevance of the hospice approach, *Palliative Medicine*, 5(1), 12–19.

Seale, C. (1991b) A comparison of hospice and conventional care, *Social Science and Medicine*, 31, 147–52.

Shaw, C.D. (1980) Aspects of audit. 1. The background, *British Medical Journal*, 280, 1256–8.

Shaw, C. (1989) *Medical Audit: A Hospital Handbook.* London: King's Fund Centre.

Sheldon, M.G. (1982) *Medical Audit in General Practice.* Occasional Paper No. 20. London: Royal College of General Practitioners.

Sisk, J. (1987) Discussion: Drummond's 'Resource allocation decisions in health care: a role for quality of life assessments?' *Journal of Chronic Disease*, 40(6), 617–19.

Slevin, M.L., Plant, H., Lynch, D. *et al.* (1988) Who should measure quality of life – the doctor or the patient? *British Journal of Cancer*, 57, 109–112.

Smith, A. (1987) Qualms about QALYS, *Lancet*, i, 1134–6.

Ward, A.W.M. (1974) Terminal care in malignant disease, *Social Science and Medicine*, 8, 413–20.

Ward, A.W.M. (1985) *Home Care Services for the Terminally Ill.* Sheffield: Medical Care Research Unit, Department of Community Medicine, University of Sheffield Medical School.

Wilkes, E. (1965) Terminal cancer at home, *Lancet*, i, 799–801.

Wilkes, E. (1984) Dying now, *Lancet*, i, 950–52.

Williams, A. (1985) Economics of coronary artery bypass grafting, *British Medical Journal*, 291, 326–9.

Working Group of the Research Unit, Royal College of Physicians (1991) Palliative care: guidelines for good practice and audit measures, *Journal of the Royal College of Physicians of London*, 25(4), 325–8.

Working Group on Terminal Care (1980) National terminal care policy (E. Wilkes, chairman). *Journal of the Royal College of General Practitioners*, 30, 466–71.

World Health Organization (1947) The constitution of the World Health Organization, *WHO Chronicle*, 1, 29.

Zimmer, J.G., Groth-Juncker, A. and McCusker, J. (1984) Effects of a physician-led home care team on terminal care, *Journal of the American Geriatrics Society*, 32(4), 288–93.

3

Informal Care and Community Care

BRENDA NEALE

Informal carers have been the subject of growing research over the past decade as their crucial role in community-based care has been recognized. This chapter explores the characteristics and demography of informal care within the context of terminal illness, and discusses the effects of community care and related policies on the informal sector. It also suggests how needs might be better assessed and services co-ordinated using the emerging principles of care management.

What is informal care?

Formal and informal care

Informal care is usually defined as that provided by spouses, other relatives, friends and neighbours, to the chronically sick and disabled, and the frail elderly. It may be characterized as caring *about* someone, rather than merely caring *for*, or tending, someone's needs. Such care is given by virtue of pre-established social relationships, and is not therefore evenly distributed (Twigg 1989). Informal care is unpaid and is motivated by altruism, long-term reciprocity and a sense of duty, which usually develop within the relatively private world of kinship. The knowledge base of informal care is rooted in the daily experience of persons and localities; it covers a wide variety of tasks requiring flexibility and adaptability, and is performed on a 24-hour basis. Formal care, in contrast, is open to all on the basis of need, and is affectively neutral. It is motivated, at least in part, by financial remuneration, and its knowledge base is rooted in professional training and clearly delineated skills, which are applied during work hours only (Twigg 1989). These differences have underpinned social policy responses to community care.

The extent of informal care

There are thought to be around 6 million carers in the UK, 1.4 million of whom devote at least 20 hours a week to caring (Green 1988). It has been estimated that two-thirds of those caring for more than 20 hours a week receive no help from either the formal or voluntary sectors, and that the total inputs from the informal care sector are greater than the combined inputs financed from central and local government (Department of Health 1989a; House of Commons 1990a).

Characteristics of informal carers

In practice, 'informal care' means care by the family – generally by one person, usually a woman – though in principle *all* members of the family may be involved. Giving care on this basis is closely bound up with family obligations and in particular with perceptions of women's 'caring' role within the family. Spouses represent over 50 per cent of carers because of their co-residence, and because ideologically marriage is regarded as the supreme caring relationship, second only to the mother–infant bond. Over 40 per cent of informal carers are themselves over retirement age.

These patterns of gender, family and age are also reported among carers of terminally ill people (Seale 1990, 1991b; Addington-Hall *et al.* 1991). Evidence suggests that an impending death may affect a high proportion of family members, and that the incidence of shared care may therefore be greater in this context than among other groups of dependents (Dand *et al.* 1991; Peace *et al.* 1992). In the majority of cases, however, the major practical part of the caring role is still likely to devolve to one family member, with other family members primarily providing emotional support (Neale 1992).

The caring role

The use of the term 'carer' implies a homogeneous group, yet no two carers' activities or needs are the same. The extent of care provided may vary from occasional help to virtually continuous care. The type of care also varies greatly. It may encompass all or some of six broad types of activity:

- personal care (also known as tending, e.g. washing, feeding, etc.);
- domestic care;
- auxiliary care (less demanding practical help such as shopping and transportation);
- social care (conversation, informal counselling, emotional support);
- basic nursing care (administering drugs and injections, changing catheters, etc.); and
- planning care (negotiating and co-ordinating support for the cared-for person).

It appears that carers may approach their role in a variety of ways; they may attempt a balancing act between caring and their other commitments, or they may become engrossed, even engulfed by their role, with an accompanying sense of stress and low morale (Lewis and Meredith 1988; Twigg and Atkin 1991). Palliative carers often attempt to cope by lowering their expectations and by 'taking each day as it comes', i.e. abandoning any future orientation or life outside the caring role (Neale 1992).

Individual characteristics such as age, sex and ethnic background may well affect the caring situation, although there is a dearth of research in these areas.

The stress of caring

Whatever the particular characteristics of carers, results from many studies indicate that a large proportion of them experience physical, emotional, social and economic burdens as a result of their responsibilities. The closer the kinship bond between carer and cared-for person, the greater the emotional strain is likely to be. When these burdens become excessive or have to be sustained over a long period of time, there is a possibility of informal care-giving breaking down or even of abusive behaviour occurring towards the cared-for person (Qureshi and Walker 1989). The social isolation of carers has been identified as an important factor both in tying the carer to the relationship, and in producing mixed feelings of resentment, bitterness and guilt (Lewis and Meredith 1988).

In palliative care, the emotional problems associated with caring are likely to be compounded by anxiety over the impending death and bereavement of the cared-for person. Moreover, patients in their last year of life have particularly high levels of dependency, resulting in severe restrictions in carers' lives (Seale 1990; Dand et al. 1991). Carers may regard the patient's pain, symptom control and anxiety as worse than either the patient or medical staff perceive it to be (Cartwright and Seale 1990). Of all the problems faced by the carer, anxiety has been rated by researchers as the greatest (Wilkes 1984b; Herd 1990; Higginson et al. 1990).

The preference among both patients and carers for home care and a home death have been well documented. Yet whether or not a patient is admitted to an institution may depend as much upon the attitudes and physical and emotional needs of the carer, or the relationship between carer and patient, as it does upon the needs and condition of the patient alone (Wilkes 1984b; Gilley 1988). The carer's lack of support and confidence – that is, social rather than medical considerations – have been identified as prime factors in the patient's admission to hospital and consequent break-down in informal care-giving (Wilkes 1984a; Haines and Booroff 1986; Walsh and Kingston 1988; Townsend *et al.* 1990; Addington-Hall *et al.* 1991). It seems that the medicalization of death has generated a high level of anxiety among ordinary people in dealing with what could more properly be regarded as a 'natural' part of the life-cycle.

Yet, for a variety of reasons, including fear of jeopardizing the support they are receiving, informal carers are often reluctant to acknowledge problems or ask for help (Lewis and Meredith 1988; Blyth 1990).

A partnership in care

The characteristics of formal and informal care, outlined above, indicate that the two sectors are not of equal status. Popular assumptions give preference to informal care. There is evidence that clients turn to the formal sector only if informal care is not available and that similar expectations hold sway in the formal sector. Yet while theoretically the affective dimension of informal care marks it out as qualitatively superior, in practice this is not necessarily the case. Informal care is an uncommandable, unspecifiable resource that is unevenly distributed. The care provided may not be adequate, either emotionally or practically (Twigg 1989). Given these problems, the affectively neutral and impartial nature of formal care may not necessarily be a disadvantage, and there is evidence that statutory and voluntary provision can be personalized and be seen to care *about* as well as care *for* its clients (James 1989; Seale 1992).

Whatever the relative merits of the two sectors, it is clear that they need to work in partnership with each other. So as to carry out their role effectively, informal carers need practical, respite, financial and emotional support for themselves, as well as holistic care for the patient which supports them indirectly. To what extent such a complex array of support is or can be provided, however, is questionable, as will be shown below.

Demographic trends

The proportion of the population over the age of 65 in the UK has increased steadily during this century, while death from infectious diseases has become rare. There are increased numbers of chronically sick and dependent people in need of care, indicating that a large proportion of the population will end their days with a terminal illness (Griffin 1991). The number of one-person households has also increased to a quarter of all households, with the elderly most likely to live alone. This adds to the practical problems of caring for them in the final stages of life.

At the same time, the proportion of the population potentially available to care has diminished. High rates of divorce and remarriage are leading to more complex family structures and the blurring of lines of responsibility for care. Reductions in family size, a declining proportion of single women in the population and changing patterns of female employment may also affect the supply of carers.

Despite these factors, there is no evidence that families are any less likely, or willing, to care for their dependent members. Patterns of kinship, affection and reciprocity are still strongly evident and most people still feel an obligation to their dependent family members, as well as a great normative pressure to care (Twigg 1989). Even so, demographic trends have placed pressures on informal carers which have added to their difficulties.

Social policy issues

The problems of informal carers have also been compounded by the recent shift towards community-based care as part of the resurgence of *laissez-faire* state policies. A decade ago, the government reduced the proportion of public expenditure going to the personal social services and encouraged the expansion of voluntary and unpaid care (Qureshi and Walker 1989). Care *in* the community has increasingly come to mean care *by* the community. Recent official reports and policy proposals have acknowledged the indispensable activities of informal carers: 'Helping carers to maintain their valuable contribution to the spectrum of care is both right and a sound investment' (Department of Health 1989a). Yet it is worth looking critically at what these ideals of carer support mean in practice.

At present, the allocation of resources is based less on individual, systematic assessments of need than on intuition, guesswork and pragmatic resource constraints. Evidence suggests, for example, that female or close family carers are less likely to receive help than either male or more distantly related carers (Arber *et al.* 1988). The extent to which the government's new proposals for community care can improve this situation is question-able. Commentators on the government's White Paper *Caring for People* (Department of Health 1989a) have criticized its rhetoric, which is not matched by properly prepared, costed and resourced proposals for carer support (House of Commons 1990a). Nor has it been backed by protective legislation; the transfer of responsibilities to local government leaves unclear the role of central government in ensuring standards of provision. There is also confusion among service providers and managers over the implications of the changes in the funding and organization of services, which the government guidelines have done little to address.

Moreover, there are problems with the new proposals for client assessment, vital interface between provision and need. From April 1993, local authorities will be required to carry out or co-ordinate assessments of individuals who may be in need (Department of Health 1989a, 1990a; National Health Service and Community Care Act 1990). Yet they will not be obliged to carry out independent assessments of carers' needs and wishes, despite the fact that they may differ from those of the cared-for person, unless the carer asks for help or is *clearly* in need of it, or there is significant disagreement between carer and patient (Department of Health 1991b). The government's proposals are not pro-active but rely on users to request help.

Given what we know of the carer's reluctance to acknowledge problems such an approach may prove unhelpful. Indeed, formal assessments may well need to be supplemented in this context by sensitive and careful probing. The government's guidelines for assessment procedures, however, do not offer the scope for such an approach. Assessment, they suggest:

> . . . should be as simple, speedy and informal as possible . . . procedures should be based upon the principle of what is the *least* that it is necessary to know . . . [and] guided by what the potential user *volunteers* as the presenting problem . . . the possible danger of wide ranging assessments is that the users are made to feel they have needs that they have never hitherto considered, thereby creating future unnecessary dependency and/or wasteful resources.
>
> (*Department of Health 1991b: 47/52–3*)

A further problem with the proposals for assessments concerns the lack of guidance on joint working between care sectors. At present, health and social care are artificially separated because of organizational and budgetary constraints. Yet at the grass roots level, the distinction between health and social care is unclear. If services are to be truly client-centred, then an overall view needs to be taken of individual needs and this distinction between the health and social components of care becomes an unnecessary hindrance (Department of Health 1990a; House of Commons 1990a). Moreover, for people with complex needs, the assessment process could be long and complicated. The problems of co-ordinating such fragmented support are substantial and, regardless of the level of resources, may give rise to unmet needs and gaps in provision. The government proposals may therefore make little practical difference to the lives of informal carers.

Care management

The way in which services are put together in 'packages' is increasingly
recognized as the key to high-quality provision. Regrettably, carers often
find themselves at the centre of a complex pattern of service delivery in which
no single person has the responsibility for the assessment, management and
co-ordination of the 'package' as a whole (Twigg *et al.* 1990).

Care management (formerly known as case management) is one way of
resolving the problems of assessment, co-ordination and effective targeting
of resources. It is a needs-led, integrated approach in which a care manager
acts as a single point of contact for a client, arranges a package of services
and has overall responsibility to ensure appropriate and effective support.
The core functions are the assessment and regular review of the needs of
the client; care planning and budgeting; arranging services; and monitoring
provision. A further function is the initial identification of people with needs,
including a system of publicity and referrals (Challis and Davies 1986;
Department of Health 1989a).

Care management involves a refinement of the key worker role in social
work. Following its importation from the USA, it has been increasingly
applied in the UK. Endorsement in subsequent policy documents is likely
to give impetus to its development, particularly as it has been found to be
cost-effective (House of Commons 1990b).

The government gives prime responsibility for the nomination of care
managers to local authorities. The potential for general practitioners (GPS)
to contribute has been stressed, given their role as gatekeepers to services
(Department of Health 1989b, 1990a). But the current bio-medical orientation of substantial numbers of GPs would necessitate a major change in
their role, which in many cases may be neither desirable nor possible (Atkin
and Twigg 1991). Moreover, the idea of care managers being independent
of service providers, thus separating the interests of users and providers,
and leaving the care manager untrammelled by organizational constraints,
has been strongly advocated (House of Commons 1990a). Certainly, there
is evidence that carers may be more open in expressing their needs to non-
service providers (Department of Health 1991d; Neale 1992). Government
policy has incorporated the idea, recommending 'a progressive separation
of the *tasks of assessment* from those of *service provision*', although it
stresses the necessity for care management staff to work within resource
constraints, and to strike a balance between meeting needs identified in
assessment, and meeting the preferences of individuals (Department of
Health 1991a). As social services departments become fewer the providers
of care and more the enablers and purchasers of it, social workers will
increasingly take on care management responsibilities.

Evaluations of care management schemes are encouraging. In the Kent
community care project, neighbours or new voluntary workers were recruited

to provide flexible forms of support to dependents and their carers. Its evaluation revealed clear benefits for carers, particularly on three outcome measures related to well-being – subjective burden, extent of strain and mental health problems. Emotional and practical support was more appropriately tailored to needs, and the anxiety of carers was relieved simply by reducing their sense of total responsibility for the cared-for person. Moreover, care management did not substitute for informal care or undermine it; carers were found to be *less* likely to reduce their support for the cared-for person (Challis and Davies 1986). The project also showed the potential for generating new models of service provision.

It is unclear from the government's proposals what the carers' role should be in care management and how they should be supported, which has led commentators to stress the necessity for carers to be involved in all stages of a care plan, particularly as their needs may differ from the cared-for person (House of Commons 1990a). Government guidance (Department of Health 1989a, 1991a, b) outlines nine different models for care management, and suggests that the various functions outlined above could be performed by different individuals. Yet this would defeat the purpose of a single co-ordinator for each client, the value of which has been well documented (Department of Health 1991c). The government's response will hardly allay these concerns:

> . . . the most likely option will be one in which skilled practitioners are used selectively for such tasks as assessment, with others delegated to support staff . . . only a minority of users with complex needs will be allocated a care manager.
>
> *(DH/SSI 1991a: 24)*

Commentators have expressed concern that the government sees care management as an administrative tool rather than the provision of an individually tailored package of care for each service user (House of Commons 1990b). The effectiveness of care management, it seems, will depend on how it is implemented at local level.

Informal palliative care: policy issues

The government's recent enlightened thinking on the value of informal care has, of course, always been a hallmark of palliative care. Since the inception of the hospice movement, the 'dying triad' (Gilley 1988) of patient, informal carer and professional has been recognized (Wilkes 1984b; Gilley 1988). An explicit aim of the hospice movement has been to treat the family as the unit of care, i.e. supporting family members through a time of stress and bereavement, and maintaining their involvement with the care of the patients. In fact, the successful growth of the hospices may be attributed in part to their ability to harness and organize the principles embodied in informal care: to care *about* their clients, rather than merely caring for them. Yet in palliative care, as in the broader field of social policy, it is worth looking critically at what these ideals mean in practice.

Hospice in-patient care

During the past decade, there have been two trends discernible in palliative care which may have affected support for carers. The first is the gradual shift towards the routinization of the larger in-patient hospices and their changing relationship with the National Health Service (NHS) (Abel 1986; James and Field 1992). Units which were set up with charitable funding, but are now managed within the NHS, show evidence of a shift in emphasis away from the psycho-social care of the family to the physical care of the patient (James 1986). A recent survey at the Leicestershire Hospice revealed that in many cases carer needs had not even been identified let alone met (Dand *et al.* 1991). In practice, then, hospices may not always fulfil their aims (see Chapter 1, this volume).

Hospices have also been affected by changes in health policy (discussed in Chapters 2 and 10, this volume), which have made audit a prerequisite to securing funding (Department of Health 1989b; the National Health Service and Community Care Act 1990). Current auditing procedures may not be sensitive enough to measure the intangible, informal qualities of care so valued in the early hospices, and the measurement of 'hard' indicators of provision, such as physical interventions and drugs administered, may also predispose towards an erosion of psycho-social support for both patient and carer.

Furthermore, if research interests are any indication of the concerns of hospice practice, then it is noticeable that researchers have rarely focused exclusively on the informal carer, except in studies of bereavement. Early research and retrospective studies have tended to elicit informal carers' views merely as a proxy for the patient (see, e.g. Parkes 1979), an approach which is questionable given that their perceptions appear to differ (Cartwright and Seale 1990). There is a tendency to view informal carers as mere extensions of the patient rather than as clients in their own right (see, e.g. Seale 1991a), with the result that the views of carers have been submerged and problems specific to them largely ignored. Some hospice practitioner guides (see, e.g. Corr and Corr 1983; Saunders 1990) also exhibit such tendencies, particularly where blanket references are made to 'the family' in a way that glosses over the problems experienced by the informal carer, and fails to explore how the problems of patient and carer may be bound up with each other (cf. Neale 1992).

Despite these trends, specialist palliative care services, whether in-patient or home-based, are still much more highly rated by carers than mainstream provision (Seale 1991b). Yet whatever the relative merits of these two sectors of care, at present less than 10 per cent of families receive specialist support, a situation unlikely to change given the high cost of such support and its almost exclusive focus on cancer sufferers. As Wilkes (1980) pointed out, it is the quality of mainstream provision which needs to be evaluated and addressed, for it is this sector of provision upon which the vast majority of families will have to depend. As yet, however, the challenge provided by the working group on terminal care (Wilkes 1980) to disseminate the principles of palliative care throughout the NHS, has still to be met.

Home-based care

The second trend within palliative care which may have affected the informal carer is the move away from in-patient care towards care in the community. On average, patients now spend some 90 per cent of their terminal year at home being cared for informally with primary health care team back-up.

The home care provided by specialist services is highly valued by both patients and their carers (Ward 1985; Higginson *et al.* 1990; Field *et al.* 1992). Yet it is not clear that such services will continue to expand at their present rate. Ward (1985) stresses that they are not necessarily cheaper to operate than in-patient units. Further, while some GPs recognize the need for increased support from specialist staff (Haines and Booroff 1986), others, particularly those who hold their own budgets, may see specialist support as an unnecessary extra expense and they may opt instead to care for their dying patients themselves (James and Field 1992). The move towards home-based care, then, indicates an increasing dependence on mainstream medical support for terminally ill people and their carers, rather than a steady expansion of specialist, multidisciplinary support.

There are a number of problems inherent in this situation. As death has become more institutionalized over the past 40 years, GPs may no longer have the degree of experience in dealing with terminally ill people and their carers that they once had (Doyle 1980). As yet, most members of primary health care teams have had little specialist training, and may have yet to grasp the hospice ideals of open communication, informed choice and intensive emotional support for both patient and carer (Addington-Hall *et al.* 1991; Seale 1992). There is evidence that GPs operate in a policy vacuum, with the result that the quality and extent of support offered varies greatly (Atkin and Twigg 1991). Moreover, time and resource constraints may necessitate a strong medical orientation, a focus on the patient and a reluctance to discuss the patient with the carer. An underlying reason for this may be the traditional emphasis within medicine on the doctor–patient relationship, and the ambiguous position of informal carers, who are regarded neither as patients nor clients in their own right (Twigg 1989). This, combined with the carer's uncertainty over the GP's remit and reluctance to ask for help, results in the 'marginalization' of the carer's own problems (Atkin and Twigg 1991).

Where support for palliative carers has been evaluated, the most widely reported finding concerns the value that carers attach to communication skills and emotional support, i.e. to the *informal* qualities of palliative care. Yet the quality of such support from mainstream medical staff is frequently inadequate (Gilley 1988; Addington-Hall *et al.* 1991). Counselling both before and after bereavement or referral to such services is noticeably lacking (Blyth 1990; Seale 1991b). Carers are rarely informed of bereavement support as a service they can utilize and are therefore unaware of its potential benefit.

Since in organizational terms palliative care is a health care speciality, the social needs of clients need to be dealt with via referrals to other agencies. Yet while GPs are expected to undertake this task (Department of Health 1989b), there are also shortfalls in these areas. In 1980, the amount of practical and respite support being received by palliative carers was minimal (Doyle 1980, 1982); a decade later, there seems to be little improvement (Herd 1990; Addington-Hall *et al.* 1991; Neale 1992), despite evidence that respite care is perhaps the biggest single need of carers (House of Commons 1990a). Moreover, most community care plans drawn up by local authorities fail to identify those in need of palliative care as a discrete client group, although the needs of carers are increasingly being recognized.

While the shift in policy towards community care is in line with clients' preferences, it has not been matched by a shift in resources. The under-resourcing of carer support has compounded the problems faced by the informal sector. In 1980, the Working Group on Terminal Care (Wilkes 1980) stressed the necessity for an expansion of statutory practical and respite help for families wishing for a continuation of home care. In 1991, Addington-Hall and colleagues echoed the plea, calling for a transfer of funds from acute hospital services to community-based services. It seems that the problems of practical and respite support for palliative carers remain largely unresolved (Griffin 1991).

Co-ordination of palliative care services

If community-based palliative care is to address the multidisciplinary needs of its clients, then it must mobilize and co-ordinate a complex array of support encompassing up to 25 different professional and voluntary groups (Blyth 1990). The emerging principles of care management, as outlined above, have obvious potential in this context through the appointment of social workers or independent care managers, or by extending the co-ordinating role of specialist nursing or administrative staff. The care management schemes referred to, much like the hospice movement, are based on co-operation and joint responsibility between the informal and formal sectors. Much of their effectiveness lies in their capacity to blur the distinction between formal and informal care, drawing on the flexibility, personal character and emotional responsiveness of the informal sector, while focusing and co-ordinating their efforts (Twigg *et al.* 1990).

The organizational framework of care management is highly conducive to client-centred provision, and may be a way for specialist palliative care services to retain and consolidate their informal qualities of care, work effectively with mainstream services, and promote good quality palliative care across diagnostic groups and care settings.

As yet, however, care management in palliative care is in its infancy and few evaluations have been made. Inter-agency relationships are disparate and fluid, making it unclear how care management can best be implemented. However, a randomized controlled trial has recently been carried out in an inner-London health district, in which two workers were appointed to co-ordinate inter-sectoral palliative care services. Community nurses were chosen for the role, although social workers had been considered. The new service, designed to be pro-active rather than reactive, was based not on referrals, but on routine identification and notification of all potential clients (MacDonald 1989). The evaluation was limited by the single site design of the project, and revealed problems for the nurses in finding structured ways to assess needs; indeed, the evaluators, as independent assessors, were rather more successful in identifying needs than the nurses had been. Overall, the new service had little positive impact on the quality of care provided (Addington-Hall *et al.* 1992). These findings lend support to the notion that the roles of needs assessors and service providers should be separated.

The recent NHS trend towards appointing regional and district co-ordinators of palliative care is recognition of the fact that fragmented support needs to be co-ordinated if it is to be effective (Trent Regional Health Authority 1988; see also Chapter 1, this volume). However, the roles, responsibilities and resources of *all* those involved in multidisciplinary teams are likely to overlap, and if muddle and conflict are to be avoided, good co-ordination is vital at *practitioner* as well as at managerial level (Blyth 1990).

Professional perceptions of carers

Twigg (1989) suggests that the level and type of support offered to informal carers depends upon professional perceptions of them as either resources, co-workers or co-clients. The practice of viewing carers as a resource and effectively rationing support on the basis of their availability or otherwise is relatively widespread. It is said to occur, for example, in the community nursing service, in the context of personal care tasks such as bathing, and in the Macmillan nursing service with its focus on emotional rather than practical support (Ward 1985; Twigg *et al.* 1990; Seale 1991a; Twigg 1992). Hunt's (1991) study of conversational interactions between specialist nurses and terminally ill cancer patients and their carers, vividly illustrates the point – the carer is assumed to be a resource which need not be substituted for.

In the resource model, formal sector policy is to continue informal care-giving for as long as possible, followed by crisis intervention when the carer can no longer cope (Blyth 1990). The model of care tends to be a residual one, responding only to deficiencies in the informal sector; it is a policy which tends to reward failure and ignore success (Twigg 1989).

Where carers are viewed as co-workers, then co-operation is envisaged between the formal and informal sectors, although given their different normative bases, the two do not easily mesh together. This approach seems to be the one most frequently adopted in government policy documents. The possibility of carers becoming their own care managers, and thus co-workers *par excellence*, has been advocated by the Carers National Association (House of Commons 1990a). This has attractions as a means of deconstructing carers as clients and empowering them to determine their own needs, and the idea been utilized with some success in the Bexley Community Care Project.

However, while many carers act as their own care managers through necessity, not all carers could, or, indeed, would wish to take such a pro-active role; and they would lose the benefit of separate and objective assessments of their needs. Moreover, while carer morale is recognized as important and support offered within this framework, the motive is *still* that of maintaining informal care-giving, rather than increasing carer well-being. Professionals may assume these two aims to be complementary but they are just as likely to be in conflict: a normal life for the patient may mean an abnormal one for the carer (House of Commons 1990a). This model is graphically illustrated by Hunt (1991) in her account of the 'word' work of specialist palliative care nurses. When carers attempted to act as 'clients' themselves, by describing their own symptoms or difficulties, the nurses discouraged the process, responding only by offering support and encouragement so that the carer would continue their co-worker responsibilities, and keep the patient at home.

The idea of the carer as co-client is one intrinsic to the early hospice movement with its focus on families as the unit of care, and an approach that has been re-advocated recently (Higginson *et al.* 1990). The policy here is not necessarily to maintain informal care-giving but to assess patient and carer separately, and relieve carers of a sense of pressure to continue if they feel unable to do so. Those that are able to care should then receive continuous support. Early identification of need is vital so that resources can be mobilized *before* the carer becomes exhausted.

Of these three models of perceiving informal carers, the co-client model would, in the majority of cases, be the most beneficial, yet there is little evidence for it in practice. At best, carers can hope to be given a choice over their role and determine for themselves the extent of their co-worker responsibilities; at worst, the norms of informal care-giving will give rise to their continued exploitation and marginalization.

References

Abel, E. (1986) The hospice movement: institutionalizing innovation, *International Journal of Health Services*, 16 (1), 71–85.

Addington-Hall, J., MacDonald, L., Anderson, H. and Freeling, P. (1991) Dying from cancer: the views of bereaved family and friends about the experiences of terminally ill patients, *Palliative Medicine*, 5, 207–214.

Addington-Hall, J., MacDonald, L., Anderson, H. *et al.* (1992) Randomised controlled trial of effects of co-ordinating care for terminally ill people, *British Medical Journal*, 305, 1317–22.

Arber, S., Gilbert, N. and Evandrou, M. (1988) Gender, household composition and receipt of domiciliary services by the elderly disabled, *Journal of Social Policy*, 17(2), 153–75.

Atkin, K. and Twigg, J. (1991) General practice and informal care: Assumptive worlds and embedded policies. Paper given at the *British Sociological Association Medical Sociology Group Annual Conference*, University of York, September.

Blyth, A. (1990) Audit of terminal care in a general practice, *British Medical Journal*, 300, 983–6.

Cartwright, A. and Seale, C. (1990) *The Natural History of a Survey*. London: Kings Fund.

Challis, D. and Davies, B. (1986) *Case Management in Community Care: An Evaluated Experiment in the Home Care of the Elderly*. Aldershot: Gower.

Corr, C. and Corr, D. (1983) *Hospice Care: Principles and Practice*. London: Faber and Faber.

Dand, P., Field, D., Ahmedzai, S. and Biswas, B. (1991) *Client Satisfaction with Care at the Leicestershire Hospice*. Occasional Paper No. 2. Sheffield: Trent Palliative Care Centre.

Department of Health (1989a) *Caring for People: Community Care in the Next Decade and Beyond*. Cmd 849. London: HMSO.

Department of Health (1989b) *Working for Patients: The Health Service Caring for the 1990's*. Cmd 555. London: HMSO.

Department of Health (1990a) *Caring for People: Community Care in the Next Decade and Beyond. Policy Guidance*. London: HMSO.

Department of Health (1990b) *The Government's Plans for the Future of Community Care*. Cmd 1343. London: HMSO.

Department of Health/Social Services Inspectorate (1991a) *Care Management and Assessment: Managers' Guide*. London: HMSO.

Department of Health/Social Services Inspectorate (1991b) *Care Management and Assessment: Practitioners' Guide*. London: HMSO.

Department of Health/Social Services Inspectorate (1991c) *Caring for People: Carer Support in the Community. Evaluation of the DH Initiative: 'Demonstration Districts for Informal Carers 1986–9'.* London: HMSO.

Department of Health/Social Services Inspectorate (1991d) *Caring for People: Getting it Right for Carers.* London: HMSO.

Doyle, D. (1980) Domiciliary terminal care, *The Practitioner*, 224, 575–82.

Doyle, D. (1982) Domiciliary terminal care: demands on statutory services, *Journal of the Royal College of General Practitioners*, 32, 285–91.

Field, D., Dand, P., Ahmedzai, S., Biswas, B. (1992) Care and information received by lay carers of terminally ill patients at the Leicestershire Hospice, *Palliative Medicine*, 6(3), 51–9.

Gilley, J. (1988) Intimacy and terminal care, *Journal of the Royal College of General Practitioners*, 38, 121–2.

Green, H. (1988) *Informal Carers: Report of the 1985 General Household Survey.* London: HMSO.

Griffin, J. (1991) *Dying with Dignity.* Studies of Current Health Problems No. 97. London: Office of Health Economics.

Haines, A. and Booroff, A. (1986) Terminal care at home: perspective from general practice, *British Medical Journal*, 292, 1051–3.

Herd, E. (1990) Terminal care in a semi-rural area, *British Journal of General Practice*, 40, 248–51.

Higginson, I., Wade, A. and McCarthy, M. (1990) Palliative care: views of patients and their families, *British Medical Journal*, 301, 277–81.

House of Commons Social Services Committee (1990a) *5th Report, Session 1989–90. Community Care: Carers.* London: HMSO.

House of Commons Social Services Committee (1990b) *6th Report, Session 1989–90. Community Care: Choice for Service Users.* London: HMSO.

Hunt, M. (1991) The identification and provision of care for the terminally ill at home by 'family' members, *Sociology of Health and Illness*, 13(3), 375–95.

James, N. (1989) Emotional labour, *Sociological Review*, 37, 15–42.

James, N. and Field, D. (1992) The routinisation of hospice: bureaucracy and charisma, *Social Science and Medicine*, 34(12), 1363–75.

James, V. (1986) Care and work in nursing the dying: a participant study of a continuing care unit. Unpublished PhD thesis, University of Aberdeen.

Lewis, J. and Meredith, B. (1988) *Daughters Who Care.* London: Routledge.

Macdonald, L. (1989) A new scheme for the care of terminally ill cancer patients, *MRC News*, 44, 12.

Neale, B. (1991) *Informal Palliative Care: a Review of Research on Needs, Standards and Service Evaluation.* Occasional Paper No. 3. Sheffield: Trent Palliative Care Centre.

Neale, B. (1992) *Informal Palliative Care in Newark: Needs and Services.* Occasional Paper, forthcoming. Sheffield: Trent Palliative Care Centre.

Parkes, C.M. (1979) Terminal care: Evaluation of an in-patient service at St. Christopher's Hospice, Part 1: views of surviving spouse on effect of the service on the patient, *Postgraduate Medical Journal*, 55, 517–22.

Peace, G., O'Keeffe, C. and Faulkner, A. (1992) Childhood cancer: changing psycho-social needs – are they being met? A review of the literature, *Journal of Cancer Care*, 1, 3–13.

Qureshi, H. and Walker, A. (1989) *The Caring Relationship: Elderly People and Their Families*. London: Macmillan.

Saunders, C. (ed.) (1990) *Hospice and Palliative Care: An Interdisciplinary Approach*. London: Edward Arnold.

Seale, C. (1990) Caring for people who die: the experience of family and friends, *Ageing and Society*, 10(4), 413–28.

Seale, C. (1991a) Death from cancer and death from other causes: the relevance of the hospice approach, *Palliative Medicine*, 5(1), 13–20.

Seale, C. (1991b) Caring for people who die. Paper presented at the *British Sociological Association Annual Conference*, Manchester, March.

Seale, C. (1992) Community nurses and the care of the dying, *Social Science and Medicine*, 34(4), 375–82.

Townsend, J., Frank, A., Fermont, D. *et al.* (1990) Terminal cancer care and patients' preferences for place of death: a prospective study, *British Medical Journal*, 301, 415–17.

Trent Regional Health Authority (1988) *No Second Chance: A Discussion Document for the Trent RHA on the Development of Terminal Care Services*. Sheffield: Trent RHA.

Twigg, J. (1989) Models of carers: how do social care agencies conceptualize their relationship with informal carers? *Journal of Social Policy*, 18(1), 53–66.

Twigg, J. (1992) Personal care and the interface between the district nursing and home help services. In B. Davies, A. Bebbington and H. Charnely (eds) *Resources, Needs and Outcomes in Community Based Care*. Aldershot: Gower.

Twigg, J. and Atkin, K. (1991) Informal care and the process of service delivery. Paper presented at the *British Sociological Association Annual Conference*, Manchester, March.

Twigg, J., Atkin, K. and Perring, C. (1990) *Carers and Services: A Review of Research*. London: HMSO/York: Social Policy Research Unit.

Walsh, S. and Kingston, R. (1988) The use of hospital beds for terminally ill cancer patients, *European Journal of Surgical Oncology*, 14, 367–70.

Ward, A. (1985) *Home Care Services for the Terminally Ill: A Report for the Nuffield Foundation*. Sheffield: Department of Community Medicine, University of Sheffield.

Wilkes, E. (1980) *Report of the Working Group on Terminal Care*. London: Standing Medical Advisory Committee, DHSS.

Wilkes, E. (ed.) (1984a) *A Source Book of Terminal Care*. Sheffield: Sheffield University Press.

Wilkes, E. (1984b) Dying now, *Lancet*, i, 950–52.

4

Developments in Bereavement Services

ANN FAULKNER

Feelings of grief may start long before the death of a patient. Relatives and patients alike have to get used to the idea of a shortened life expectancy, uncertainty, and often a good deal of worry and concern. These issues need to be addressed in order to formulate an overall policy on both palliative care and bereavement services which will properly meet the needs of those requiring them.

In the report of the Working Group on Terminal Care (Wilkes 1980), little mention is made of a national policy on bereavement services. However, the summary of recommendations does address two items that are concerned with bereavement and one with education. First, it is suggested that advice and support should be given to the relatives of terminally ill individuals both before and after death, though a clear idea of what this advice should be is not given. Secondly, it is suggested that hospitals should have facilities for relatives such as simple meals, a room to talk and overnight accommodation, but there is little mention of what happens after the death of the patient. In terms of education, it is recommended that greater emphasis should be given to the psychological aspects of dying and bereavement in basic nurse training courses, which should also include an introduction to counselling. There are no recommendations suggesting that staff other than nurses should be given this specific training, though it is suggested that terminal care units should have the capacity to educate and inform by linking units to nursing and medical schools.

A more recent document on the care of people with terminal illness makes even less reference to bereavement services, stating that 'The staff of nursing homes continue contact with relatives of those who have died in their homes, only to the extent that they wish to do so' and 'In a recognised hospice, there should normally be satisfactory provision of bereavement and counselling services for a patient's family and friends. It is regarded as an integral part of the hospice service' (NAHAT 1991: 29).

What is the reality? In a study of relatives and friends, Addington-Hall *et al*. (1991) found general dissatisfaction with the care of terminally ill individuals and an associated belief that nurses were 'too busy' or 'too rushed' to meet the needs for effective care and information. The public, in general, appear to be very forgiving of health professionals, but many issues need to be addressed, for with the lack of a clear government policy on bereavement services and a matching lack of commitment from the National Health Service (NHS), it is not surprising that there is no clear rationale for bereavement services across the country. The issues that need to be addressed include clear decisions on what bereavement work should involve, when it should take place, who it should involve and how the outcomes should be monitored. It would then be possible to reduce the areas of dissatisfaction described by Addington-Hall *et al*. (1991)

The present

Local commitment

There has been a growing commitment to the needs of bereaved individuals at a local level. This has resulted in hospital nurses being sent to patients' funerals, the introduction of bereavement visiting by nurses, volunteers and/or others, and commitment to group activities in some areas. To date, if a patient has died in the community, it is much more likely that the family will have been visited after the death than if that patient had died in hospital, but this is changing in some areas. Similarly, hospices appear to be more committed to bereavement work than general hospitals, though there is no clear defining line between the two. In workshops described by Maguire and Faulkner (1988a), health care workers varied enormously in their involvement in bereavement work. At a recent workshop, one nurse from a hospice had attended a funeral most weeks for the previous few months, whereas others had not been to a funeral at all, and there is quite a divergence of thinking as to whether in fact attending funerals should be part of bereavement work.

In some areas, bereavement visiting is a standard follow-up to a death, whereas in others this is left to voluntary services, many hospices for example having a cohort of bereavement visitors, most of whom have been bereaved themselves. There is, at present, no statutory obligation to visit, or assess, bereaved individuals in any area of health care. Where services are offered by health care workers, it is usually because the institution in which they work is committed to the concept. The service is offered by community nurses, social workers, volunteers and, less often, by hospital staff.

Volunteers provide the backbone of bereavement work and may be attached to a hospice, the church or a voluntary organization such as CRUSE or the National Association of Bereavement Services. This inevitably leads to a patchy and variable approach to work with bereaved people.

Risks

Without a clear policy on bereavement, there are obviously attendant risks to the current situation. Both those who are bereaved and those who visit bereaved individuals are at risk.

Bereaved individuals

Currently, an individual who is bereaved may or may not be visited by either a health professional or a trained bereavement volunteer. If they do receive a visit, there is absolutely no guarantee that the person who visits them will actually be skilled in the ability to communicate with and, if necessary, counsel them. Nor can it be assumed that the visitor will be able to recognize those bereaved individuals who are unable to cope effectively with their grief and who may need specialist help to reach Worden's (1992) final state of recovery from loss, i.e. to be open to a new relationship. Although most bereaved individuals do cope with their grief with the support of family and friends, there is no guarantee that the small number of those at risk will be recognized or even visited for an assessment of their ability to work through their grief without specialist intervention.

There is also the risk that a bereaved individual may be 'triggered' by the lack of focus of the visitor's interview. This can occur because the recent death may be linked with other losses, guilt or trauma. In a recent workshop, a nurse gave the example of Dorothy, a spinster, who had cared for her mother during her mother's final illness. Her loss when her mother died was compounded by guilt about the way she had treated her mother during adolescence and further complicated because she had not dealt with an unhappy love affair prior to her mother's illness. An untrained bereavement volunteer did not assess Dorothy or try to put her loss into context. A thoughtless remark by the visitor about 'a time to go' triggered Dorothy's memory of herself in adolescence telling her mother that she wished her dead. The visitor could neither understand the resultant devastation nor deal with it. In this case, the nurse was at a loss as to how to 'pick up the pieces' or indeed if more specialist help was needed. Helping someone work through their more serious grief reactions requires preparation and skill, yet training is often minimal.

Dependency, seen in psychoanalytic terms to date from oral dependence in babyhood, may also occur, which can be a problem for both the bereaved individual and the visitor, since the family and social support which is so vital to adaptation, will be excluded in favour of the support offered by the bereavement visitor. This often occurs in the absence of a contractual arrangement where the function of visiting is clearly spelt out and times for review agreed between both parties.

Typically, all attention that surrounds death diminishes after the funeral, and the bereaved individual can begin to feel very alone. Friends and relatives may not know what to say (Buckman 1991) and so avoid the issue. A friendly and understanding bereavement visitor offers solace and support, so generating a dependence on the part of the bereaved individual which becomes increasingly important.

Visitors

The dependency of bereaved individuals is probably one of the greater risks faced by bereavement visitors. If attempts are made to withdraw the support, bereaved individuals face a new loss and may become afraid, angry and distressed to the point of engendering guilt and thus prolonging the association with the visitor. Society in general does not encourage bereaved people to express their grief. Worden (1992) suggests that of the four tasks of bereavement, first one has to accept the death and, secondly, one has to feel the pain. The latter requires that the bereaved individual is able to talk about his or her feelings and his or her reactions to the loss of a loved one, yet in Western society there is little encouragement from an individual's social circle to talk or express feelings, and those who put on a 'public' face and suppress their grief are rewarded and seen to be coping well. In such cases, bereavement visitors who offer support and counselling subsequently find themselves in the role of friend rather than professional. This carries inherent risks in terms of the cost to the carer of a number of very dependent 'friends' rather than clients from whom the professional can 'switch off' at the end of the working day.

A further risk for bereavement visitors who allow or unwittingly encourage dependency is that of transference. In psychoanalytic terms, when transference occurs, unconscious feelings and wishes originally directed towards an important individual are projected onto a therapist. This allows the therapist to 'work through' unresolved business with the patient, but in the bereavement situation it can result in the visitor becoming out of their depth as they are cast into the role of the dead person. An example of this was given by a nurse who had been supportive to a family before the death of the wife, aged 35. She recalls hugging the husband after the death, attending the funeral and starting bereavement visits, usually in the evening when the husband came home from work. Her moment of truth came one evening when the bereaved husband opened the front door and she saw behind him the candlelit table-for-two, bottle of wine, and heard the soft music. She admits to turning on her heel and running but feeling very guilty about it.

The concepts of dependency and transference are not generally taught to those involved in palliative care, since they are seen to be associated with psychiatric care. As a result, they may not easily be recognized by bereavement visitors who may feel that the phenomenon is due to some shortcoming in themselves, for example their inability to deal with it. The resultant risk of encouraging dependency and the possibility of transference is that the load on the visitor becomes out of proportion to other work that is done. This has implications not only for time management, but for the risk of burn out (Bernard 1989).

Co-ordinating services

Current attempts at co-ordinating services are made by voluntary associations. For example, the National Association of Bereavement Services (NABS) is a relatively new organization set up to co-ordinate the many unsupported bereavement services that exist throughout the country. This association, started in 1988, has become a charity. Its aims and objectives include compiling a national register of existing services and to provide fora, highlight gaps in provision, pressure for new services and undertake educational activities for counsellors, co-ordinators and professional workers. The association also undertakes to research and debate matters relating to bereavement, loss and terminal illness, and to disseminate their results. This national initiative is probably the first of its kind. Other attempts to standardize services have been made by organizations such as CRUSE, which started as an organization for bereaved widows but now undertakes training activities and concerns itself with all areas of bereavement. These and similar organizations depend on contributions from the public to maintain their services and are successful because of voluntary rather than statutory support.

What evidence is there that national concern over setting up effective bereavement services is necessary? Earnshaw-Smith and Yorkstone (1989) used a predictive questionnaire to assess the risk of poor outcome of 181 individuals after bereavement. Those respondents predicted to have poor outcome were assigned to two groups in a random fashion. One of the groups was given the support of the bereavement service at St. Christopher's Hospice in London, among whom the risk of abnormal reactions to grief was reduced. Among the second, unsupported group, however, a significant association was found between high risk and poor outcome.

Pottinger (1991) studied 40 relatives of cancer patients to discover their needs, both emotional and practical. The services meeting the emotional needs of the relatives were seen to be the most important. However, the results indicated that although the cancer unit staff seemed to be responding to those relatives who were distressed, this support did not alleviate the distress of those family members. The relatives who did not receive support but had desired it seemed highly anxious and distressed. Such findings remind us that setting up a service is only the beginning of effective bereavement work.

The general picture to date suggests that where bereavement care is given, it is still very much seen as being 'done to' rather than empowering individuals to make an informed choice about what they need, who they need it from and what they expect in terms of outcome.

Improving bereavement services

· The main problem in the bereavement services at present is the lack of agreement in the health service of what should be offered, by whom and for how long. This has resulted in a hotch-potch of services offered by committed and willing organizations but without clear guidelines to ensure that the services offered actually help the bereaved, and do not impose too great a burden on those who visit them.

Before bereavement services can be improved, it must be made clear what it is that bereaved individuals require from the service and what is needed by those who work with them. Too often in the past, 'needs' have been established without consultation with those for whom a service is created. Now, with district health authorities taking on the responsibility of assessing health needs, more emphasis will be placed on the skills of assessment (Faulkner 1992). The Working Group on Terminal Care (Wilkes 1980) paid little attention to the actual needs of bereaved individuals, beyond suggesting that 'advice and support should be given to the relatives of the terminally ill both before and after death' (Wilkes 1980: 467). It is argued here that if that advice and support is going to be appropriate, then we must assess the actual needs of every individual bereaved person; similarly with the recommendation that greater emphasis should be placed on the psychological aspects of dying and bereavement. The suggestion is that this element should be incorporated into basic nurse training courses, which should also include an introduction to counselling. In this area, knowledge is more certain, for there is considerable research to suggest that nurses lack the skills to communicate effectively with their patients (see, e.g. Faulkner 1980; Macleod Clark 1982). More recently, Faulkner and Maguire's work on the evaluation of skills before and after teaching has shown that little in the way of communication skills is brought to the teaching situation, but that both nurses and doctors can learn very quickly to improve their skills (Faulkner 1992).

Assessing the needs of bereaved individuals

Pottinger (1991), who not only studied bereaved individuals but also their adjustment to the imminent loss of their loved ones, found the demand for emotional support to be greater than that for practical informative instruction.

There is increasing interest in the concept of empowerment for those who need the help of health care professionals. In what way can those who are to be bereaved become empowered? Often their major concerns are simply that they do not have the power to make their loved one better, to reverse the situation, or to control what is happening in their family. This need for some control in a difficult situation, and for some way of dealing with the uncertainty, often goes unrecognized by health professionals who may unwittingly foster the idea of helplessness by trying to take over the care of the dying patient to relieve the pressure on the relative.

Kline-Bell (1992) describes empowerment as the ability to liberate an individual to deal with his or her own grief and which must involve giving some control back to both patient and family. This notion may cause difficulties for some health professionals, who may find that what is right for a particular individual may not match what they themselves feel to be right. It must be acknowledged that this is a problem faced by health professionals and not necessarily dying patients, and their families.

One could argue that there is little choice in dying, since it is almost impossible to predict or control the time of death except in suicide. In fact, there are a number of choices for those who are dying and those who care for them which should be made on the basis of realistic information rather than advice. These choices include where the patient will die, yet such decisions are often made by clinicians or managers without an assessment of the patient and family, and the possibility of meeting their stated needs. It is, for example, consistently shown that patients who are dying would prefer to die in their own home (Copperman 1983); yet more people die in hospitals and hospices than in their own homes.

Hospices are increasingly moving towards a policy of respite care rather than adhering to their original aim of providing a place where people can die with dignity. Further change is necessary in the matter of choice. Some hospices, for example, have a two-week rule, i.e. a patient must return home after a two-week stay no matter what the state of health or feelings of either the patient or family. This certainly mitigates against the notion of empowerment or individuality in palliative care. These and other rules can cause tremendous problems, particularly for those families where coping at home with a dying relative is extraordinarily difficult.

How the patient dies is also important, and certainly should involve choice; both choice as to where, if possible, and choice of who with. For these choices to be made and the family to feel empowered, then talking about death and potential death can no longer be treated as taboo. This is an area in which health professionals can help both patients and their families to come to terms with reality in a sensitive way. Unfortunately, health professionals, patients and family members are all often guilty of avoiding the matter. Dying patients are even reassured by doctors and loved ones that things will improve and have begun to plan their non-existent futures. If such collusion continues, then the grieving process will be much more difficult for family and friends. In their desire to protect their loved ones from the truth, relatives and friends may deny themselves the chance to say 'goodbye' and not observe the wishes of the person who has died.

Promoting openness within a family is not always easy. Close relatives often argue that they know the patient better than the health professional, and if the dying person was to be told the situation as it really was, they would give up there and then. In this situation, the health professional would find it difficult to disagree, but such collusion needs to be ended if at all possible. Such an approach frees relatives and will hopefully leave them trusting the professional to find out how the dying person feels, something that relatives find difficult to cope with. In effect, most collusion is a two-way process. Few dying patients truly deny that they are dying, but attempt to protect their loved ones (Maguire and Faulkner 1988b).

When such collusion is broken and the family members are able to talk to each other about the situation as it really is, then issues such as where the death will take place and who will know in advance can be discussed and each person is able to feel that he or she is actively involved. The outcome can be surprising. Recently, for example, a patient in a London hospice died as she wanted to die, sitting up in bed with a glass of pink champagne in one hand and a smoked salmon sandwich in the other, her cat lying at the bottom of the bed over her feet. Most health professionals would not find this a particulary dignified way of dying unless it was explained to them that this was what the patient wanted.

The process of dying can have a considerable impact on those who are left behind when trying to cope with their loss. Poor bereavement care can lead to unhappy memories and fuel the feelings of guilt which are so often an element of grieving. Improving the care of those who are dying should lead to the improved care of those who are bereaved, since many of the problems of bereavement are linked to the circumstances surrounding the final illness and death.

The needs of bereavement workers

If those who are dying and their families are to exert some control over the way death occurs, where it occurs and what part family members play, then health professionals who are involved with bereavement work will also have needs that must be met before they are able to offer the service that is required. These include knowledge of the psychological and physical aspects of death, dying and bereavement. It also requires a positive attitude to the care of those who are dying and the bereaved, which will enable empowerment of the key players. Finally, but just as important, the skill will be required to assess a situation, an individual and the problems inherent in any individual's fight to regain some sense of normality after a major loss.

Knowledge

Too often, bereavement visits commence before individuals are ready to discuss their loss, how they are coping and how they see their future. For the first few days following a bereavement, most people find that normal life is temporarily suspended; they describe themselves as having been 'in a dream' or 'on automatic pilot'. In this respect, the funeral is often an aid, as it is something that has to be concentrated on, with forms to be filled out, the undertaker to be mobilized, flowers to be ordered and relatives to be informed. There is a lot involved to help keep the bereaved person on a fairly even keel.

Real feelings of grief and loss normally start to come to the surface once the funeral is over and the bereaved individual is alone. Things are quiet and something, usually quite small, triggers the bereaved person to start feeling the pain (Worden 1992). It may be catching sight of a photograph of the person who has died or seeing a television programme that they used to watch together. Whatever the cause, the bereaved individual will describe starting to cry and feeling unable to stop, or feeling depths of misery and just not being able to tune in to other things.

There are no set time limits for the stages of grief, but it seems that within 6–8 weeks of a death, most people who are coping adequately with their loss are able to describe a positive change in their grieving, no matter how slight. Parkes and Weiss (1983) describe this as being able to face reminders of loss without being overcome by grief, pain or remorse. This emotional acceptance comes slowly but the bereaved individual is usually able to give examples: 'I can watch his favourite programme without crying now – at first I couldn't bear to have the TV on.' On the other hand, the risk of suicide by those who are unable to cope appears after about 3 months.

Knowledge of the normal range of grief reactions allows the bereavement visitor to assess the level of coping within normal limits at a time when the relative is able to talk. It is also necessary to be able to discriminate between those individuals who will be able to cope – with or without extra help – from those who will not. For this small minority, the visitor will need to know the signs of abnormal reactions to loss.

Attitudes

Attitudes towards bereavement work should be positively geared towards the expressed needs of the bereaved individual. This may seem obvious, but many bereavement workers visit their clients long after they should be moving towards Worden's (1992) third and fourth stages of grieving, i.e. accepting life goes on without their loved one and finally being open to new relationships. It can be very rewarding to feel needed and those who are bereaved, particularly those who live alone and do not have much social contact, may become very dependent on the visitor who is able to cheer them up. Nurses in particular find it difficult to disengage from such a situation. In workshops such as those described by Maguire and Faulkner (1988a), a problem commonly expressed is that nurses are asked to visit bereaved individuals without any idea of the purpose of the visit, the need or frequency of subsequent visits or how to ensure that the bereaved person does not become dependent on them.

Those involved in bereavement work need to recognize this risk and to take a very professional approach to their interactions with bereaved people. This means agreeing contracts with those who need more than one assessment visit and being prepared to mobilize family support where this is appropriate. Most of those who are bereaved manage their bereavement quite normally with help from family and their own social network. Those in most need are the few individuals who have little support and who are at risk of being unable to cope with their grief.

Skills

As bereavement work is a professional activity, professional skills are required so as to assess the bereaved person's ability to cope, to evaluate the outcome of support and to refer where necessary for more expert help. Bereavement workers need to learn the skills of assessing where an individual 'is at': these skills are often felt to be innate. Faulkner (1985) found that a majority of nurse educators believed that it was not possible to operate in society without effective skills of communication, and so these skills did not need to be taught. Such an argument suggests that talking to those who are dying and those who are bereaved is no more than a social exercise, where in fact it is argued here that professional communication is very different from social interaction, if only because the health professional has to raise subjects that are normally taboo (Faulkner 1988). In an on-going study to evaluate the assessment skills of health professionals before and after a skills-based workshop, Faulkner (1992) suggests that few of them exhibit the skills necessary to identify another individual's concerns before tuition.

A lay person may offer comfort to a bereaved friend or acquaintance but may not feel comfortable asking specific questions which help the bereaved person to explore their feelings, e.g. how they felt when they realized that death had occurred, how they felt at the funeral when they were saying goodbye for the last time, and how they felt afterwards when it finally dawned on them that their loved one would never return. Allowing an individual to express their feelings, to feel the pain and to start moving towards accepting life without their loved one is a very skilled process that has to be learned. It certainly should be part of every health professional's education, although at the moment this is not the case. There are, however, signs of change, in that communication as a subject is now an examinable part of the nursing curriculum. Evaluation is also important in terms of learning to set goals and measuring the effect of interventions such as counselling. Without these skills, bereavement work will remain a very 'hit and miss' activity.

The future

It is likely that we will see a more co-ordinated bereavement service in the future, probably due to the efforts of the voluntary sector, which will exert pressure to persuade government that bereavement care is part of an effective health service. Should this happen, all health professionals will need to be taught professional communications skills, and those who are directly involved in bereavement work will need to be very carefully selected, trained and monitored. Currently, those who take on bereavement work are not necessarily supervised and evaluated. However, this is essential in the future if the service is to be effective. The service should be properly monitored and evaluated by the professional bodies involved. Only then can we provide a properly funded, co-ordinated service to help those who are bereaved to cope better and to reduce the morbidity of those who have problems. Finally, there are financial implications: in an already over-stretched health service, it will take considerable vision for the policy makers to release money for a service that is currently reliant on the goodwill and commitment of volunteers.

In this chapter, much of which is based on experience of working with those involved in bereavement work, it has been shown that the level of care available to bereaved people falls far short of the ideal. A service needs to be developed within the NHS, albeit partly supported by voluntary activity, that is properly funded, properly co-ordinated and properly evaluated. This can only happen if considerably more work is undertaken to identify the real needs of dying patients and their close relatives and friends. If the ideal were to be achieved, no bereaved individual would struggle with unresolved grief without help at the appropriate level.

References

Addington-Hall, J., MacDonald, L.D., Anderson, H.R. and Freeling, P. (1991) Dying from cancer: the views of bereaved family and friends about the experience of terminally ill patients, *Palliative Medicine*, 5, 207–214.

Bernard, P. (1989) *Counselling Skills for Health Professionals*. London: Chapman and Hall.

Buckman, R. (1991) *I Don't Know What to Say: How to Support Someone Who is Dying*. London: Papermac.

Copperman, H. (1983) *Dying at Home*. Chichester: John Wiley.

Earnshaw-Smith, E. and Yorkstone, P. (1986) *Setting Up and Running a Bereavement Service*. Kent: Bishop and Sons.

Faulkner, A. (1980) Communication and the nurse, *Nursing Times*, 76, 21.

Faulkner, A. (1985) *Communication in Nurse Education: Survey of Schools of Nursing in England, Wales and N. Ireland and of Tutors in Colleges of Nursing in Scotland*. London: Health Education Council.

Faulkner, A. (1988) Effective communication, *Senior Nurse*, 8(3), 5–6.

Faulkner, A. (1992) The evaluation of training programmes for communication skills in palliative care, *Journal of Cancer Care*, 1(2), 75–78.

Kline-Bell, H. (1992) Healing grief for the planet by hope, love and empowerment. Paper given at the *ADEC Conference*, April, Boston, Mass.

Macleod Clark, J. (1982) Nurse–patient verbal interaction. Unpublished PhD thesis, University of London.

Maguire, P. and Faulkner A. (1988a) How to improve the counselling skills of doctors and nurses in cancer care, *British Medical Journal*, 297, 847–9.

Maguire, P. and Faulkner, A. (1988b) Communicating with cancer patients: Handling uncertainty, collusion and denial, *British Medical Journal*, 297, 972–4.

National Association of Health Authorities and Trusts (1991) *Care of People with Terminal Illness*. Report by a Joint Advisory Group. Birmingham: National Association of Health Authorities and Trusts.

Parkes, C.M. and Weiss, R.S. (1983) *Recovery from Bereavement*. New York: Basic Books.

Pottinger, A.M. (1991) Grieving relatives' perception of their needs and adjustment in a continuing care unit, *Palliative Medicine*, 5, 117–21.

Wilkes, E. (1980) *Report of the Working Group on Terminal Care*. London: Standing Medical Advisory Committee, DHSS.

Worden, J.W. (1992) *Grief Counselling and Grief Therapy*, 2nd edn. London: Routledge.

5

HIV/AIDS: Lessons for Policy and Practice

NEIL SMALL

By the mid-1980s, in the early epicentre of the AIDS epidemic, San Francisco's Castro District, it was hard to remember 'a time before the sickness'. HIV and AIDS had changed individuals and had changed the mores of the community. Leon McKusick, a San Franciscan psychotherapist, summed it up in this way: 'It's my hypothesis that the community has been going through the stages that individuals are said to go through when faced by a life threatening disease: denial, rage, bargaining and acceptance' (quoted in Fitzgerald 1987: 114).

This chapter considers how both individuals and their communities have responded to HIV and AIDS and specifically to those people dying from AIDS. I will argue that there are medical, epidemiological and social factors that construct responses to AIDS. All of these have impacted upon the specific needs of those dying and of those offering them care. While I would argue that the similarities outweigh the differences in the experience of dying and in the care of the dying as regards those people dying of AIDS and those with other terminal illnesses, the context of that death does exhibit important differences. These differences will be considered in this chapter. I will also consider the specifics of the response in the UK and will concentrate on three initiatives: London Lighthouse, the Mildmay Mission Hospital (also in London) and Milestone House in Edinburgh. My aim is to examine what those offering care to those dying from AIDS have learned from services oriented to other illnesses and what the AIDS experience can contribute to policy and practice in the overall care of dying people.

The context of AIDS

There is AIDS and there is the fear of AIDS. This, of course, AIDS shares with other illnesses. Consider:

> For most of the fortunate citizens of the United States, the pale rider of pestilence is now retired, and the cadaverous rider of hunger is too obese to maintain his seat. We must now face different riders, one in the shape of a mushroom cloud, and one in the shape of a crab.
>
> (*Shimkin 1980: 1*)

James Patterson argues that the USA has been suffering from cancerphobia which has had a 'tenacious grip' on the American popular imagination. It 'loomed as an alien, surreptitious, and voracious invader that seemed to attack anybody, anywhere, and to advance relentlessly until it killed its victims and impoverished their families' (Patterson 1987: 310). Patterson sees fear of one disease as being eclipsed only when another arrives to replace it. Perhaps it was to be AIDS that would shift the phobia from cancer, just as cancer had dislodged tuberculosis. Indeed, the rhetoric around AIDS talked up that fear – it would 'probably prove to be the plague of the millennium' (the claim of one researcher cited in Lieberson 1986). In 1985, the head of the World Health Organization (WHO) was able to say that, 'we stand nakedly in front of a very serious pandemic as mortal as any pandemic there ever has been' (*New York Times*, 23 December).

Indeed, by 1992, the pandemic was spreading and proving as mortal as feared; or at least on a worldwide scale it was proving as mortal as feared. Initial projections as to the rate of spread of HIV and the incidence of AIDS in Western industrialized countries had proved overly pessimistic. Also evident by 1992 was a developing sophistication in these countries in the treatment of the symptomatic infections that collectively constitute the syndrome of AIDS. There was the real possibility that a future for AIDS care would have to include conceptualizing some of those with the virus as exhibiting chronic illness. They would then require the panoply of care services that such situations necessitate. But in the rest of the world, the scenario was different. WHO reported that in the last nine months of 1991, one million people had contracted HIV worldwide and they were projecting rates of infection of between 5 and 10 million in India alone by the year 2000. Worldwide, WHO estimates between 12 and 15 million people will be HIV positive by the end of the century. Poverty appears to impact on both the rates of infection and its speed of progression. For example, an HIV

positive pregnant woman who lives in Africa or Asia has a one in two chance
of passing on HIV to her child; in the West, the figure is one in eight. Life-
expectancy after diagnosis is, in part, determined by poverty or its absence
(Drucker 1990).

Clinical care and its management

There are two important aspects to care that must be considered here. First,
the use of anti-viral drugs following the introduction of AZT after a short
period of clinical trials in the USA in 1987. In early 1992, such drugs – AZT
and those with a similar effect – represent the only licensed treatment
specifically directed at HIV. They are controversial. Summarizing the complex debates that surround them, we see the manufacturers claiming that
they delay the onset of AIDS and prolong life. Critics argue that the data on
which such claims are based are contaminated, that AZT has carcinogenic
side-effects, that the huge profits generated by AZT have prompted the
development of copycat drugs rather than the pursuit of other research
possibilities. Further critics argue that claims as to the benefits of AZT
for unsymptomatic but HIV positive people are unproved and that the
side-effects of the drug are such as to impact on the quality of life of
those taking it (John Lawrentson, quoted on Channel 4's *Dispatches*, 12
February 1992).

The second area of clinical advance is in the treatment of those opportunistic infections that are most commonly manifest in AIDS and that prove
to be the cause of death. Here there has been major progress in slowing the
progression of such infections and in ameliorating some of their effects.
Treatment for pneumocystis carinii (PCP), for example, means that less time
has to be spent having in-patient treatment. Treatment for pulmonary
Karposi's sarcoma (KS) means that there is a shift from a median survival
of 3 months to one of 8 months, with much longer periods for some people
(Sweeney *et al.* 1991).

In brief, we can project a medium-term future that sees AIDS in the West as
more of a chronic condition requiring some periods of in-patient care but mix-
ing these with times when care in the home and out-patient care dominate.
These periods of ill-health will be interspersed with periods of relative good
health. At present, this is the reality of living with AIDS for many people. In
the future, the length of time a person lives with AIDS will increase. This will
have implications for the sorts of care that will be required.

The changing pattern of AIDS

I will complete these introductory sections on the context of AIDS with
a note on its changing distribution. In the UK, the early history of AIDS

was dominated by its overwhelming impact on gay men. The numbers also reflected a dominance of cases in the London area. Figures published in January 1992 on cumulative totals of British reports of AIDS showed a total of 4197 cases in which it is probable that the virus was contracted via sexual intercourse between men, of whom 2650 had died. In addition, 83 men in such a category also reported injecting drugs, 53 of whom had died. There were also 290 haemophiliacs, 76 recipients of infected blood products, 49 children, 442 people infected via heterosexual sex (of which 48 had partners in other 'at-risk groups' and 344 of whom were exposed abroad) and 245 injecting drug users (176 men and 69 women, 141 of whom had died). Sixty nine cases were recorded as of undetermined origin. Of the 5451 cases in total, 3391 had died (Department of Health Press Release, 29 January 1992).

However, the likely future pattern of AIDS is different. The number of people reported as being HIV positive was 16 828 (14 746 men, 1952 women and 130 gender not stated). The government, however, estimates that there are approximately 30 000 people who are HIV positive (*World AIDS* 1991). Many of these people have been infected via injecting drug use. Estimates of people injecting drugs who are infected with HIV vary between 2 per cent in some regions to 70 per cent in Edinburgh (Terrence Higgins Trust Medical Briefing 1991). More injecting drug users will develop AIDS as will more women and more children. The geographic dispersal will be greater – London will still have a high incidence but pockets of infection will exist elsewhere (most notably, on current known distributions, in the Lothian region).

The context for looking at the care of people with AIDS is one of a developing world epidemic within which AIDS will be increasingly categorized as a disease of poverty. There is little scope for the use of anti-viral drugs or for the treatment of opportunistic infection in countries where per capita health expenditure is in single figures. However, in the West, and specifically in the UK, treatments are being developed, survival times are lengthening and living with AIDS as a chronic, but infectious condition is becoming a likely scenario for many people. The pattern of distribution will change, as will the characteristics of those with AIDS. It is likely though that in the medium term, the dominant characteristics of people with AIDS will include their relative youth and their having attributed to them a stigma – drug-user or male homosexual. It is also likely that many people with AIDS will die. It is to one area of the care of those dying that I now turn.

The hospice movement pre-AIDS

In 1969, there were 16 in-patient and one domiciliary nursing team specializing in the care of dying people. The growth of provision was largely inspired by the example of St Christopher's Hospice in Sydenham, London (Seale 1991). Hospice pioneers had two objectives: to provide a service neglected by others and to challenge the 'great taboo subject of our age', death, and so encourage dying people, their families and all those caring for them (for a full range of the hospice services available in the UK in 1992, see Table 1.2, p. 23).

Such an approach, in practice, meant that as well as offering care, the hospice movement possessed many of the characteristics of a missionary movement with charismatic leaders seeking to promote a strategy that would overturn the errors of the past and contribute to a different discourse on care and a different approach to death. Furthermore, there was an overt belief in the colonizing potential of the movement. Not only in pain relief, but in its emphasis on care rather than technical excellence, on the whole person rather than on the sick person and on the importance of incorporating the family and friends into the overall provision of care, would the hospice ideal spread (Young 1981).[1]

Consider Dame Cicely Saunders who, in establishing St Christopher's in 1967 outside the National Health Service (NHS), had the clear intention of moving back into the NHS the attitudes and knowledge that would be gained. Dame Cicely was concerned to reconcile the science of sophisticated treatment with the art of caring – 'competence alongside compassion' (Saunders *et al.* 1981: 4). The time was right in 1967 for the successful launch of the first hospice. There was a great deal of academic and popular concern with issues surrounding dying and with the visibility of a group of people for whom the advances of modern clinical treatment were no longer effective. However clever medicine was becoming, there were still the incurables and their presence seemed to prompt some to question the over-riding dominance of cure over care, of treatment over compassion. The time was also right because of the energy and commitment of a small group of founders and their tenacity in starting a building fund in 1964 and then opening in 1967. The expansion of services to care for dying people included a number of hospices outside the NHS, the growth of the longer-established charitable foundations like the Marie Curie and Sue Ryder Foundations, continuing care units established by the National Society for Cancer Relief and subsequently maintained by the NHS, the development of home care teams and the emergence of hospital support teams which would advise on the care of those dying in acute hospital wards. From the initial stone thrown into the pond, it was hoped ripples would spread to all areas of terminal care, that services would improve even for those not immediately within the orbit of the new specialists.

By 1980, the prevailing climate had changed once more. The NHS was experiencing a real cut in its resources and the pressures that resulted in terms of resource allocation coincided with a 'value for money' ethos that prompted a critical look at the level of resources available in hospice care.

The result was to prompt a concentration on developing integrated systems of care building on existing facilities (Wilkes 1980). New hospices, many argued, should not be the priority. It might be hard to finance and staff them. Perhaps a more cost-effective way that could still achieve high patient satisfaction would be to develop home care teams. Existing hospices would benefit from the scrutiny of detailed research. In short, a continuing drive towards expansion might be at the cost of not being able to maintain the standards so far achieved.

Hospices have developed expertise in pain control and in establishing regimes that both patients and relatives found satisfying when contrasted with hospital wards. They have systems of staff support and a strong sense of mission. However, they excited some jealousy (for their level of resource perhaps) from other professionals and a sense in the public view of being equated with hopelessness (Hillier 1983). They had concentrated very largely on cancer and by the mid-1980s were being criticized for a failure to respond to, for example, long-term neurological disease or chronic diseases such as renal failure, lung or cardiac conditions. Seale (1991) argues that the development of services should properly be termed terminal cancer care services as opposed to care for the dying as a whole.

As well as a wish that services diversify and as well as the concerns over costs and over the need for more research, two further pressures were evident as the hospice movement entered the 1980s. First, a changing demography, specifically an ageing of the population, meant that many who die live alone at the time of their final illness (i.e. the hospice concern with the involvement of spouses may not be so relevant). For many of these people, pain may not be as acute but is likely to be longer lasting and require different regimes of response. Secondly, a movement whose rationale was innovation and whose moving force was the energy of its pioneers ran the risk of becoming ossified. The innovator may have become the establishment (James 1986; Paradis and Cummings 1986).

> Early on it was clear who the villains and the heroes were, where the challenges lay, what were the pitfalls to be avoided. There was the good work and it was easy to devote one's life . . . I think now we have passed that stage and ahead lie many diverse paths, many confusions of a subtler nature.
>
> (*Torrens 1981:194*)

The arrival of AIDS

Early in 1986, a group of men and women, all either diagnosed with HIV, ARC or AIDS or close to people who were, met to discuss the need for additional voluntary service provision in London. It was a meeting that was eventually to lead to the official opening of London Lighthouse on 23

November 1988, based in a £4.85 million purpose-designed building near Ladbrook Grove. London Lighthouse was to be a major residential and support centre for the growing number of people with HIV, ARC and AIDS and those seeking to offer them care and support.

The first hospice or continuing care unit for people with AIDS in Europe had opened in February 1988 in a refurbished third-floor ward in Mildmay Mission Hospital in East London. Mildmay had been operating since 1866, when it began to offer a service to counter a cholera epidemic. It moved to its present site in 1892 and has offered medical, social and spiritual care to those from its neighbourhood since then.

In December, 1988, representatives from a group of statutory and voluntary organizations met and established the Waverley Trust whose stated purpose was to 'promote the welfare of, care for, aid and assist persons residing in Lothian Region with HIV-related illness and their relatives and dependents'. Two years later, in February 1991, Milestone House, the UK's first purpose-built hospice for people with AIDS/HIV took in its first resident. Milestone House is sited in the woodland grounds of Edinburgh's City Hospital.

These three facilities, all contributing to the continuing development of services for those people with HIV and AIDS and their carers, all draw on the accumulated experience of the hospice movement but also modify and add to established practice. They each have different origins, the first with a self-help ethos, the second the expansion of a spiritually inspired mission into a new area and the third from a realization among service providers that a new initiative was needed.

All exist outside the NHS but get substantial funds from the public sector. Milestone House estimates its annual running costs at £1 million. It receives £350,000 from both Lothian Regional Council and Lothian Health Board. That leaves just short of £1000 per day to be raised elsewhere. London Lighthouse began with 'a good idea and £700 in the bank'. They began energetically fund-raising and received help from the J. Paul Getty Charitable Trust, a £700,000 two-year interest-free loan and a gift of £50,000, a gift matched by another charity. The 22 months from the resulting purchase of a property to its opening saw £4.85 million being raised, half from central and local government and half from a combination of charitable, corporate and individual fund-raising. Mildmay has a long history, but in recent years has suffered from precarious finances. Indeed, in 1982, the hospital was closed. After vigorous protests it was reopened in May 1984 as an independent charitable hospital that has to be financially viable.[2]

When the Lighthouse initiative was taking shape, there was a concentration of people with AIDS in London. By the end of 1986, 77.5 per cent of the total number of people diagnosed were either living, or had been treated, in one of the four London regional health authorities, with one of these – North West Thames – having 64 per cent (Spence 1989: 179). Hospitals in the London regions were reporting problems in that there were only acute care beds available for an increasingly large group of patients who needed nursing care but of a different sort to that on offer. At the same time, the early British pioneers of the Terrence Higgins Trust and Body Positive were pointing to the need to expand information, counselling and support services – for which demands were considerable. These pushes from service providers were occurring at the same time as a pull from patients and their immediate carers. The sorts of experience that had spurred the St Christopher's pioneers was occurring again, or occurring still among different communities. St Christopher's had responded to Glaser and Strauss (1965) with their observations about terminally ill cancer patients being relegated to side rooms on a hospital ward, alone and denied both awareness and support. Now there were many accounts that sounded similar: 'After a day or so people began wearing gloves, masks and gowns and these full body-suits, and there was a nurse stationed outside my room at all times' (Mordaunt 1989: 84–5). Indeed, the Terrence Higgins Trust was set up as a voluntary organization to provide support, counselling and information for those concerned with AIDS and HIV infection following the death of Terrence Higgins, one of the first people in the UK to die from AIDS. Body Positive is a national campaigning and support group for people who have had a positive HIV antibody test and also draws on direct experience of the strengths and weaknesses in systems of care.

Staff at Mildmay emphasize the problems people encountered in acute hospitals and the problems of trying to care for someone in their own home. Two examples illustrate:

> One is of a young man terrorised by the fear of persecution in his flat and by the fear of rejection should he leave it. The second is of a man discharged from his acute bed to the care of his parents. While there out patient symptom control was good but his parents, who could not accept their son's homosexuality, would not allow his partner to visit.
>
> (Sims and Moss 1991: 2–3)

Lothian, which embraces Edinburgh, has the highest prevalence of known HIV in the UK. Estimates are that 1 in 100 men and 1 in 250 women aged between 15 and 45 are HIV positive. Nineteen per cent of known HIV positive women in the UK live in Edinburgh. Eighty children have been born to HIV positive mothers. Forty per cent of the UK's HIV positive children live in this area. By June 1991, there had been 122 cases of AIDS in the Edinburgh catchment area; 52 had died with an average life expectancy after a diagnosis of AIDS of two years. In comparison with much of the rest of the UK, Lothian had a high proportion of people who contracted HIV from sharing needles. One response to this regional scenario was that of the voluntary body Scottish AIDS Monitor, which drew up the original proposals for a residential unit which it believed was much needed and which became Milestone House.

Developing practice in the USA

Each of the three ventures introduced above could look to the established hospice movement for guidance. They also had the experience, specifically in relation to AIDS, that had been developed in the USA. Mildmay acknowledges utilizing the experience of Edinburgh City Hospital as they began to see both drug users and children requiring terminal care. In turn, Edinburgh had looked to the USA (Sims and Moss 1991: ch. 10).

The history of the hospice movement in the USA had emphasized its contribution as being an oppositional one, posing community over professional dominance and the expertise of nursing over doctors' authority (Abel 1986; Mor 1987). Some initiatives had been directly modelled on Elizabeth Kubler-Ross's (1969) work, for example the Shanti Project in California which was established in 1975 and which early in the AIDS epidemic in San Francisco provided, in its weekly support group meeting, 'about the only services available to those stricken with the terrifying novel diseases' (Shilts 1987: 123).

In 1982, the Shanti Project was given a grant by San Francisco's Board of Supervisors to finance grief counselling and personal support for people with AIDS. The following year Shanti was allocated funds to provide a service to homeless people with AIDS and to fund support staff for a rapidly developing network of volunteers. By 1984, some commentators were reporting the creation of a Shanti-led culture of sanctification surrounding death. AIDS funerals were becoming social events, videotapes made by the deceased some time before death were played, nobody seemed to just die – they 'passed over' after having spent their last days doing 'white light meditations' with their Shanti Project volunteer (see Shilts 1987: 427, 515). Indeed, Kubler-Ross (1987), in writing specifically about AIDS while not ignoring the pain of dying or the loss and grief of the bereaved, speaks of death as a step in a journey: 'you are going where others have been, I have seen them go, it is good'.

But Kubler-Ross also acknowledges the hostility to people with AIDS in a detailed account of her difficulties in establishing a hospice for children. That hostility was very widespread. Sometimes it manifest itself in outright attack, sometimes in a determination to ignore the epidemic. For example, the New York-based organization Gay Men's Health Crisis was pioneering education and support both for people with AIDS and their carers and for doctors and nurses encountering AIDS in their work. By 1983, they were training 50 new volunteers every month, they ran 20 training sessions a month for clinicians and nurses and had enlisted 300 clinical volunteers. But they got no help from the city when seeking more adequate premises, or help to set up hospices, alternative care facilities or clinics (Shilts 1987: 380).

The US experience, therefore, showed two things. First, that the greatest resource in the response to HIV and AIDS would be people, and particularly those people who were, or felt, touched by the epidemic. Secondly, that some lessons could be learned from the past but that many new things had to be devised to meet the specifics of this epidemic.

The British initiative

The London Lighthouse in particular represents an attempt to build on the tradition of the hospice movement in it aims to achieve a continuum of care and to emphasize adding to quality of life as opposed to 'just' managing death. In these areas it echoes hospices of the past. It also does so in appearing to be part of a developing social movement, not only in offering a paradigm for care but in making a statement about acceptance and a need to combat denial and prejudice. Where it demonstrates initiative is in its integrated model of care and its ability to adapt hospices for a new client group. It also appears to have been able to challenge the failing of some palliative care, which appears as a sort of adjunct to medically constructed hospital regimes.

An integrated model of care means a variety of different services offered from the same organization. The Lighthouse has a residential unit of 23 beds. Within this it offers palliative care, which totals about 5 per cent of the people who use the unit; respite care, which can become palliative if there is a sudden deterioration (a not uncommon feature of the syndrome); and, thirdly, convalescence. Pressure of demand means that there can be a short wait before admission for some people, usually between one and two weeks. Day care has places for ten people per day, some of whom will have neurological or psychological difficulties. Neighbourhood teams offer care in their own homes for 100 people. There is a drop-in advice and support service, a counselling service, an educational unit, a very nice place to have lunch and countless visitors from all over the world. The integrated model of care also means that conventional medical care is available as well as a range of complementary therapies. It means that considerable emphasis is given to psychological and emotional care and that the involvement of families, partners and friends is supported and encouraged. It also means that the Lighthouse has its own mortuary, viewing room and facilities for ceremonies after death.

Five hundred people work at the Lighthouse, of which 160 are paid workers. In any week between 1500 and 2000 people use the building in one way or another. Three features of the building itself must be noted. First, it is in a central London neighbourhood that was initially hostile and then won over when it finally accepted and actively supported this establishment in its midst. Secondly, its architecture is of a sort that emphasizes welcome (the front portico is meant to replicate arms reaching out) and integrates the residential unit into the life of the whole centre by a system of aerial walkways via which residents can see what goes on below and so choose to determine the extent to which they will involve themselves in the social milieu they are presented with. The third aspect of the building is its comfort and its taste. This reflects a commitment by central and local government and the NHS who together fund 75 per cent of the revenue budget of £4 million a year. But it especially reflects the fund-raising and voluntary contributions of its many supporters. The grand piano in the Ian McKellan room and, when I was there, the backdrop of Elton John music, are only the most visible signs of this welcome largesse.

Mildmay's residential unit was opened in February 1988 and by March 1991 had given care to 461 people with AIDS. This represented 10.4 per cent of the total number diagnosed as having AIDS in the UK.[3] Like the Lighthouse, some in the unit will require palliative care with its emphasis on symptom control, relief of pain and facilitating the comfort of the patient to enable an improved quality of life. Some patients will be unable to manage at home and can be admitted for long-stay terminal care for a possible period of 6–9 months. This service is provided in such a way that at any one time the number of long-stay patients on the unit is always less than one-third of the total number. Some will move at regular intervals between home and their care centre and so will require a service that can keep in touch with them and respond to their changing needs. Other patients (Mildmay uses this term, one they describe as everybody involved being most comfortable with) are admitted for respite care from the community for a maximum of four weeks to provide a break for themselves and their carers. Others come from acute hospital units for a maximum of four weeks of rehabilitative care.

Milestone House had 74 people staying in its first six months, 33 of whom were there more than once. The average length of stay was 10 days, with the longest 35 and the shortest one day. Fourteen of the 74 patients died; seven in Milestone House, three at home and four in hospital. Like the others, Milestone House offers convalescence, respite and terminal care, as well as care for their residents and their carers when they are outside the hospice. Respite care is for up to two weeks and convalescence for four weeks. Terminal care, because of the nature of the conditions associated with AIDS, can be for longer than in many hospices, where cancer predominates. Although Milestone House does not profess a facility for acute care, there is a recognition of the complexity of problems associated with AIDS and those present in its terminal stages. The multi-faceted treatment now being offered as acute care might, in drug treatment regimes for example, need to be continued within the hospice (for example, to counteract cardiac problems or developing blindness). In this environment, there is also a recognition of the contribution of complementary therapies. One example cited in Milestone House's introductory leaflet concerns the control of the chronic diarrhoea that is so often associated with AIDS with a homeopathic intervention (candida nosode).

Philosophies and frustrations

The hospice movement has always carried with it a determining philosophy through which the activities of caring for terminally ill people assumed a significance wider than its immediate impact. 'Hospice is a philosophy, not a facility. It is an approach to the giving of care, rather than a place in which services are offered' (Corr and Corr 1983: xi). Many writers emphasize that hospice care is not just about cancer, nor is it just about care of dying people. If it concentrated on these areas this is not untypical of any new movement in care-giving that emphasizes a particular subset of the overall population in its early days. In essence, what characterizes hospice care is its programme to maximize present quality of living.

Three other things enter the frame: first, a religious imperative (Mildmay's logo reads 'He sent them to preach and to heal the sick'); secondly, a concern to put right the bad practices of the present and the past, a reformist imperative; thirdly, a social change imperative to be achieved by presenting the hospice as a paradigm for a new way to relate to the individual in need.

In the London Lighthouse, there is a continuation of this emphasis on philosophy not just facility. The Lighthouse sees itself as offering a place of safety and a challenge to attitudes and service provision. The very image of 'Lighthouse', accentuated by the graphics it utilizes, seems to imply illuminating the darkness around. But this wish to illuminate is not a simple wish to replicate the model of care that has been developed at the Lighthouse. The Lighthouse is seen as a specialist facility that will develop a considerable expertise. In some places, such an approach offers the best response for people with AIDS, but in others the pattern of need and of service availability should encourage a different form of care. The dissemination of the continuum of care as a method and a commitment to acceptance as a guiding principle remains central within any organizational framework.

One feels at the Lighthouse a pressure from outsiders to cast the facility as ideal. The consequent dangers are three-fold. First, it will be easy to say 'we can never achieve what has been achieved here' and so take refuge in the quiescence such idealizations engender. Secondly, it ignores the way the Lighthouse model grew organically (albeit quickly) as new needs and new resources were identified. It is a mistake to reproduce mechanistically what has emerged in this way in other places, where the same conditions are not evident. Thirdly, it undervalues the achievements of others in the variety of settings throughout the country in which good practice and commitment are evident, sometimes despite the institutional and attitudinal framework in which the individual has to practise.

The dangers of idealization appear to be vigorously contested at the Lighthouse. The stream of visitors which passes through are invited to consider their own practice, scrutinize their own organizations and do something original. Visitors are not given a template. This is true of overseas visitors also. There has been a decision to enter into partnership with one other facility in each continent – the Sao Paulo connection seems most advanced, there are contacts in India, and so on. Mildmay also lists requests for consultancies from eleven countries and has been advising staff from a ten-bed specialist AIDS unit in Poland. All the UK's AIDS hospices are involved in research, clinical teaching and in wider educational programmes. This they share with the original hospices.

There is a second sort of idealization that must be considered. This is an idealization of dying or 'the dying'. Consider the harshest critic of Mother Teresa's home for dying people at Kalighat in Calcutta;

> Mother Theresa's policy is not one of intervention. God decides who lives and who dies. People are better off in heaven than in the operating theatre. Thus, instead of using her influence and income to finance a properly equipped hospital, Mother Theresa and her Sisters of Charity continue to give aspirin to patients with cancer, linctus to those with T.B., and glucose drips with old needles rinsed in cold water to those in comas. And everybody, regardless of creed, gets a good Catholic funeral.
>
> (*Loudon 1992: 7*)

Further, hospices can be weighed down by a sense of challenging a social construct that says in contemporary Western culture that death is something sanitized and denied. 'In our achievement orientated Western countries death is curiously equated with failure' (Yalom 1978). It is too much to ask hospices, busy enough with doing what they do, to also do what the rest of us will not do.

The practice in Mildmay will provide an example of how far this, and the other AIDS hospices I have discussed, are from the criticism of a lack of effective intervention. The skills used in pain relief are pronounced and are patient-centred. There is an avoidance of defining what is acceptable pain for a patient – they are given appropriate autonomy in this area. But at times it is necessary to give treatments not normally given in a terminal care setting.[4] The expertise that is developed and made available both in the hospice and via community services is considerable. As to combatting a sense of 'mission' to hold societies responsible for reconsidering death, Douglas Crimp (1987: 6–7) sums up the dominant approach: 'We don't need to transcend the epidemic; we need to end it'.

If this weight of social expectations is one frustration for hospices, a second is the strain placed on staff. This has two possible results. There might occur a routinization of work, such that actions were carried out, targets met and so on but without a sense of the real engagement that in many ways is what separates the hospice from some of the places it stands critical of. Secondly, there might be a high turnover of staff and a consequent breakdown of continuity and of accumulating expertise.

In terms of their involvement with AIDS, all three of the hospices I have considered are new and very much in a phase of initiative and expansion. Mildmay's expansion into offering a specialist continuing care unit for mothers with their babies and young children is just one example. All recognize the enthusiasm of staff but also the demands made upon them. Those demands centre on a sense of grief that might be more pronounced because many of those dying are relatively young. The demands also cross occupational boundaries. Milestone House emphasizes flexibility and approachability:

> It does not matter whether a resident tells her troubles to the dietitian weighing her, the porter shifting her furniture, the nurse settling her for sleep, the night steward at four o'clock in the morning or the social worker over lunch. All will listen sympathetically.
>
> (*Milestone House Brochure, n.d.: 7*)

The Lighthouse has a system of support groups for staff and a very low rate of staff turnover.

The hospice setting has features acting in favour of the morale of staff, certainly when contrasted with acute care hospitals:

> The lack of a biomedical response to AIDS offers nursing the opportunity . . . to prove what nursing is worth and to demonstrate that although the eventual outcome cannot be changed, the path to the outcome can be made less rigorous and more tolerable through nursing's interventions.
>
> (*Wells, in the foreword to Pratt 1989*)

It could be argued further that the very thing which can lead to strain and grief, the death of people one has got to know quite well, encompasses that which can sustain the worker. Many of the frustrations for carers come from a lack of contact with patients and a lack of continuity of care with a resulting objectification of the person and a sense of pointless repetition in the work that one does. Such circumstances do not seem to apply in these hospices. (See Chapter 1, this volume, for a discussion of related issues.)

The future

The AIDS hospices that are currently in existence may move from a preoccupation with innovation to one of consolidation. They face two challenges determined by that changing picture of AIDS described in my introduction and one challenge in the short- to medium-term arising out of new ways of organizing and funding health and community care.

The absolute increase in numbers and the increase in average time from diagnosis to death will require a development of services that is both quantitative and qualitative. There will be a push and pull effect to encourage less hospital care. The push will be from clinicians and managers who see care on an acute ward for those who need palliative, terminal, respite or rehabilitative care as both inappropriate and wasteful of resources. The pull will be from people with AIDS and their carers who want to live at home as long as is possible. These changes will require the development of services specifically for people with AIDS but also the integration of people with AIDS into existing service provision in hospices and via care in the community. The task for the future must be to ensure that this integration does not occur at the cost of losing the initiatives and insights developed in the specialist services.

There will be a more widespread distribution of AIDS throughout the country and an increasingly diversified population in need of services. The overwhelming dominance of London and the preponderance of gay men will be less evident as time goes by. Palliative care will have to address the needs of women and of children. It will have to accommodate heterosexuals and people who contract HIV via injecting drug use. The Lighthouse is making every effort to encourage use by a variety of people, to make the environment welcoming. The same is true of Mildmay and Milestone House. The need will be to create some harmony out of the diversities of culture and of need that will be apparent.

It is likely that some harmony will arise from the shared experience of illness and death. Indeed, such experiences can transcend a preoccupation with categories like age, sexuality and social class. But social categories do influence forms of cultural practice and do help define the nature of social need. Two studies of HIV positive people provide an illustration. Dixon (1990), writing about Dundee, found that of those who were HIV positive, 80 per cent were in the age range 20–29 years, 35 per cent were women and 90 per cent had been infected via injecting drug use. Their main needs were basic – money, beds and blankets were top of the list. In contrast, a study of HIV positive people at a London hospital (McCann 1990b) found a group of gay men with a higher age profile and with a significantly higher average social class status. They also had financial problems – ill health and financial strain seem inexorably linked. But they had good access to statutory and voluntary sector organizations and the financial problems were not of the order of those found in Dundee.

Culturally, London Lighthouse and Milestone House have been aware of the strains that can be created between a group of gay men and their carers and the forms of cultural and personal expression dominant in the group of those infected via injecting drug use. As yet, there has been an imbalance in favour of the former group. But, as we have seen above, that might well change and the style and nature of hospice regimes may have to respond accordingly.

Changes in the organization of the NHS presented in the White Paper *Working for Patients* (Department of Health 1989a) are likely to have an impact upon the development of specialist hospices that exist outside the NHS but are in part supported by funds from it (see Chapter 10, this volume). Further, the new proposals for care in the community summarized in the White Paper *Caring for People: Community Care in the Next Decade and Beyond* (Department of Health 1989b) will also impact on the continuum of care that is necessary for people living with AIDS.

Working for Patients encouraged a split betwen purchasers and providers of health care. This provides an opportunity and a potential problem for non-statutory facilities. The opportunity is for them to 'sell' a high-quality but cost-competitive service to the purchasing authorities without being disadvantaged by their structural position outside the NHS. The potential problem is that some purchasing authorities might decide not to pay even if the hospice wished to offer a service. New arrangements for the funding and overseeing of community care are likely to have repercussions on those areas of counselling support and domiciliary care currently offered by AIDS hospices. This will be a time of challenge and of opportunity in which there does seem to be some chance for the continued development of responsive services. But there is also a concern that there might be a prevailing austerity which will act to the detriment of the voluntary and independent sector of care providers seeking to anticipate need.

Underpinning the future of policy and practice for people with AIDS is a determining construct of stigma and marginalization. This acts as a formidable barrier. It is a barrier making more difficult the acceptance into existing service provision of people living with AIDS. It is a barrier that will slow down the diffusion of lessons learned in the specialist hospices into general service provision: the advantages of a continuum of care policy; the development of liaison between the voluntary and statutory services; the importance of self-help and of advocacy, and so on. The future care of people with AIDS will require a shift from services developed in response to a crisis to those more fitting for a siege (Munk quoted in McCann 1990a: 423). This will be achieved if the struggle can be against the virus and not also against the denial and hostility of others.

Acknowledgement

I would like to thank Christopher Spence, Director of London Lighthouse, for his generosity both of his time and of material written about the Lighthouse.

Notes

1 For a critique of the changing form of the hospice and the relationship between bureaucracy and charisma, see James and Field (1992).
2 The changing legislative context for health and social care in the UK will involve hospices in a market-oriented structure in which individual hospices will have to negotiate specific service agreements with health authorities (see Department of Health 1989a, b).
3 Figures for admissions: February 1988–March 1989, 56; April 1989–March 1990, 154; April 1990–March 1991, 251 (from *Mildmay's Business Prospectus*, n.d.). If readmissions are included, the figures become 67, 193 and 314, respectively.
4 For example, injections to prevent the progression to blindness in patients with cytomegalovirus retinitis, treatments involving nebularized Pentamidine as a prophylaxis against *Pneumocystis carinii* and Total Parenteral Nutrition to patients with cryptosporidial diarrhoea or obstructive Kaposi's sarcoma (Sims and Moss 1991: 11).

References

Abel, J.M. (1986) The hospice movement: institutionalising innovation, *International Journal of Health Services*, 16, 71–85.
Corr, C.A. and Corr, D.M. (eds) (1983) *Hospice Care: Principles and Practice*. London: Faber and Faber.
Crimp, D. (1987) AIDS: Cultural analysis/cultural activism, *October*, No. 43, Winter.
Department of Health (1989a) *Working for Patients*. Cmd 555. London: HMSO.
Department of Health (1989b) *Caring for People*: *Community Care in the Next Decade and Beyond*. Cmd 849. London: HMSO.
Dixon, P. (1990) Changing patterns in AIDS home care. Paper presented at the conference on *AIDS; The Challenge for the Community*, 18–20 April, St Davids Hall, Cardiff. Royal College of Nursing/British Medical Association.
Drucker, E. (1990) Epidemic in the war zone: AIDS and community survival in New York City, *International Journal of Health Services*, 20, 601–615.
Fitzgerald, F (1987) *Cities on a Hill*. London: Picador.
Glaser, B.G. and Strauss, A.L. (1965) *Awareness of Dying*. Chicago, Ill: Aldine.
Hillier, E.R. (1983) Terminal care in the United Kindom. In C.A. Corr and D.M. Corr (eds) *Hospice Care: Principles and Practice*. London: Faber and Faber.
James, N. and Field, D. (1992) The routinization of hospice: bureaucracy and charisma, *Social Science and Medicine*, 34(12), 1363–75.
James, V. (1986) Care and work in nursing the dying: a participant study of a continuing care unit. PhD thesis, University of Aberdeen.
Kubler-Ross, E. (1969) *On Death and Dying*. New York: Macmillan.
Kubler-Ross, E. (1987) *AIDS: The Ultimate Challenge*. London: Collier Macmillan.
Lieberson, J. (1986) The reality of AIDS, *New York Review of Books*, 32, 43–8.
Loudon, M. (1992) Heaven can wait. *The Observer*, 3 May.

McCann, K. (1990a) Care in the community and by the community, *AIDS Care*, 2(4), 421–4.

McCann, K. (1990b) *The Role of Informal Carers and Volunteers in Providing Community Care for Gay Men Who are HIV Positive*. London: Institute for Social Studies in Medical Care.

Mildmay Business Prospectus (n.d.) Mildmay Mission Hospital, Hackney Road, London E2 7NA.

Milestone House Brochure (n.d.) 113 Oxgangs Road North, Edinburgh EH14 1EB.

Mor, V. (1987) *Hospice Care Systems: Structure, Process, Costs and Outcome*. New York: Springer.

Mordaunt, J. (1989) *Facing up to AIDS*. Dublin: The O'Brien Press.

Paradis, L.F. and Cummings, S.B. (1986) The evolution of hospices in America: towards organisational homogeneity, *Journal of Health and Social Behaviour*, 27, 370–86.

Patterson, J.T. (1987) *The Dread Disease: Cancer and Modern American Culture*. London: Harvard University Press.

Pratt, R. (1989) *AIDS: A Strategy for Nursing Care*, 2nd edn. London: Edward Arnold.

Saunders, Dame C., Summers, D.H. and Teller, N. (eds) (1981) *Hospice – The Living Idea*. London: Edward Arnold.

Seale, C. (1991) Caring for people who die. Paper presented at the *British Sociological Association Conference on Health and Society*, March, University of Manchester.

Shilts, R. (1987) *And the Band Played On*. Harmondsworth: Penguin.

Shimkin, M. (1980) *Science and Cancer*. Washington.

Sims, R. and Moss, V. (1991) *Terminal Care for People with AIDS*. London: Edward Arnold.

Spence, C. (1989) Responding to a metropolitan health crisis, *Community Development Journal*, 24(3), 177–84.

Sweeney, J., Peters, B.S. and Main, J. (1991) Clinical care and management, *AIDS Care*, 3(4), 457–60.

Torrens, P. (1981) Achievement, failure and the future: hospice analyzed. In Dame C. Saunders, D.H. Summers and N. Teller (eds) *Hospice: The Living Idea*. London: Edward Arnold.

Wilkes, E. (1980) *The Report of the Working Group on Terminal Care of the Standing Committee on Cancer*. London: HMSO.

World AIDS (1991) No. 17, September. London: Panos.

Yalom, I. (1978) *Existential Psychotherapy*. New York: Basic Books.

Young, Sir G. (1981) Hospice and health care. In Dame C. Saunders, D.H. Summers and N. Teller (eds) *Hospice: The Living Idea*. London: Edward Arnold.

6

Cultural Issues in Terminal Care

SHIRLEY FIRTH

In the UK, medical and social work professionals are likely to encounter people from a wide range of ethnic, religious and cultural backgrounds. An understanding of their beliefs about health and illness, life and death, can improve care-giving, by providing information about specific needs and problems. It will also help in the provision of an appropriate service (Taylor 1990). This is particularly important with reference to terminally ill patients with strong religious traditions, because it will influence the way they respond to treatment and the way they die. By increasing sensitivity and awareness, it can be seen that the patients and their families are not just 'problems' or stereotypes. They are unique individuals, often with an important contribution to make in understanding the value of established social and religious traditions at the time of death and bereavement.

The principal focus in this chapter will be on Hindu, Sikh and Muslim approaches to death and bereavement, exploring some of the issues which confront Asian patients, their families and medical staff. After looking at some problems of understanding and communication, Hindu, Sikh and Muslim approaches to death and mourning will be explored, along with issues of change which confront them in the UK.

Understanding and communication

For Hindus, Muslims and Sikhs, religion plays a very large part in beliefs and practices around death. While there is a common core of beliefs in each religious community, it is important to recognize that there is also an immense variety of languages, regional traditions, sects, social classes and education. Many South Asians are British-born and very Anglicized, whereas others live in tightly knit groups maintaining a 'village' atmosphere and speaking little English. Some have come directly from the subcontinent; many others from East Africa as a result of the Africanization policies after independence. All these factors will impinge on the ways they approach their own health and the health services. They are also likely to have an important bearing on the definable 'health needs' of these groups (Donaldson and Parsons 1990; Taylor 1990).

Despite their very different traditions, South Asians share some common presuppositions about the nature of family life, marriage and the wider community. On the subcontinent, they tend to live in extended families in which adult family members play a significant role, so that the loss of a 'cousin-brother' may be as distressing as that of a sibling. The elderly are usually cared for in this context. With a lower life-expectancy, death may be a familiar occurrence. Children are not usually kept away from dying people or excluded from the domestic part of the funeral and mourning procedures.

In the UK, this ideal of caring for elderly people in the extended family may not be realized in practice. Donaldson and Johnson (1990) indicate that elderly people face the additional problems of age, racial discrimination, not having access to services and not speaking English. They may be brought to the UK by their sons when they can afford it, but house size rarely makes it possible to live as a full extended family. Social mobility may mean that relatives may not live near each other, or even their own communities. If both partners work, elderly people may feel isolated, bored and lonely instead of feeling they have a valuable role to play in the family and community. If the parent requires care, the daughter-in-law may remain at home to cope with this alone; in other cases, the social services may be expected to help, or, if finances permit, the parent may be sent to a private nursing home where no-one speaks their language.

Recent immigrants unfamiliar with British medical care or the social and legal system may have problems at times of illness and death because of a lack of understanding of procedures, problems of communication and difficulties in obtaining religious and social support from their own communities. If medical and social work professionals display ignorance and lack of sensitivity or understanding regarding their personal history, religious beliefs and cultural traditions, or demonstrate either overt or unconscious racist attitudes, these can increase the anxiety and fear accompanying illness and hospitalization. Professionals who are unfamiliar with the patients' backgrounds and have little time to find out about their religious or social needs may also have problems with different attitudes to women, to modesty, to food and to religious practices. Different family patterns, particularly the role of the extended family, are often seen as 'disruptive' and 'noisy' on wards.

Good communication, as we have seen elsewhere in this volume, is essential to assess patients' needs and to make a correct diagnosis. It is also important for the patient, as Rees (1990: 306) points out: 'Next to pain, poor communication is the most important source of distress to the dying patient. Poor communication is often the result of haste, of being focused on the next patient or visit instead of the present problem.' Communication problems are not only due to the fact that doctor or nurse and patient and family speak different languages. Even if the patient and family members are articulate in English, there may be different forms of non-verbal communication or of using English. There may be different role expectations or goals, and there may also be stereotypes which preclude understanding (McAvoy and Sayeed 1990). Interpreters may not be readily available or may be inadequate. Sometimes the family have to depend on quite a young child to act as interpreter, particularly in the case of women patients. This practice, according to Rack (1990: 66), is 'unethical, unprofessional, uncivilized and totally unacceptable.' The use of other relatives, particularly the husband, may also be problematic, as McNaught (1990: 35) indicates: 'Reliance on family members tends to reduce the ability of the practitioner to act in his patient's best interest on issues where there is family conflict or misunderstanding' (see also Rack 1990: 299). McAvoy and Sayeed (1990) provide useful guidelines for good communication and recommend the use of trained patient advocates and link workers from ethnic minorities. These are a bridge between patients and professionals, and can also help with education and staff training.

Impersonal treatment by some professionals, coupled perhaps with unfamiliar technology, which can be bewildering and alarming to white Britons, may be more so to those who do not know what is being done to them nor have the concepts to cope with it. There may also be new and unfamiliar concepts on both sides. Depression and sadness, for example, may be explained in terms of a physical pain in the liver by Turkish Muslims (Antes 1989). Chinese patients may show anxiety at having blood removed as it is thought to generate weakness; one Chinese Vietnamese couple with a jaundiced baby were told they should have it tested because it was 'yellow' and flatly refused to permit it because their experience of persecution led them to fear the blood would be used in witchcraft against them. Concepts such as 'brain death' may be very hard to understand in the face of an apparently alive individual who is breathing on a respirator.

Sometimes it is felt that a lack of sensitivity on the part of doctors and nurses is racist, particularly when assumptions are made about the patient's or relative's capacity to understand what is going on (McAvoy and Donaldson 1990; Rathwell and Philips 1986). Generalizations and stereotypes about religion, cultural groupings, race or colour come into this category. Donovan (1986: 129) reports situations where inaccurate diagnoses were based on assumptions about the cultural background of Asian women; they were made to feel their child's illness was their own fault and medical decisions were made without consulting them. Patients or their relatives may be accused of 'making a fuss' when they ask for more attention or display emotion. Patients who are 'difficult' or who cannot communicate may receive less attention than those who respond 'normally'. Remarks to the effect that 'if they come here they should adapt to our ways' are not infrequently heard. Checklists with information about the beliefs and practices of ethnic minority religions can hinder as much as they help if they reinforce stereotypes. It should not be assumed, for example, that all Muslims object to the body of a relative being handled; some would wish nurses to clean up vomit and haemorrhages before the family see it.

Caring for dying people

If the death of a South Asian is anticipated it is important, in theory, to inform the dying person and/or the relatives so that both spiritual and practical preparations can be set in motion. In practice, this is not so simple. The attachments between members of the nuclear family may be very intense, particularly between parents and adult children who live with them. Several Asian doctors have described the dilemmas they face in having to inform relatives that a parent or other relative is dying, as the consequence might be emotional collapse or hysteria. If the dying person is not aware of the terminal nature of the illness, the information might lead to loss of hope, particularly in the case of a premature death, and relatives might withhold information from a dying person in case they gave up. A Hindu might believe untimely death was due to bad *karma*, a Muslim that it was the will of God, and thus not put up a fight in the way the medical staff and family would wish them to. All of these factors can compound the difficulties associated with a 'closed awareness context'.

It is common, on the Indian subcontinent, to send people home when they are about to die, as hospital is regarded as a place to be cured, and home is where you should die with the loving support and assistance of the family. As a result, some patients also wish to return to their country of origin to die (Rees 1990). In many hospitals on the subcontinent, provision is made for the family to stay with the patient, prepare the correct food and undertake much of the physical and emotional care of the patient. In the UK, while hospitals may be valued as a good place to be from the perspective of the best treatment, there may be concern about adequate emotional and spiritual support for dying patients. Asians tend to have higher expectations of medical care in the UK than in the Third World, and the doctor's word is more likely to be taken on trust, so the disillusion is greater if the patient dies. There may also be a desire to consult alternative therapists such as *hakims* (Muslim practitioners) or *vaids* (Ayurvedic specialists) (Qureshi 1989; Rees 1990). These may be felt to have a greater understanding of Asian concepts of wellness and wholeness, be more able to advise on lifestyle and diet as well as spiritual practice, and be more aware of the patient in the context of the whole family.

When relatives know that death is likely, they will want to be with the person and perform any last services, prayers and rites for them. This is regarded as a sacred religious and moral duty.

For Hindus, a good death is a conscious, willing and peaceful one in old age. Many Hindus know when they are going to die, even to the day, and prepare for it by saying goodbye to family members, dealing with unfinished economic and family business, and meditating on God. The signs of a good death are a peaceful expression and slightly open mouth or eyes; a bad death is characterized by pain, vomit or the passing of urine or faeces. Such signs, even if the death otherwise seems to be a good one, indicate the person has some negative *karma* (the consequences of good and bad deeds) and may cause distress to the family. Ideally, death should take place on the floor, with the head to the north, in order to enable the soul to be released easily. It is therefore helpful, if asked, to allow the dying person to be placed on a mattress on the floor; cases have been known in England of elderly patients lying on the floor and being placed back in bed by uncomprehending nurses. At the point of death, Ganges water and *tulsi* (basil) leaf should be placed in the dying person's mouth. One should die with the name of God on the lips, as the thoughts at the point of death determine one's destination. It is important for family members to be present to help facilitate this, by chanting *Ram Ram* or *Om* at the point of death, singing favourite hymns, or reading the *Bhagavad Gita*. The family, especially the sons, have a sacred obligation to perform the correct rituals at and after death. If these are not done, it can mean that the soul of the deceased fails to move onto its next life and brings misfortune to the family. An elderly Gujarati woman was in hospital with terminal cancer when the doctor said he wanted to switch off the life-support machine, but he refused to allow the family to give the old lady Ganges water 'Because the shock might kill her'. Because the correct rituals were not performed, the family believe that the soul of the aunt will be a restless ghost for seven generations. The doctor also had a point in believing that the giving of Ganges water might prove very disturbing to the aunt, and careful communication about expectations might have saved a great deal of anxiety on both sides.

Sikhs have a similar model of a good death, for which the patient should be spiritually prepared, so they will wish to be with a dying relative to facilitate it. At the point of death, the mind should be fixed on God by reading the scriptures, the *Guru Granth Sahib*, singing the evening prayer, *Kirtan Sohila*, or the *Sukkhmani Sahib*. Holy water, *amrit*, may be placed in the ears and mouth if the dying person can swallow. As the person dies, *Waheguru* (wonderful Lord) should be repeated in the ears.

Muslims believe that life and death at any age are in God's hands, and this belief will affect the way in which illness, death and bereavement are approached. Physical and psychological pain in dying people may be seen as a punishment, have a purgative role, or be sent by God in order to compensate the patient in heaven (Antes 1989; Rahman 1989). Qureshi (1989: 165) points out that a Muslim 'believes in fate and the will of Allah to the extent that he will accept any consequence of the disease or treatment that may follow', and since the doctor's skill to heal is given by Allah, treatment will be more effective if backed by the phrase 'Allah will heal you' (see also Rahman 1989).

Death, for Muslims, should, ideally, take place at home and with the family. Some Indian Muslims believe that death should take place on the floor, but this is not Islamic. A dying person should be enabled to deal with family affairs, especially making a will. At the point of death, the patient should be propped up or the head should be turned to face Mecca, and should affirm the unity of God by saying *Kalimat Ashshahadah* – there is none worthy of worship except God'. Forgiveness and mercy from God should be sought. Other people should read the *Qur'an*, particularly the Surah Yasin, to help the dying person's mind to be fixed on God.

Treatment and care

There are usually few problems of a religious or cultural nature associated with the use of medical treatments, except that Muslims will not take medication such as insulin containing pork substances and Hindus will not take beef extracts. Muslims may also refuse medications containing alcohol, including surgical spirit. Many Muslims also have problems accepting medication, including an inhaler or injections, during the hours of fasting (dawn to dusk) in Ramadan. If the times of drug-taking cannot be adjusted accordingly, exemptions can be obtained, although the Imam may have to be consulted for permission (Qureshi 1989). Many elderly Hindus who anticipate death will fast as a spiritual discipline and also to ensure the body will have minimal discharge at death. Strict dietary taboos may mean that patients will refuse to eat off plates which might have been contaminated by forbidden foodstuffs, but may have difficulty communicating this. Patients who are capable of continuing prayer life will need extra water for ablutions, and also to wash the genital area after using the bedpan and urinal. Strict rules about modesty and allowing patients to be touched by opposite sex nurses and doctors should be respected as far as possible.

For Sikhs, the five K's, symbols of Sikhism (shorts, bangle, uncut hair, comb and dagger), are so important they need to be kept by patients even if they cannot be worn, as in surgery. If a Sikh has a head operation, for example, the comb should be kept near by and never removed without consultation. The *kara*, the steel bangle, can be taped in place. If it has to be removed for surgical reasons, this needs to be explained carefully to the patient, who can wear it on the other arm. Drips should be placed in the left arm. If the patient is used to wearing the *kirpan*, the sword (often in miniature form), this too should be left on. It should not be removed, nor should any part of the body be shaved for surgery, without discussing the matter with the patient and his or her relatives. The shorts symbolize modesty, and some Sikhs will never remove one without, at the same time, putting on another, so one leg is always inside the garment. It is particularly important to respect the modesty of older Sikhs in this regard (Neuberger 1987).

Ending or prolonging life

All the communities under discussion believe that life is sacred and should never be artificially ended. *The Islamic Code of Medical Ethics* states that: 'A Doctor shall not take away life even when motivated by mercy'. This is prohibited because it is not one of the legitimate indications for killing (Antes 1989: 186). However, the boundaries between active 'killing' and 'allowing to die' are acknowledged by Asian, as by other doctors, to be hard to draw. Some doctors would always treat aggressively to prolong life, whereas others would support, in principle, the switching off of a life-support machine when it is clear that death is imminent or the person is brain-dead. *The Islamic Code of Medical Ethics* reminds doctors that the aim is to maintain the process of life rather than the process of dying (Antes 1989). See Chapter 7, this volume, for a wider discussion of these issues.

After death

The laying out of the body is regarded as an important religious and social obligation. With hospital deaths, Hindus and Sikhs do not usually object to the body being straightened and cleaned; the ritual bathing will take place later. Many Muslims object to the body being touched by someone of a different faith or the opposite sex. If this is absolutely necessary (e.g. in the absence of relatives or friends), disposable gloves should be worn. The face should be turned towards Mecca. If the family is present they should always be consulted first.

Post-mortems create great anxiety, particularly for Muslims, as the post mortem seems to deny that death is God's will. Since there is said to be a level of consciousness still in the body, cutting open the head or violating privacy by blocking the lower passages is abhorrent. However, in some circumstances, the family wish to know the cause of death. The issues should always be discussed carefully with the relatives to ensure mutual understanding.

Muslims lay out the body of the same sex in the local mosque or at the undertaker's according to strict rules, after the heir's permission has been given. It should be done immediately after the death so that the body is no longer impure and the mourners can resume their prayers. After gently bathing it with soap, and three times ritually, it is placed in a shroud, *kafan*, made of three pieces of white calico for men, and five pieces for women, before the last viewing by the family.

Hindus wash and dress the body of someone of the same sex immediately before the cremation to purify it for the fire. If they have had to wait several days it can be quite difficult. This is done at the local undertakers. There are caste and family traditions concerning how this is done: a man will be dressed in the clothes he normally wears, a young single or married woman in a red sari or *salvar kameze*, a widow in white, covered by a cloth or shawl. The body is then placed in a coffin and taken to the family home.

Sikhs follow similar procedures to Hindus. The body is bathed and dressed by family members and close friends with the five K's, as in life, then placed in a coffin and taken by hearse to the family home (Henley 1979; Neuberger 1987).

Funerals

Hindus, Sikhs and Muslims have to face major changes in the timing of funerals because of difficulties in arranging for immediate cremation or burial. For Hindus, the focus of the funeral has shifted from the open pyre, as in India, to the home, where the body is displayed for the final viewing. Specialist funeral priests are not available in the UK, and if no other priest is available, the ritual is conducted by a local Brahmin or senior caste member. While the pandit chants from the scriptures, the chief mourner (normally the eldest son) performs the rituals. Herbs, sandalwood, clarified butter and flowers may be placed on the body. Ganges water and *tulsi* are put in the mouth. The family and friends circumambulate the coffin to bid farewell and it is closed and taken to the crematorium. The National Council of Hindu Temples, and some local temples, have devised services for use at the crematorium, which are very different from the orthodox Sanskrit rituals, but are useful in the absence of a priest. Everyone follows, as a social duty, although Gujarati women usually do not go. After a few prayers and a homily, the eldest or youngest son pushes the button, or may push the coffin into the cremator. The mourners return to the house of the deceased, where there may be further prayers, readings and hymn singing.

Hindu children are not normally cremated under the age of three or four, as they have unformed personalities and are too pure to require the ritual purification of fire. They may be buried with little ceremony in a special corner of the cemetery, or with a pandit saying some prayers.

Sikhs also take the body home for a final viewing, where family members and women friends circumambulate the coffin. It is then taken to the gurdwara for prayers led by the *granthi* (reader) or a senior member of the community, before being taken to the crematorium for a short service. The eldest son or male relative presses the button or pushes in the coffin. There are further prayers at the gurdwara before the mourners return home for a meal. Very young children have a simplified service, and may be buried instead of cremated, but this is not part of Sikh teaching.

Muslims are enjoined to bury their dead immediately, so that any delays caused by local bureaucracy create a great deal of distress. There are also religious objections to coffins, as Islamic law requires the body to be laid on the earth resting on its right side facing Mecca. Some local authorities have given permission to bury without one; and in other cases compromises are worked out with the funeral directors. Male relatives or friends carry the body to the mosque or cemetery for the funeral prayers (*salat-ul-janazah*), which are said without the usual bowing and prostration (Prickett 1980). Women are not allowed to attend. At the graveside, verses from the *Qur'an* are recited, including Surah 20: 55: 'From the (earth) did We create you, and into it shall We return you, and from it shall We bring you out once again.'

In some Muslim communities, there is a special fund to help with the burial and mourning expenses, and the community will take all responsibility for the arrangements, transport and post-burial meal.

Mourning

The set period of mourning, which has both religious and cultural aspects, is of great therapeutic value in providing a framework for the legitimate expression of grief and allowing a period of time of up to a year, with rituals as 'markers', for adjusting to the new personal and social situation in which a member of the family is no longer present.

All the religions under discussion discourage too much weeping. Hindus believe it hinders the progress of the soul because of the attachment of the survivors. The Sikh Gurus say that the deceased has gone to God, so excessive grief is inappropriate. Islam allows weeping for three days but not beyond that, and wailing is forbidden. Nevertheless, wailing is still practised in certain villages and may occur in hospital settings. There are also fewer cultural taboos to showing emotion, so a great deal of distress may be shown on the death and this may disturb and embarrass staff and other patients. Its therapeutic value needs to be recognized. A separate room for this purpose is helpful.

Asian communities can provide a strong network for support. Family, friends and neighbours provide food, accommodation for visitors, help with funeral and mourning arrangements, and care for children. If this network is absent, as in the case of new immigrants, or those who have moved away, there may be a great sense of isolation. It is important to ensure that bereaved families have an adequate support system and, if necessary, for social workers to help those who are isolated to link up with the nearest mosque, gurdwara or temple of their particular sect or community. A list of religious organizations and leaders facilitates this.

It is obligatory among Asians to pay their respects and express their regrets. Furniture is removed and sheets spread on the floor. In Muslim and many Sikh and Hindu homes, the men and women will sit in different rooms. The deceased are talked about, scriptures may be read, and the mourners reminded of their religious teaching. Hindus and Sikhs may sing hymns. Condolence visits from non-Asian friends or professional contacts are greatly appreciated. It is enough to express one's sincere regrets and sit quietly with the bereaved. Shoes are usually removed at the door, and in Muslim households women should cover their heads with a scarf or shawl in the presence of men. This should also be done in Sikh homes when the *Guru Granth Sahib* is being read. In most Hindu homes, food and drink are not offered to guests as this is regarded as a time of great impurity. If they are offered it is an especial courtesy.

The official period of mourning for Muslims is three days, when the family and friends provide food. After this there may be prayers and readings of the *Qur'an* for 40 days, when the grave is visited every Friday. A widow is in *iddat* for 4 months and 10 days to ensure she is not pregnant and to protect her if she is. Some strict Muslims will not go out at all during this period, but Shi'as allow a widow to resume normal life provided she has no social contact with men. After this time, she may remarry. A young widow in *iddat*, who is without the support of family and community, may be extremely isolated, especially if she has young children and it is important if a Muslim man has died in hospital to ensure that the widow has got support.

The mourning period for Hindus lasts between 10 and 16 days. The family lead an ascetic lifestyle, eating plain food brought by relatives and friends, although in the UK they may have to begin cooking sooner than they would in India. On the tenth to twelfth day, a series of rituals create a new spiritual body for the deceased, who becomes an ancestor. If a priest who knows the ritual is unobtainable, the family may have this done in India. Ashes may be taken to the River Ganges, or thrown into the sea or a river here, although there are problems over the legality of the latter (Poulter 1990). Further rituals occur at intervals throughout the first year, which allow a gradual return to normality. Widows normally stay indoors for 3–6 months, and then gradually return to a life in which their status is drastically changed, although they have more freedom than in the past. In many communities, she will not be able to remarry. Each year there is a ceremony called *shraddha* on the anniversary of the death, and during a two-week period in the autumn, the deceased are remembered by offering gifts to Brahmins and to charity.

Sikhs follow a similar pattern to Hindus, although theoretically there is no pollution, and the religious rituals are different. The holy book, *Guru Granth Sahib*, may be read regularly over a week or it may be read continuously without stopping for three days, at the end of which the eldest son is given a turban, *pagri*, by the wife's relatives, as a sign that he is now the head of the household. Young widows can remarry.

South Asian widows whose own relatives are in India can feel lonely and isolated, especially if relations with the husband's family are poor. Young widows may feel pressure, especially from older women, to conform to expected norms, and they may be blamed for their husband's death.

Issues of change

Apart from problems of misunderstanding and communication, the main issues for Asians are: being absent at the time of death, not being permitted to perform the correct religious prayers or rituals at death, feeling control is taken out of their hands after death – particularly with respect to post-mortems – and the changes in timing for burial or cremation. There are religious objections to the delay, but traditional mourning patterns are also disrupted, as in South Asia mourning begins after an immediate burial or cremation. Paying people to deal with the body and the need to place the body 'in a box' are also greatly disliked.

Asian communities themselves are undergoing changes. Second- and third-generation Asians may feel alienated from the more traditional aspects of their communities, yet feel disorientated at the time of a death if they do not know what should be done. They may feel uncomfortable with traditional expressions of grief, yet get a sense of cohesion and strength from the community. Extended families, because of social mobility, may fragment, although loyalties remain strong. Expectations may change, and traditional customs, such as viewing the body or banning women from attending the crematorium, may be objected to.

Where there is an extended family, the authoritarian structure may create dependencies which make separation difficult at the time of bereavement. There are also powerful taboos against expressing anger against a parent, or against a husband, which may make grieving more difficult. For some Asians, this may take the form of depression and withdrawal. While it is essential to be cautious about the use of such terms as 'guilt' in a non-Christian context, it should be recognized that for Asians the failure to perform adequate religious rituals may have more serious implications than remorse, particularly for Hindus, who have a sacred obligation to obey parents. To neglect this could have long-term ramifications for the welfare and safety of the entire family, as the ghost of the unhappy person could create sickness or misfortune, plus negative *karma* for the neglectful son.

Conclusion

In the National Health Service, particularly with reference to hospital care, there may be difficulties of communication and understanding, racism and a lack of facilities to enable a dying Asian to receive the sort of religious and emotional support that is needed. Medical staff may also have problems coping with these needs within existing structures, or of recognizing unconscious prejudice or ignorance. Asians do not expect professionals to know all the answers, but to be sensitive, willing to learn and respectful of their traditions and beliefs: 'Carers don't have an idea about cultural diversity – but they only need to listen for a few minutes, to be sensitive' (Sikh doctor). This sensitivity needs to be manifested from the outset – over the details of nursing care, respect for different beliefs and, finally, over openness and willingness to communicate with patients and relatives so that mutual compromises can be made and no-one dies alone.

It is essential to ensure that adequate interpreters are available, who can deal not only with translating the language and medical terminology, but also understand the cultural tradition on both sides. In the hospital situation, the provision of a private room for dying patients can minimize the 'disruption' caused by religious rituals and relatives, and if communication is good, the need for restricting numbers can be explained. A willingness on the part of professionals to get to know Asians outside the hospital or surgery can only increase mutual respect and understanding. A multicultural component on in-service courses, particularly those on death and bereavement, helps to develop awareness and sensitivity, not only – as tends to be the case – for nurses and social workers, but for doctors as well.

Despite the changes faced by many Asians, the strength and cohesion of the community becomes most apparent at the time of death and bereavement, when the strong social bonds and religious traditions provide meaning and support. Structured mourning provides a mechanism for the expression of grief, as well as reinforcing social bonds, and the alternation between religious readings, prayers, talking and weeping can be very therapeutic.

High-quality palliative care, as championed by the hospice movement, has placed a major premium on the holistic approach. It is vitally important, as palliative care develops, that it should be made available to *all* sections of the community, regardless of age, diagnosis or ethnic group. The holistic, patient-centred approach is part of the Asian traditions we have been discussing, and they have as much to contribute as to receive.

Acknowledgements

My gratitude to the following: Rahim Bashir, Parveen Damani, Piara Singh Sambhi, Dr Kanwaljit Kaur Singh, Dr Yashvir Sunak, Dr Desai, Dr Amrit Bening, Dr Harcharan Sanir, Darshan Singh and members of the Asian communities. First-hand accounts and examples are based on interviews by the writer.

References

Antes, P. (1989) Medicine and the living tradition of Islam. In L.E. Sulivan (ed.) *Healing and Restoring: Health and Medicine in the World's Religions*, pp. 173–202. New York; Macmillan.

Donaldson, L. and Johnson, M. (1990) Elderly Asians. In B. McAvoy and L.J. Donaldson (eds) *Health Care for Asians*, pp. 237–49. Oxford: Oxford Medical Publications.

Donaldson, L. and Parsons, L. (1990) Asians in Britain: the population and its characteristics. In B. McAvoy and L.J. Donaldson (eds) *Health Care for Asians*, pp. 72–92. Oxford: Oxford Medical Publications.

Donovan, J. (1986) Black people's health: a different approach. In T. Rathwell and D. Phillips (eds) *Health, Race and Ethnicity*, pp. 117–36. London: Croom Helm.

Henley, A. (1979) *Asian Patients in Hospital and at Home*. London: King Edward's Hospital Fund for London.

McAvoy, B. and Donaldson, L. (eds) (1990) *Health Care for Asians*. Oxford Medical Publications: Oxford University Press.

McAvoy, B. and Sayeed, A. (1990) Communication. In B. McAvoy and L.J. Donaldson (eds) *Health Care for Asians*, pp. 57–71. Oxford: Oxford Medical Publications.

McNaught, A. (1990) Organization and delivery of care. In B. McAvoy and L.J. Donaldson (eds) *Health Care for Asians*, pp. 31–9. Oxford: Oxford Medical Publications.

Neuberger, J. (1987) *Caring for Dying People of Different Faiths*. London: Auston Cornish.

Poulter, S. (1986) *English Law and Ethnic Minority Customs*. London: Butterworth.

Poulter, S. (1990) *Asian Traditions and English Law*. Runnymede Trust and Trentham Books.

Prickett, J. (ed.) (1980) *Death*. Living Faiths Series. London: Butterworth.

Qureshi, B. (1989) *Transcultural Medicine: Dealing with Patients from Different Cultures*. Dordrecht: Kluwer Academic.

Rack, P. (1990) Psychological/psychiatric disorders. In B. McAvoy and L.J. Donaldson (eds) *Health Care for Asians*, pp. 290–303. Oxford: Oxford Medical Publications.

Rahman, F. (1989) Islam and health/medicine: a historical perspective. In L.E. Sulivan (ed.) *Healing and Restoring: Health and Medicine in the World's Religions*, pp. 149–72. New York: Macmillan.

Rathwell, T. and Philips, D. (eds) (1986) *Health, Race and Ethnicity*. London: Croom Helm.

Rees, D. (1990) Terminal care and bereavement. In B. McAvoy and L.J. Donaldson (eds) *Health Care for Asians*, Oxford: Oxford Medical Publications.

Taylor, C. (1990) Asians in Britain – origins and lifestyles. In B. McAvoy and L.J. Donaldson (eds) *Health Care for Asians*, pp. 3–27. Oxford: Oxford Medical Publications.

7

Euthanasia

TONY CROWTHER

Western society no longer takes the view that suffering is an acceptable and inevitable part of living. Whether the cause is physical or psychological, ways of avoiding such suffering are increasingly being examined and tested. One method, which may be seen as an easy way out, is by speeding up death in some fashion; a further way is for individuals to make a living will or advance directive for medical care. There are considerable difficulties in both these areas, and these will be discussed in due course.

With the achievements of the hospice movement in the field of palliative care, much of the relevance of euthanasia for the patient with cancer is reduced. However, this continued care and expansion of care has highlighted the problems that are met with in other areas of medicine. For example, in the field of geriatrics, with the very frail patient and the demented patient; in neurology we increasingly see advanced prolonged but progressive neurological deterioration; with improved neonatal survival, and improved survival after major trauma and following severe infections, we sometimes have further ethical problems to address. Advances in anaesthesia with the concomitant extension of surgical practice, as well as progress in new radiotherapy techniques and chemotherapy regimes, are also being highlighted and questioned as a result of attitudes associated with palliative care (see also Chapter 8 this volume).

There is a lot of confusion and misunderstanding when the meaning of euthanasia is considered. On the one hand, surely most human beings agree with a definition of euthanasia as an easy, gentle, painless death; on the other hand, what is often difficult to clarify and understand is the means by which that good death can be achieved. This whole subject enters the realms of religion, philosophy and medicine, intertwined with ethical, moral and social issues.

The *Concise Oxford Dictionary* definition of euthanasia (Gk. eu – well; thanatos – death) varies, but even as long ago as 1932 the word was defined as 'Gentle and easy death; bringing about this, especially in the case of incurable and painful disease'. This definition continued in the 1956 and 1979 editions. Another dictionary published in 1969 gives the meaning as 'painless death; practice (sometimes advocated) of putting incurable invalids painlessly to death' (*Penguin English Dictionary*). A further definition is quite unequivocal, giving the meaning as 'the bringing about of a gentle and easy death for a person suffering from a painful incurable disease' (*St Michael Oxford Dictionary* 1981). An authoritative publication of 1989 (*Oxford English Dictionary*) subdivides the meaning, thus making it somewhat more clear:

(a) a gentle and easy death;
(b) the means of bringing about a gentle and easy death;
(c) the action of inducing a gentle and easy death.

It seems sensible, therefore, as well as important, to define what we mean by the word euthanasia before entering a discussion on the subject. It can be useful to introduce an additional or defining word but even that is not necessarily enough to indicate a precise meaning. Phrases such as active euthanasia, pro-active euthanasia, passive euthanasia, non-directive euthanasia, voluntary euthanasia, involuntary euthanasia, non-voluntary euthanasia, imposed euthanasia, mercy killing, mercy dying and assisted suicide are often used. Such a broad range of terms highlights our unease and lack of agreement about what constitutes 'euthanasia'.

Today, various phrases have evolved to convey certain definitive meanings (British Medical Association 1988):

1. *Presence or absence of the agreement of the subject*
   • *Voluntary* euthanasia is that which is requested by the subject or agreed by him or her when proposed by others.
   • *Imposed* euthanasia is that which is not agreed to by the subject and consists of:
     – *Involuntary* euthanasia, where the agreement of the subject could be obtained but is not.
     – *Non-voluntary* euthanasia, where the agreement of the subject cannot be obtained because of unconsciousness or otherwise and therefore the subject is unable to express agreement verbally or rationally.

2. *The means by which death may be administered*
   • *Active* (positive or direct) euthanasia is where death is produced deliberately or actively by positive means.
   • *Passive* (negative or indirect) euthanasia is where death is deliberately produced by withholding or withdrawing the ordinary means of nutrition for the subject or the treatment of the subject's clinical condition.

Despite these apparently clear definitions, further ambiguity exists and should be recognized if continued misunderstanding is to be avoided. The term 'passive euthanasia' may be used to describe that produced by the physical neglect of the basic needs of the subject by withholding necessary effective treatment. Alternatively, it may describe the decision to let nature take its course as the patient approaches death and not to use futile or ineffective treatment which may also be burdensome to the patient. The latter sense is commonly used in the USA and in the Netherlands but would generally be regarded in the UK as good medical practice rather than euthanasia. It could be called 'mercy dying' as opposed to 'mercy killing' (Twycross 1981).

Having looked at some of the difficulties in giving an acceptable meaning to the word 'euthanasia', we should perhaps look at where society is now with regard to the realities of the subject before looking a little into the future.

Thoughts on why we are where we are now

Why, as a society, are we increasingly having to address the possibility of active euthanasia?

Social attitudes and experiences

In the West, death and suffering are much less frequent now compared with a century or so ago. We are much less experienced at seeing and handling death, which increasingly is something that happens to the elderly with whom it is so much more acceptable and normal. Though less frequent, death at a younger age does happen and is difficult to accept, particularly when this is as a result of disease as opposed to an accident. Since we as a society are less well equipped to cope with death, it is perhaps not surprising that we seek ways to avoid the distress associated with it.

In a strange way, one can highlight this attitude by the comparison of hospices with top security prison hospitals. Both types of institution are looking after a section of the community which society as a whole does not wish to be involved with. Yet there would be no shortage of criticism if the care in these places was not of the highest order. In one sense, this is correct; on the other hand, such places can be considered to be society's way of providing an uncomfortable area of necessary care even at very considerable cost.

A recently viewed comic compilation of children's drawings and expressions on *Facts of Love* had its last page on death. Nigel, aged 8, was quoted

as saying 'it would be nice if when you died you blew away like a leaf so
people wouldn't have to clean up after you'. Perhaps society is looking at
death and suffering in this way so that by some form of euthanasia the
whole process will be made tolerable and decent. Whether this is for the
benefit of the patient or society is obviously open to debate; possibly both
may feel more comfortable.

Protagonists for active euthanasia develop their arguments from a variety
of fronts: compassion for the patient; the patient's right to die; social
progress (eugenic obligation); and economic necessity. The assumptions
taken in adopting those arguments in favour of active euthanasia are many
and varied. A recent article by Wilkinson (1990) has summarized many of
the arguments in the following way:

(a) *Philosophical*
   1. Human beings have the right to die.
   2. The value of human life is measurable.
   3. Human life can be dealt with in the same way as animal life.
   4. Suffering can have no beneficial function.
   5. A clear motive of compassion can be guaranteed.
   6. A request for euthanasia is always rational and reliable.

(b) *Medical*
   7. Medical diagnosis and prognosis are always certain.
   8. Effective alternative methods for relief of suffering are not
      available.
   9. Euthanasia is a justifiable duty of a doctor.

(c) *Legal*
   10. The legalization of euthanasia can control its abuse.
   11. Euthanasia can be clearly distinguished from murder.

From the number and significant nature of these assumptions, it is obvious
that they cannot be ignored and that any decision to legalize the practice of
euthanasia is one which will have important moral, legal, social and professional implications.

Antagonists of active euthanasia similarly present their case from basic
arguments which clearly adopt a different interpretation or non-acceptance
of all of these eleven assumptions. In more general terms, there are at least
five arguments against the practice of euthanasia:

1. It is too radical. Euthanasia destroys the problem rather than solving it.
   Destroying the life of a patient deprives him or her of hope and any
   opportunity to regret or reverse the decision. It is dangerously final.
2. It is ethically undesirable. It is difficult to distinguish euthanasia from
   murder. Murder is a sin according to religious teaching and society
   regards it as a crime.
3. It is legally inadmissible. Legislation on euthanasia may be expected to

fail to control its abuse or to provide appropriate safeguards for its practice (cf. the law on abortion in the UK). The legal problem is how to distinguish euthanasia from murder when, although the motive may be different, the intention to kill is undoubtedly present.

4. It is practically unworkable. Doctors are trained to preserve life not destroy it. It is assumed that, in the event of legalized euthanasia, it would be administered by doctors. This would seriously alter the important relationship between doctors and their patients.
5. It is increasingly unnecessary. Until the advent of the hospice movement, doctors had no guidance and little experience in the alleviation of distressing symptoms arising from incurable disease. The situation is very different today and the consideration of the use of euthanasia is increasingly unnecessary and outdated.

To acknowledge this debate is to recognize that society has a difficult problem which it is trying hard to solve. Perhaps the characteristic English compromise will be achieved, but in the meantime the debate will continue in many areas.

Attitudes of carers

As medicine has advanced and become rather more a science than an art, so the profession has increasingly pursued the scientific path with considerable dedication and achievement. This progress has tended to leave behind the necessary skills of communication, kindness and understanding for a sick fellow human being. This overall paucity of humaneness is more acceptable when the outcome is cure, but actually magnifies the distress when a cure is not possible. No-one can deny the tremendous advances in medicine, but similarly there can be no denying that understanding attitudes have not advanced or even kept pace; one might suggest that they have been sacrificed in the name of 'progress'. A reminder that 'patients are not there for doctors, rather doctors are there for patients' is simple and telling.

Medical progress has produced two further problems for the caring professions and for society. Patients can now be kept alive by artificial means for far longer than in the past; without these techniques, death would occur much earlier. At the same time, the ability to make an accurate forecast of the outcome, following resuscitation and the use of artificial maintenance of life, has not yet been acquired. This results in remarkable and wonderful successes but also many tragedies. A lack of improvement in the patient's condition can result in a distressing clinical situation for patient and family with extremely difficult ethical and moral decisions to be made. There are several well-known examples of this picture that have been reported in lurid detail by the national press. It is not right to comment here on these cases since, without a full knowledge of the details of each individual case, it is at worst dangerous and at best meddlesome to do so. Further progress in this area will be made, but in the meantime the caring professions and society have got to address the problem in one way or another.

The currently accepted translation of the Hippocratic Oath gives a warning about administering lethal medicines and having any part in the planning of such a use. The second and third sentences in the second paragraph read as follows:

> I will follow that system of regimen which, according to my ability and judgement, I consider for the benefit of my patients, and abstain from whatever is deleterious and mischievous. I will give no deadly medicine to anyone if asked, nor suggest any such council; and in like manner I will not give to a woman a pessary to produce abortion.
> (*British Medical Association 1984: 69*)

In the poem 'The Latest Decalogue', Clough (1819–61) strives to make his own modifications to the Ten Commandments and writes the lines 'thou shalt not kill; but needst not strive officiously to keep alive'. These lines probably have more poignancy and relevance now than a century and a half ago; certainly this is a consideration doctors in modern times need to address. Such thoughts could be summarized with this remark, overheard from a patient talking to a friend:

> I have two appointments tomorrow and I can only manage one. I have an appointment with my hairdresser and one with my oncologist. The trouble is I know my hairdresser will make me feel better and very much doubt whether my oncologist will.

The recent case of Dr Nigel Cox highlights the difficulty facing doctors, the criminal law and the medical profession's governing body, the General Medical Council. Dr Cox had given an injection of potassium chloride to one of his patients thereby ending her life; he said that he had used the drug to relieve and ease the final moments of the patient. On 21 September 1992, Dr Cox was convicted at Winchester Crown Court of an offence of attempted murder and was sentenced to twelve months' imprisonment, sentence being suspended for twelve months. A panel of the Council's Professional Conduct Committee considered this conviction in November 1992. The Committee's decision took into account the law under which he had been convicted, the predicament of the patient and her family, the distress of a doctor who has looked after his patient for a long time and finds that in the terminal stages of illness the patient suffers extreme pain, and that the doctor acted in good faith in what was thought to be in the best interests of his dying patient, although evidence from a number of experts was critical of the use of a lethal injection. It also took account of the evidence of the clinical situation in what was an exceptional case and particularly of the sentence pronounced by the court, tempering justice with mercy. The president announced that the Committee (president and chairman, seven medical members and two lay members) having considered erasure from the Register or the suspension of his registration, proposed to follow the same course as the criminal court and concluded the case.

It is possible that this range of complex issues could lead on to a parliamentary bill for active euthanasia; this is certainly one way in which a democratic society can deal with the problem.

Changes in Western society

Society appears to be dedicated to speed and efficiency. This is something which is difficult to argue against but it has a damaging effect when applied to human relationships and care as opposed to areas of pure economy. In its turn, the economics of caring have an effect on the attitudes of carers and therefore on those needing the care.

While we must try to avoid inefficiency and waste, we must be careful to give time and space to those needing care and to those who are doing the caring. If this is not achieved, then the arguments for deliberacy in euthanasia will grow stronger into a demand for such legislation. On the other side of this argument, it may be that such demands will result in a modification of our attitudes for speed and efficiency in this area of care. As long as it is not too late for this to be appreciated and acted upon, then much good should come out of it.

Alongside this speed and efficiency, there moves impersonalization in our society. Large is not beautiful. It may be economically more efficient, but personal acknowledgement tends to suffer. Individuals easily lose some of their identity; this need for personal identity is something we all have and we require it to be nurtured in a diversity of ways.

The death of elderly people is generally accepted as being inevitable. However, premature death is not often experienced within any one family, so when it happens we are not equipped to deal with it, either physically or emotionally. The means of helping the patient and family in this situation has to be addressed by society.

For many sociological reasons, families are split up geographically, economically and emotionally. There is good evidence that individuals in families continue to care for one another. But this, in the context of more widespread families, brings into focus other forms of social caring. Active euthanasia could be considered to be one of those forms of caring.

Whether this dedication to speed and efficiency, with impersonalization and reduced family ties, constitutes an advancement in society or a destructive evolution is very much open to debate. If it is thought to be the former, then society should think carefully about passive euthanasia; if it is thought to be the latter, then active euthanasia could well be a part of that evolutionary process.

Changes in medical attitudes

The medical profession is not exempt from this dedication to speed and efficiency. As a result of this, one hears patients say that they at times feel abandoned. In a personal communication, I have the story of an American solicitor who was booked to have a repeat hip replacement in a highly prestigious orthopaedic unit. He duly registered at the hospital reception desk to be told that he should follow coloured floor markers and that he would receive further instructions from computers as he arrived at each door. This he did, duly receiving further instructions at each of these doors until finally he was told by a computer to go into a particular room, undress and get into bed. There he waited for seven hours before he was seen by a doctor. He said that he felt 'intimidated by the system' and 'abandoned'. Patients with terminal illness may for various reasons find themselves in acute medical or surgical wards where, correctly, the staff are dedicated to their acute roles. Yet frequently such patients say that they feel 'abandoned'.

A dedication to advancement and expertise leads to a feeling of failure when faced with a patient with an incurable disease. This sense of failure tends to be communicated secondarily to the patient and it also often results in the reduction of the physician's input to the patient (nothing can actively be done and so the whole situation becomes embarrassing and uncomfortable).

The selection of professional carers applying for training (particularly in medicine) has for some years now concentrated on academic ability and less on suitable character and personality. This has to some extent been appreciated as wrong and a better balance between academic ability and general character and suitability is being achieved. Good communication not only needs the ability, both natural and acquired, but it requires time, inclination and honesty. These are valuable elements which are not always available and the resulting lack of communication simply magnifies the problems of the patient, the family and other carers.

What to do: the future

Palliative care

Those of us who work in this field are often involved in the care of people in distressing situations, either fundamentally medical or fundamentally social in origin, but frequently a combination of both. While acknowledging the importance of palliative care, it is however a restricted and quite specialized area. It is also one that is generally very well received and much appreciated by patient and carer alike. Stemming from this encouragement and confidence it is important that those working in palliative care pass on their expertise and attitudes to health care workers in other fields so that they in turn adopt a more caring and understanding attitude to their patients and families. Continuing education is vital to allow the adoption or even revival of these attitudes in order to reverse some of the trends mentioned earlier.

Research in the whole range of palliative care, while far from easy to perform, must be done and the results disseminated widely among professional carers. In this way, these carers can keep up to date, avoid complacency and be stimulated to continue their work with patients and their families, adopting these other attitudes to their particular field of work.

Communication is important in health care. Good communication between professional carers themselves, between patients and relatives, between the carers and the patient, and also between the carers and the relatives is an important element to a better and more understanding care. The education of professional carers in communication skills must be available and be an important element in their training. These skills can and must be taught, since lack of information, misunderstanding and misinformation are potent stimulators of anxiety, apprehension and frank fear both in the patient and in their relatives. These sensations seriously undermine attempts at symptom control and therefore contribute significantly to the distress of the patient and naturally of the relatives. Similarly, a well-trained professional can facilitate improved communication between patients and their relatives with a resultant diminution of anxiety levels. Better communication will break down those barriers of lies which so commonly make the caring of a loved one very much more difficult than it need be. The result is of benefit to the patient during the final stages of their illness and also to the relatives during these stages and in their bereavement.

Speaking generally, hospices and hospice attitudes are a very strong antidote to active euthanasia. On two separate occasions, I have had members of Exit (Voluntary Euthanasia Society) in the audience for postgraduate workshops. In each case after the talk, the slides to demonstrate some of the points and a question and answer session, the individual doctors concerned have identified themselves and what they believed in, going on to state quite openly that if patients were looked after in the way that had just been discussed Exit would not need to exist. It seems highly commendable to say this and also seems to carry a very important message regarding levels of care and active euthanasia.

Governments are increasingly having to address the question of legislation for some form of euthanasia. The British government has in recent years encouraged the expansion of the hospice movement (see Chapter 10, this volume). This could well be one way of reducing the demand for the issue to be addressed by way of the statute books. In early 1992, there was an Early Day Motion in the House of Commons which set out both to praise all those working in the hospice movement and in palliative care and to seek to mobilize parliamentary opinion against the decriminalization of euthanasia. In total, 181 members of Parliament signed this 'Salute to the Hospice Movement', which was further expanded as follows:

> That this House salutes the success of all those involved in the hospice movement and in palliative care; congratulates those who care for the terminally ill and the dying on the great progress which has been achieved in the development of palliative medicine in the United Kingdom; notes with profound concern the fact that in the Netherlands euthanasia now accounts for 3,700 deaths each year of which more than 1,000 are as a result of involuntary euthanasia; and registers its opposition to the decriminalisation of euthanasia in this country.
>
> (*House of Commons 1992*)

In a reply to a letter from a Member of Parliament to the Minister for Health in January 1992 drawing attention to the Early Day Motion, the minister made reference to the extra financial support that the government had allocated to the voluntary hospice movement in 1990–91 and 1991–92. These allocations were specifically to enable these hospices to increase the provision of care and support for terminally ill people and their families. The minister went on to say that there is sympathy for those who fear becoming seriously incapacitated and that no-one should have to face the prospect of suffering and loss of dignity. However, the letter says, euthanasia raises very difficult problems for all those concerned with the care of the sick. Any doctor while taking account of the patient's wishes and attempting to relieve suffering is bound by the law and by his or her professional ethics and cannot be required to take action which conflicts with either. The latter finishes with a sentence saying 'the Government has no plans to change the criminal law in this area'.

However, it seems to me that on some occasions hospice attitudes, hospice care and hospice treatments may shorten life. If the patient is made comfortable and is looked after in a dignified way, then it seems that this is not euthanasia but rather it is good ethical care. Very rarely, but nevertheless on occasions, we must walk a tightrope between a predominantly passive role, allowing the patient to suffer, and one of deliberacy which would seem illegal and unnecessary.

There are three areas which can be considered here:

1. A patient who has struggled with various medical and social problems at home or, on occasions, in a busy acute hospital ward, on admission to a hospice may well be able to relax with security, better symptom control and round-the-clock nursing. This feeling that the struggle to survive can safely be cast aside does mean that some patients die relatively quickly after admission. On the other hand, I can see no point in the patient being kept alive by poor symptom control, fear, uncertainty and isolation. This is not euthanasia, however, since there is no element of deliberacy.

2. The timing of standing back from further acute procedures to prolong life is vitally important. If that treatment is not likely to improve quality of life and, with all the evidence available, the patient's life is very near the end, then perhaps one should stand back. No one person should take this decision but they should be guided by as many carers as possible, close relatives certainly (but we must remember not to leave them to feel that they made the decision) and, on appropriate occasions, the patient him or herself (when the patient is well enough to be involved). It is also important to remember that the decision may have to be reversed if the patient's condition does not continue to deteriorate at the rate that was expected – it is not necessarily a once and for all decision. The obvious broad example of this is the use or non-use of antibiotics for a presumed final chest infection. If death follows quickly, then that seems kind and caring, but if life continues, then the decision will have to be reconsidered.

3. Severe symptoms, particularly pain in one of its mantles, may need high or very high doses of drugs to achieve control. It is possible that with very high doses the life of the patient may be shortened. Again it seems at best unreasonable and at worst immoral to leave a patient with gross symptoms that are uncontrolled. The important thing to remember in my view is, that as long as the primary use of the correct drugs in a suitable dose and at appropriate intervals is to achieve better symptom control for the patient then, if life is shortened as a secondary manifestation, that is preferable to leaving the patient to suffer. Again it is important that no one person takes these decisions without adequate and truthful communication with other carers and the patient's relatives and, on occasions, the patient. It is these sorts of decisions that are vitally important and, what is more, they should not be made in private. With such considered decisions being made, deliberate euthanasia should not need any real thought, and the need for euthanasia is therefore lessened considerably. If we stand back too far from these ethical decisions, then society is more likely to demand some form of deliberate euthanasia from its governing body.

Society

In October 1969, the British government published *The Patient's Charter* with the intention of creating a better National Health Service (NHS). There were then added three new patients' rights from 1 April 1992, thus making a total of ten. However, while the charter is a central part of the government's programme to improve and modernize the delivery of the service to the public, it is much more about standards of service, efficiency and good value for money than about a basic service with a deep commitment to care for the needs of patients in social, psychological and compassionate contexts. It is difficult to combine efficiency and compassion within that service. It can be done, but it is generally easier to achieve in smaller units that are economically not 'good value for money'.

Hospices are generally held high as examples of dedicated compassionate care, but the cost per patient in in-patient units is high because of the high staffing levels needed to achieve and maintain these standards of care. They therefore tend to be centres of excellence, giving a small percentage of patients a dedicated expensive service. Additionally, they also provide a considerable teaching role to professionals in training. In this way, hospices have a vital role to play in society in being leaders by example and by education of the total dedicated care of terminally ill patients, their relatives and other lay carers.

The financial and other support that the public gives to hospices is commendable, but it also underlines how important hospices are felt to be and the need for the continuance of their services. The dedicated support that society gives to the hospice movement is important in a material way, but it is important also to observe it as a commitment by society to the care of its terminally ill members.

The living will or advance directive

In recent years, there has been considerable interest shown in our society in the making of living wills, sometimes known as advance directives. Such a document is drawn up by an individual, witnessed to make it more authentic, and lays out in some detail what should or should not be done for that individual in the event of some serious illness or injury. There are several forms, but they are all basically the same and three examples are given in Appendices 1, 2 and 3.

A living will has several advantages, not least that it makes plain the person's thoughts on not wanting their life prolonged needlessly and their wish to avoid unnecessary suffering. It helps medical advisors looking after the patient at any significant time to communicate the medical situation to relatives or other next of kin and for them to consider the advice given to them in the light of the document.

There are, however, several disadvantages, not least that similar to a last will and testament, it does not exonerate anyone from the obligation to behave within the law of the land. Therefore, it is a help and a guide to all those involved in the patient's care, rather than a mandate to act to shorten life. It may help with decisions when such a patient has a poor quality of life and is developing fatal complications. It may be easier for all concerned when such decisions involving the use of life-prolonging rather than life-saving skills or the withholding of those skills have to be made; that is still no reason to break the criminal law.

A further disadvantage is that a living will is usually drawn up while the patient is in good health. However, it may well be that their view on their continued existence, albeit limited by illness or injury, has changed. Life frequently becomes very precious even though severely limited; the human will to live is frequently stronger in limited health than when taken for granted in normal health. It therefore follows that it is difficult to forecast in health what one's feelings would be with regard to the circumstances leading up to death.

One must add to this the fact that the outcome of medical skills and technology, particularly when dealing with trauma and other acute medical emergencies, is uncertain at the time of initial delivery. In other words, resuscitation in serious trauma has not got a predictable outcome; some patients do remarkably well and others remarkably badly. A living will really cannot help anyone at this point of care, but could be a help once the outcome of the clinical state is more clear.

Even with widespread malignant disease or advanced neurological destructive disease, it is almost always difficult to predict the time of death. As this time may have a bearing on the quality of life of the patient, decisions on allowing the approach of death without hindrance are fraught with difficulty. Professional carers need to understand that the decision to let 'nature take its course' taken with close friends or relatives (the patient also, if appropriate) assumes that the deterioration in the patient's condition that has helped make that decision will continue; if such deterioration does not continue as expected, this may dictate a change in the patient's management and a reversal of the passive role. The situation requires regular review and communication with those close friends or relatives (remembering, if appropriate, the patient), so that kind, considerate and legal decisions are taken. This ensures minimal suffering for the patient and family but at the same time correct and ethical medical care for the patient. This, in my view, is what the patient is asking for when making a living will.

Enduring Power of Attorney

A Power of Attorney is a legal document which proves to anyone concerned that the person who has made such a document has given to a named person rights for that person to act on their behalf. Such powers can be limited or can be completely free of any restrictions and therefore apply to all that person's affairs.

Until recently, the ordinary Power of Attorney was only valid while the person giving it was of full mental capacity and capable of giving instructions. In the event that the person became unable to supervise the attorney then the power came to an end – just at the time when it was probably most needed. This is obviously a particular difficulty with health matters. One can now make an Enduring Power of Attorney which does not come to an end because of subsequent mental incapacity. You are able, therefore, to give your instructions while you are capable of doing so, in anticipation of a time when you may not be so capable. It is wise for the person making the Absolute Power of Attorney to discuss the detail of the person or persons who are to be made attorneys with other members of their family, since they can oppose the appointment.

While there are many disadvantages to a living will, one backed up with an Absolute Power of Attorney should make as sure as possible that decisions regarding undue and pointless prolongation of life will be taken in the way the patient wanted. In the face of a life-threatening turn of events, due consideration of the patient's further management can be given by the carers, since these will have been appointed, and therefore trusted, by the patient.

Neither a living will alone nor one with an Enduring Power of Attorney gives anyone the right to break the criminal law, but the two together do help considerably when it comes down to considered medical knowledge suggesting that further efforts to prolong the life are futile and an insult to human dignity.

Bill of euthanasia

This possibility has been mentioned earlier, but in view of what has been discussed there are a few further points that require to be considered with regard to such an important subject.

No civilized society has up to now legalized mercy killing (*British Medical Journal* 1992). The Netherlands is probably as close as any country to that position, but the government there has shied away from the issue, preferring that the law turn a blind eye to certain doctors who are prepared to actively help patients, with their relatives' approval, to die. The doctors appear to operate openly but with very strict criteria before that help is made available. It is of course debatable whether this is the correct way to handle the situation.

On the other hand, there is little doubt that in several countries public opinion is substantially behind the legalization of active euthanasia and in some countries this is on the increase. The British Social Attitudes Survey has included a question on this subject over a number of years. In 1983, 1984 and 1989 this took the form: 'Suppose a person has a painful incurable disease. Do you think that doctors should be allowed by law to end the patient's life if the patient requests it?' There were remarkably few 'don't knows' (less than 1 per cent in any year), with the following figures for 'yes' and 'no':

	1983	1984	1989
Yes	76.9%	75.1%	78.7%
No	22.5%	23.7%	20.0%

Statistically this suggests a very small change in attitude, but that the population holds firm views (SCPR 1992).

However, also in the UK, National Opinion Poll found that agreement with the statement 'Some people say that the law should allow adults to receive medical help to an immediate peaceful death if they suffer from an incurable physical illness that is intolerable to them, provided that they have previously requested such help in writing', rose from 69 per cent in 1976 to 72 per cent in 1985 and to 75 per cent in 1989. A similar statement in the USA was supported by 62 per cent in 1986 and 68 per cent in 1991 (polled by the Roper Organization). In Canada and Australia, figures are available over a longer time-scale and therefore are even more significant. To a similar statement in Canada, the affirmative response rose from 48 per cent in 1968 to 78 per cent in 1990 (Gallup Canada, Toronto) and in Australia from 47 per cent in 1962 to 73 per cent in 1991 (Morgan Gallup Poll, Melbourne).

The medical and legal professions cannot ignore these statistics. Active euthanasia is an act of premeditated homicide, which surely has to be unacceptable. However, if a parliament decided a change in the law was needed as a result of pressure from public opinion, a special defence mechanism would be needed that could be used to validate and give justification to such a procedure.

In some countries, there are books available for purchase giving explicit details of how a person should plan and expedite the end of their own life or that of someone else. A recent one in the USA has proved popular with large sales and the resulting difficulty in obtaining a copy (Humphry 1991). This gives explicit details as well as compelling arguments in favour of shortening life should the patient so desire.

There are of course advantages to having legalized active euthanasia, the first being that of economy. It is expensive for society to look after these groups of patients. The cost of the care and of the expertise that are needed, with additionally the costs of drugs, dressings and appliances, is considerable. This is a significant economic burden on society, whether this is financed through statutory funding or commercially through insurance. In societies where the rationing of care is a growing issue, the economic aspects of euthanasia must be addressed.

A further advantage is that legalized active euthanasia would to a large extent remove the responsibility of the medical profession for the possible poor outcome from attempted resuscitation. If these procedures are undertaken without due consideration of the possibility that recovery might not be reasonable, then in that circumstance the patient can always be actively helped to die. One can of course argue whether this would be an advantage or a disadvantage to the profession and to the patient and family.

The disadvantages of such a bill of euthanasia range from opposition based in religious attitudes and beliefs in the sanctity of life to exactly when and by whom such an act should be performed and under what exact circumstances it is to be enforced. These alone are difficult areas to address in a positive and strictly controlled way. In the event of legislation being formulated, there are fears of abuse for reasons of gain or easing of responsibilities. There is also the question of differing interpretations of those rules (cf. the abortion law in the UK) and the difficulties of resisting pressures from the patient's family and friends (this could be directed at the medical advisors as well as at the patients themselves).

There is a further compelling disadvantage which arises from the fact that it is extremely difficult or even impossible to forecast how one would feel towards living when faced with a terminal illness when in good health. It is too easy to simply say mercy killing would be the answer when considering the questions from a stance of good health and often with little or no experience of strictly limited life. Those professionals working with terminally ill people find that it is very rare indeed for patients genuinely to want their life shortened; in the vast majority of cases, even though the horizons of life may be very limited, life is precious both to the patients and to their friends and relatives. Much more often the suggestion of wanting life terminated is a cry for help with symptoms and personal distress in the knowledge that it is safe to suggest it and communicate in that way.

In conclusion, this is clearly an extremely complex and emotive subject with both moral and legal issues on the agenda. To an extent, the very structure of our society as we know it is being endangered with possible far-reaching effects following these deliberations. It is quite possible that the legal structures to a bill of active euthanasia would be too restrictive and rigid; on the other hand, tight legal control would be vital.

Attention to good medical practice is perhaps the most important way forward. The keeping of a balance between expertise and humane attitudes as well as improved communication and understanding between professionals themselves, between the professionals and the patient, relatives and friends, and indeed facilitating these between the patient and those relatives and friends, are all fundamentally and vitally important.

Many governments are looking to others for a lead. The recently formed National Council for Hospice and Specialist Palliative Care Services in the UK has considered the issue of euthanasia very early in its existence. It was felt by the National Council that many countries are looking to the UK for a lead, since the modern hospice movement, with its fundamental attitudes of care, started here about 30 years ago. A statement of policy on euthanasia was made public in 1992 and reads as follows:

> The National Council for Hospice and Specialist Palliative Care Services has been asked to make a statement on active voluntary euthanasia. This is defined as direct killing of patients at their own request to prevent further suffering.
> Council believes that the issue of active voluntary euthanasia with

all the complex legal and ethical problems it presents is entirely separate from the provision of good palliative care. Council deplores the linking of the two statements on good palliative care for the terminally ill.

Hospice and palliative care services aim to promote comprehensive care for those with progressive advanced disease and a short life expectancy in order to achieve the best possible quality of life. This provision of care recognises and meets the needs of relatives and thus also involves professional advice and support of the close family and friends of the patient.

Council affirms that the intention of good and appropriate palliative care is to relieve the physical, emotional, social and spiritual suffering of such patients, whilst respecting their individuality, and does so without intent to shorten life.

In this context Council believes there is no place for the direct killing of patients at their own request.

It is of interest to compare the second paragraph of this statement with the wording of the Early Day Motion mentioned earlier in the chapter.

Euthanasia is an issue on which many people have firm opinions. It is vitally important, in the discussions on this fascinating and complicated subject, that the definitions of the words involved are clearly understood. Without an understanding of these meanings, the discussions lose their importance and relevance. While in a sense society has to sort out the complexities of euthanasia, this will come about as a result of different groups, institutions and individuals responding to the dilemmas it poses in quite varying ways, according to the interests they are seeking to promote. There seems little doubt that the debate on such an important issue will continue well into the future as attitudes change and understanding evolves.

Appendix 1

To whom it may concern

Copies of this document are located with my personal documents, my general practitioner, my next of kin or with (specify name, address and occupation as applicable) _____

DECLARATION

Although I wish those entrusted with my treatment during future grave illness to care for me as best they can, I fear gross dependency, dementia or equivalent indignity more than death. I therefore request that this be borne in mind and absolve my doctors from any liability due to their not using all therapies of marginal benefit in my case, whereby the prolongation of dying rather than of living may well result.

I reserve the right to revoke this document at any time.

Signed: _____   Name: (caps) _____

                             Address: _____

                             _____

                             _____

I witnessed the signing of the above document. I am satisfied that the full meaning of the document was clearly understood. I will not be a significant beneficiary in the will of the above-named.

Signed: _____   Signed: _____

Name: (caps) _____   Name: (caps) _____

Address: _____   Address: _____

_____   _____

_____   _____

Appendix 2

To my family, my physicians, my lawyer, and all others whom it may concern.

If the time comes when I can no longer take part in decisions for my own future, let this statement stand as an expression of my wishes and directions, while I am still of sound mind.

If at such a time the situation should arise in which there is no reasonable expectation of my recovery from extreme physical or mental disability, I direct that I be allowed to die and not be kept alive by medications, artificial means or 'heroic measure'. I do, however, ask that medication be mercifully administered to me to alleviate suffering even though this may shorten my remaining life.

This statement is made after careful consideration and is in accordance with my strong convictions and beliefs. I want the wishes and directions here expressed carried out to the extent permitted by law. In so far as they are legally enforceable, I hope that those to whom this Will is addressed will regard themselves as morally bound by these provisions.

Signed _____   Date _____

Witness _____

Witness _____

Copies of this request have been given to:

Spouse/next of kin   ☐

Children   ☐

Parents   ☐

Solicitor   ☐

General Practitioner   ☐

Parson/Priest   ☐

Hospital Consultant(s)   ☐

Dying with Dignity, Toronto, Canada

Appendix 3

ADVANCE DIRECTIVE

TO MY FAMILY, MY PHYSICIAN AND ALL OTHER PERSONS CONCERNED

THIS DIRECTIVE is made by me _____

_____

_____

at a time when I am of sound mind and after careful consideration.

I DECLARE that if at any time the following circumstances exist, namely:

1. I suffer from one or more of the conditions mentioned in the schedule; and

2. I have become unable to participate effectively in decisions about my medical care; and

3. two independent physicians (one a consultant) are of the

opinion that I am unlikely to recover from illness or impairment involving severe distress or incapacity for rational existence,

THEN AND IN THOSE CIRCUMSTANCES my directions are as follows:

1. that I am not to be subjected to any medical intervention or treatment aimed at prolonging or sustaining my life;
2. that any distressing symptoms (including any caused by lack of food or fluid) are to be fully controlled by appropriate analgesic or other treatment, even though that treatment may shorten my life.

I consent to anything proposed to be done or omitted in compliance with the directions expressed above and absolve my medical attendants from any civil liability arising out of such acts or omissions.

I wish it to be understood that I fear degeneration and indignity far more than I fear death. I ask my medical attendants to bear this statement in mind when considering what my intentions would be in any uncertain situation.

I RESERVE the right to revoke this DIRECTIVE at any time, but unless I do so it should be taken to represent my continuing directions.

SCHEDULE

A Advanced disseminated malignant disease.
B Severe immune deficiency.
C Advanced degenerative disease of the nervous system.
D Severe and lasting brain damage due to injury, stroke, disease or other cause.
E Senile or pre-senile dementia, whether Alzheimer's, multi-infarct or other.
F Any other condition of comparable gravity.

Signed _____

Date   _____

WE TESTIFY that the above-named signed this Directive in our presence, and made it clear to us that he/she understood what it meant. We do not know of any pressure being brought on him/her to make such a directive and we believe it was made by his/her own wish. So far as we are aware we do not stand to gain from his/her death.

Witnessed by:

Signature _____   Signature _____

Name _____   Name _____

Address _____   Address _____

_____   _____

_____   _____

Voluntary Euthanasia Society, London

References

British Medical Association (1984) *Handbook of Medical Ethics*. London: BMA.

British Medical Association (1988) *Euthanasia: The Report of the Working Party to Review the British Medical Association's Guidance on Euthanasia*. London: BMA.

British Medical Journal (1992) Euthanasia round the world, *British Medical Journal*, 304, 7–10.

Social and Community Planning Research (1992) *British Social Attitudes Cumulative Sourcebook*, first six surveys. Aldershot: Gower.

Humphry, D. (1991) *Final Exit: The Practicalities of Self-deliverance and Assisted Suicide for the Dying*. Eugene, OR: The Hemlock Society.

House of Commons (1992) *Notices of Motions*, 20 January, No. 43, 1571.

The Patients Charter (1969) HMSO 51–1003, 10/91, C5,000. London: HMSO.

Twycross, R.G. (1981) Euthanasia. In A.S. Duncan, G.R. Dunstan and R.B. Welbourn (eds) *Dictionary of Medical Ethics*, pp. 164–7. London: Darton, Longman and Todd.

Wilkinson, J. (1990) Ethics of euthanasia, *Palliative Medicine*, 4, 81–6.

8

The Medicalization of Dying

Editor's note: In this chapter, two authors present short essays on the complex issue of the extent to which the care of dying people is being inappropriately 'medicalized'. In order to do this, we have gone to an established independent hospice and sought the views of the senior doctor and senior nurse. The result is not intended to polarize the main issues, but rather to illustrate the wide range of views currently in evidence. Both writers speak from substantial experience and offer us a lively exploration of the medicalization thesis.

A NURSE'S VIEW

BRONWEN BISWAS

There is evidence to indicate that the recent expansion of the hospice movement has seen the increasing medicalization of hospice care (Johnson *et al.* 1990; James and Field 1992). This development, I would suggest, poses a very real threat to the fundamental principles on which the movement was founded. As the Matron of the Leicestershire Hospice since it opened seven years ago, it appears to me that although this process of medicalization began slowly, it is fast gathering momentum. This acceleration has been greatly influenced by the subtle shift in recent years, from what was initially referred to as terminal care, to what is now known as palliative care, culminating in 1987 with the recognition by the Royal College of Physicians, of palliative medicine as a sub-speciality of general medicine. The enthusiastic 'amateur' hospice doctors of the past are fast disappearing to be replaced by career grade doctors, who have had a formal training prior to taking up medical director/consultant grade posts. This new breed is recognized and accepted by their counterparts within the National Health Service (NHS) as specialists in their own right, with all the status and prestige accruing to such expertise.

I intend in this chapter to begin by examining the impact the hospice movement has had on the care of dying people and go on to define what is meant by the terms medicalization, palliative and terminal care. I will then look at the contribution made by education and research and the national cancer charities as well as the place of investigations in terminal care. Finally, I will attempt to draw some conclusions from the issues that arise in order that the way forward for the future may be less confusing.

What impact has the hospice movement had on the care of dying people?

It was the committed belief of Dame Cicely Saunders, founder of the modern hospice movement, that the care of dying people could be greatly improved by the alleviation of emotional, spiritual and social distress, as well as physical suffering, which became the driving force for the movement. As Elizabeth Earnshaw-Smith stated, 'the achievements to be looked for are not merely in physical ease and improvement, though they may be considerable, but in the use of the time given by these to deal with past problems, enjoy present opportunities and probe future plans for the family who must live on afterwards' (quoted in Saunders and Baines 1983: 1). It is both interesting and significant to note that when Dame Cicely opened St Christopher's Hospice in 1967, she brought to it the skills she had acquired from her training in three disciplines – social work, nursing and medicine. According to Sir George Young, 'the initial achievements of the pioneers of terminal care in opening up the whole subject (of death and dying) for examination, research and debate cannot be underestimated' (quoted in Saunders *et al.* 1981: 1). The hospice movement has, therefore, been instrumental in dramatically improving the care of dying patients in the UK. The original aim of the movement was to create a new approach to the care of dying people and it was a response to the perceived unmet needs of dying patients and their families within the mainstream of care provided by the NHS.

There are several elements which are unique about this approach. First, there was a recognition that dying was not a symptom, but a process, and that individuals required much more than physical care if they were to be supported through it. Secondly, it was also recognized that family and friends had an important role to play, as the impact upon them, during and after the patient's death, was considerable. The patient and family combined was seen as the unit of care, not the patient alone, and the major givers of care were family, friends, nurses, volunteers, chaplains, bereavement counsellors, not only doctors. Thirdly, in order to meet the wide-ranging individual needs of each patient and family, a contribution from many disciplines was required, including medicine. These individual needs encompass the emotional, spiritual and social aspects of human beings, as well as the physical ones. The patient and family benefited most when all the agencies involved combined equally to form a cohesive team. Fourthly, there was a recognition that death need not be viewed as a totally negative experience, in terms of failure, but that it could be an enriching one for all those involved. The patient, family and carers may discover that they have a range of inner resources that had never emerged before. As a result, for some patients and families, the quality of family relationships improved and attitudes to life changed, as individuals actively searched for a meaning in order to make sense of the situation they found themselves in.

What do we mean by 'medicalization' in the hospice context?

It is important at this point to define clearly what is meant by the term 'medicalization'. At its simplest, it means the increasing dominance within the hospice movement of doctors, for instance in full-time medical director posts. This is in contrast to the early days when doctors were merely one member of a team of equals, often on a part-time basis. Associated with the increasing dominance of doctors is the incorporation of the traditional 'medical model', used in other aspects of medicine. The main elements of the medical model are the search for objective, discernible signs of disease, its diagnosis and treatment.

The emphasis within the medical model is on biological explanations and biological treatments and the focus of care is on the pathology within the individual, that is, the part, rather than the whole, individual. Care in this context is determined by the patient's physical condition, dictated by the physical symptoms, which in turn leads to care being doctor-led. In contrast, the hospice definition of care emphasizes a wider, holistic approach where the patient's physical, social, psychological and spiritual needs are attended to and care is patient-led. Hence, the effect of medicalization on hospice care is to shift the emphasis of both the theory and delivery of care, as I shall attempt to argue.

Are the terms 'palliative care' and 'terminal care' synonymous?

In my view, the above terms are not synonymous. The difference is clearly highlighted by Penson and Fisher, who define palliative care as 'a broad band of care, indeterminate in length, which should start the moment cancer is diagnosed, or even before. When there is a gleam of apprehension in the patient's eye'. They go on to suggest 'that it is at this point that the District Nurse should be introduced to the family concerned, even though the care required initially might only be intermittent'. Terminal care, they state, 'is only part of the palliative care programme and comes at the end of life, that is in the last hours or days. Important and demanding though it is, it is usually the least difficult part of total care' (Penson and Fisher 1991: 3). The question is, least difficult for whom? I presume 'least difficult' for the doctor, certainly not for the patient, relatives, nurses, counsellors or chaplain.

The objective of palliative care, according to Penson and Fisher (1991: 3), is 'to improve the quality of the preceding days, weeks, months and years and by so doing, quite possibly increase the quality of those weeks, months and years'. This definition clearly blurs the distinctions between medicine, surgery, oncology, palliative and terminal care.

There are many medical and surgical patients who cannot be totally cured, but who learn to live with their disease for many years, but this is very different from patients who are actually in the process of dying from their disease. Palliation is the relief of symptoms, and the logical extension of this view is that death is a symptom, and with increased expertise in palliation techniques, death can be alleviated altogether.

Terminal care, on the other hand, acknowledges that death is a process, not a symptom and, as the only certainty in life, cannot be avoided. If the process of dying is to have any value or meaning, it must be recognized that it involves more than a collection of physical symptoms. No-one would contend that there is not a need for distressing symptoms to be relieved, or that symptom control is not an important part of terminal care, but as Michael Kearney (1992: 44) points out, it is 'the ability to actively control, or at least contain, the distressing symptom, so creating an environment of safety and trust, which is the necessary pre-requisite to any loosening and opening to the deep level of experience'. This statement points to there being value in the actual process of dying.

The shift from terminal care to the much wider area of palliative care is a shift in emphasis which alters the original concept of improving care of dying people. Palliative care shifts the focus of attention away from death and there is a real danger that by talking about and focusing upon palliation, people may stop talking about and confronting the fact that the individual is going to die.

Have research and education contributed to medicalization?

Yes, in some ways I think they have. Dame Cicely Saunders had to move outside the NHS so as to create a new approach and new models of care for dying people. As she herself said, 'we moved out [of the NHS] so that attitudes and knowledge could move back in' (Saunders *et al.* 1981: 4). It is her committed belief that education is the key to the dissemination of these new attitudes and knowledge throughout the medical and nursing establishment, in order that care for all dying patients should improve, no matter where they are cared for – at home or in hospitals. Dame Cicely never envisaged all dying patients being cared for in hospices, but fervently believed that the hospice philosophy could be used in a variety of settings – the home, hospitals, residential and nursing homes – and did not rely on a purpose-built building. Over the past 30 years, terminal care, especially for cancer patients, has markedly improved in all these settings.

The dissemination of the philosophy of terminal care has led, as James and Field (1992) have observed, to others having adapted the initial ideals and grafted them onto already existing organizations and traditions. Here, I think, lies a danger. From this adaptation of the original ideals comes the drive to push back the frontiers of terminal care, away from dealing solely with dying patients, to include those patients who, although they cannot be cured, have nevertheless many months or years of life left.

The urgent need for improved methods of pain and symptom control initially led to this becoming a prolific area for research. There were already existing methods of research in other areas of medicine which could be applied and the results contributed to the gradual acceptance of the speciality throughout the medical establishment. It followed that these research findings formed the basis of a wide range of education programmes which resulted in changes in clinical practice in both nursing and medicine. The continuing cycle of practice, research and education, leading to changes in clinical practice shifted the emphasis to symptom control which overshadowed the philosophy of care. Research and education were especially appealing to doctors, but also to some nurses, hence palliative care was born.

There is no doubt that education has proved to be the vital key to the dissemination of knowledge which has greatly improved the care for dying people, but there is an inherent difficulty for hospices in maintaining their philosophy as they become accepted by the traditional medical and nursing establishment within the NHS. As James and Field (1992: 1368) comment: 'having originated outside the health care establishment as a critic of the standards and practices of terminal care within the National Health Service hospitals and elsewhere, the hospice movement, as a result of its success, has now become part of the mainstream of health care provision, an example of good practice in terminal care and an influential player in policy making'.

The crucial question which must now be asked is *at what cost?* And, as the hospice movement joins forces with the NHS, will the hospice model be so diluted, aided by palliative medicine, that the 'traditional bio-medical emphasis on physical interventions and professional dominance re-assert themselves?' (James and Field 1992: 1370).

Is there a role for investigations in terminal care, or is this 'creeping medicalization'?

There is evidence to support the idea that the use of investigations in terminal care is a form of creeping medicalization. Johnson *et al.* (1990: 792) found that 'more use was made of invasive procedures and that patients were more likely to be referred for palliative surgery and organ donation in hospices, where there is a full-time consultant or medical director' in post. The extensive use of medical investigation was found to be linked directly to the level of medical input and the danger is that they become routine rather than selective. Another important finding from this study was 'a significant trend for units with such medical support to see themselves as technical and those without to see themselves as non-technical' (ibid.).

In this study, 'technical' and 'non-technical' referred to how staff in the units classified themselves: technical units were described as pain relief centres, or specialist medical/nursing units; non-technical units were described as peaceful havens, home from home, a place for compassion and dignity. Staff in units which have part-time medical input see themselves as more like a nursing home, whereas those with a full-time medical presence see themselves as active units. There is clearly a role for investigations, such as X-rays and blood tests, but it is important that the reason for undertaking any investigation is that it is appropriate for that particular patient, rather than a case of standard practice.

Have the national cancer charities contributed to the medicalization process?

Help the Hospices, an organization which has played a significant role in gaining government recognition for the value of hospice care, states in a paper defining hospice care that 'all patients should be under the constant clinical supervision of a doctor and should not receive medical care only at the discretion of the senior nurse at the time. Medical staff should be on call at all times and should have experience in palliative medicine' (Help the Hospices 1990: 5). Many hospices started with part-time medical cover, with nurses providing most of the care, in partnership with family members, volunteers and other disciplines. Many patients who die have very few physical symptoms, but they and their family still need skilled nursing care. There is a question of balance here. Good medical care can enhance the overall quality of care given to the dying patient and the family, but it should not be seen as the most important component of that care.

Another national charity that has played an important role in improving the care of dying people has been Cancer Relief MacMillan Fund. It has also played a significant role in shifting the focus from terminal to palliative care by its creation of medical lectureships and senior nursing posts. This professionalization has also provided the opportunity for a recognized career structure in both medicine and nursing. The benefits have been a quicker dissemination of knowledge and a beneficial change in attitudes towards dying people, but the costs have been an acceleration of palliative medicine and the danger of the re-emergence of the medical model.

Medicine, unlike nursing, has a particular structural problem in that it is difficult for doctors to move between specialities. With the introduction of formal training programmes, it is possible for doctors to enter the field of terminal care when they are relatively young and there is a greater possibility of them being trapped in a small speciality for 30 years. The enthusiastic amateurs of the past had the advantage of entering hospice work later in their careers having spent time in other fields. The new breed of medical director needs more than terminal care to avoid burnout or boredom, hence the drive towards palliative care.

Government recognition of the value of hospice care has led to the provision of substantial government funding, and provided the impetus for the formation of the National Council for Hospice and Specialist Palliative Care Services. A crucial part of its role is that it is to be recognized as the official channel for communication between government and the movement. There is a need to be vigilant in order that government funding and the power it commands does not dictate and distort the care. Apart from being the recognized voice of the movement, it is also concerned with the setting of standards and encouraging the use of audit, by which the quality and cost-effectiveness of hospice care can be judged. This drive to introduce NHS audit measures, which rely heavily on numbers, throughput, bed occupancy and turnover, poses a threat. Hospice care is more concerned with 'effective communication, empathy and feelings of satisfaction' (James and Field 1992), areas for which there are not very precise audit measures. There is, therefore, a danger from the 'imposition of crude measures of quality and cost effectiveness which may damage or subvert hospice practice' (James and Field 1992). These measures, which tend to concentrate on physical symptoms because they are easier to assess, rather than the emotional or spiritual aspects, lead back towards the medical model and provide an incomplete measure of total hospice care. One present dilemma for the hospice movement is that failure to use these measures may result in failure to obtain much needed funding.

Conclusion

Palliative medicine has become the major driving force behind the shift from terminal to palliative care. If terminal care is not to be consumed by the broader speciality of palliative care, then thought should be given to their clear separation rather than their merger. There are, I would suggest, two distinct specialities, rather like two fingers on the same hand. Although they lie next to one another and are joined at the base, they are also two separate entities. On this basis, palliative care could concentrate on those patients who can be enabled to live with their disease for many months or years, whereas terminal care could focus on those patients who are in the final stages of life.

There is no doubt that medicine in the field of terminal care has, over the past years, resulted in great improvement in the care for dying people, especially in the area of symptom control. But a solution must be found to prevent dying patients and their families becoming the 'cinderella' of palliative medicine. The hospice movement put death on the agenda, but palliative care has the capacity to relegate it to the sidelines. Can those involved in terminal care allow this to happen? I for one, very much hope not.

References

Help the Hospices (1990) *Hospice Care: Definitions and Qualifications*. Working Paper. London: Help the Hospices.

James, N. and Field, D. (1992) The routinization of hospice: charisma and bureaucratization, *Social Science and Medicine*, 34(12), 1363–75.

Johnson, I.S., Rogers, C., Biswas, B. and Ahmedzai, S. (1990) What do hospices do? A survey of hospices in the United Kingdom and Republic of Ireland, *British Medical Journal*, 300, 791–3.

Kearney, M. (1992) Palliative medicine: just another specialty? *Palliative Medicine*, 6(1), 39–46.

Penson, J. and Fisher, R. (1991) *Palliative Care for People with Cancer*. Leeds: Edward Arnold.

Saunders, C. and Baines, M. (1983) *Living with Dying: The Management of Terminal Illness*. Oxford: Oxford Medical Publications.

Saunders, C., Summers, D. and Teller, N. (1981) *Hospice – The Living Idea*. Leeds: Edward Arnold.

A DOCTOR'S VIEW

SAM AHMEDZAI

It is an interesting paradox of the ageing population in a typical Western society such as the UK, that as we have more old people, it has become less common to say that an elderly person has died of 'old age'. Nearly always we identify a medical diagnosis, and the assumption is that the person has died from a disease, despite medical intervention. Has this arisen because modern medicine has 'medicalized' death and dying? And, if so, how does this affect our attitudes towards dying people, and the provision of care? In this essay, I will explore these themes and I will discuss what benefits or disadvantages may arise from the process of medicalization. I shall focus particularly but not exclusively on those dying from malignancy, and on the contribution of hospices and the emerging speciality of palliative medicine. My biased viewpoint is that of a doctor working in this new speciality, but I do not pretend to be representative of all my colleagues.

What is meant by 'medicalization'?

It is important first to establish what is meant by 'medicalization'. In my view, it is the consequence of adopting the medical model of thinking about illness and health, which is based on an understanding (however incomplete) of pathological processes. It is assumed that as the human body is an organism, all disease states can be understood in terms of immunological, biochemical, degenerative or (increasingly) genetic malfunctions.

The World Health Organization (WHO) has stated that health is more than the absence of disease – it is the complete physical, psychological and social state of well-being. The medical model, however, is founded on the negative aspects of disease and illness rather than the positive dimensions of health. It is therefore possible that the medicalization of health care can lead to a relatively restricted view of the human condition, instead of one based on the concept of well-being. This has led not surprisingly to medicalization being seen as a narrow, non-humane approach to caring for people.

In practice, the medical model can be applied in many dimensions of function (physical, social, sexual, etc.), classifying significant deviations from the norm as symptoms. In this admittedly piecemeal and multi-system fashion, medicalization may give the appearance of being holistic – that is, based on the whole person rather than on one system or organ. The end result may be that a person who is dying is seen comprehensively (pseudo-holistically) as a failing organism, with many malfunctions that may be ameliorated.

Provided that the ultimate malfunction (i.e. death) is itself not denied, might this lead to an acceptable method of care?

It is important to appreciate that medicalization does not mean the deployment of only medically trained staff. It is possible, and fashionable, for other disciplines (e.g. nursing and physiotherapy) to adopt the disease- or problem-led approach. However, doctors have a unique place in the introduction and establishment of new ideas and methods of practice, because in most Western societies they are traditionally granted a superior professional status. It is noteworthy that two of the most influential figures in the adoption of modern principles of care for dying people – Saunders and Wilkes – are medically qualified. It is appropriate that other disciplines should assert their place in the provision of care, as well as in the study and teaching of care of dying people. It is acknowledged that good palliative care needs teamwork – but the question of who should lead the team is usually avoided.

Another issue that is often mistakenly seen as synonymous with medicalization is the use of technological aids in diagnosis and care. It is ironic that one of the greatest contributions made by hospices in the field of symptom control has been the dissemination of the battery-powered syringe driver (Johnson and Patterson 1992). This unobtrusive but patently technological device has replaced the intravenous infusion for many situations requiring parenteral (i.e. non-oral) medication, but even though the syringe driver can be hidden under the pillow it remains a use of technology. There is also currently a creeping re-introduction of intravenous infusion therapy in hospice care, for the management of hypercalcaemia with bisphosphonate drugs. Since this line of therapy is seen primarily as palliative – that is symptom-relieving rather than life-prolonging – it is accepted in hospices where a few years ago intravenous treatments would have been banned. As more of the difficult symptoms and syndromes of the terminal stages of life become potentially palliatable, will we see more examples of invasive and technological therapies being assimilated into previously low-tech hospice care? If so, does that process represent intrusive medicalization, or the rational application of a better understood and safer therapy to a wider pool of patients who may benefit?

The role of hospice principles in the care of dying people

It is impossible to contemplate the recent changes in attitudes and practice of care for the dying without acknowledging the role of hospices. However, the basic hospice concept is ages old – being based on the post-Roman sense of 'hospitality', or welcoming guests who need shelter, warmth, food and tending (Saunders 1987). What is new is that these humane actions are now less substantive and more conceptual – so that it is often stated that hospice is not bricks and mortar, but a philosophy of care. Interestingly, hospices for dying people were first being established in the UK and Ireland in the last century, at the time when many of our large hospitals were also being built from public subscription. Intriguingly, the second phase of hospice building – from the opening of St Christopher's in 1967, and again based on voluntary giving – came when society and the professions were beginning to see clearly the flaws in the National Health Service (NHS).

An important tenet of hospice care is the multidisciplinary approach. This is the origin of the need for teamwork and, as mentioned above, itself leads to the question of which discipline leads the team. The predominance of nurses in the hands-on aspects of care, and the high nurse–patient ratios in most hospice in-patient services, have led naturally to a tendency for nurses to challenge the previously 'superior' position of doctors. Is it appropriate to use the relative numbers of staff, or even which group spends most time with the patient and family, as the yardstick for who should lead or dominate in the power stakes? Or are these just as illogical or arbitrary as perpetuation of the historical importance of medical men in the health services?

It is again ironic that alongside the humanistic message of treating dying people with respect, the other initial contribution of modern hospice care was the introduction of rational scientific practice in the area of symptom control. In British health care, most clinical diagnoses which lead to initiation of drug treatment or other interventions such as surgery or radiotherapy are made by doctors. Similarly, it is at present only doctors who can actually prescribe drugs and perform surgical procedures. However, this position may change, as in other countries nurses have assumed greater powers in prescribing and in the administration of intravenous therapy. Could this assertion of intellectual and technical skills by nurses apply in the area of hospice care in the future? And would that be seen (and regretted) as another form of medicalization? Some of the other disciplines involved in the care of dying people, e.g. physiotherapy and occupational therapy, already have considerable autonomy over their access to patients and their kinds of intervention. Might these professions also one day challenge both the doctors and nurses for leadership of the hospice team?

The wide recognition and respect now given to hospices in British society can paradoxically serve to undermine their original value, which was to be a constructive reaction to the worst aspects of inhumane health care delivery. Hospices are now seen as important parts of most communities, but in response to the changing management of the NHS and its method of funding in particular, they are also seen to be entering into partnership with the same system that they broke away from. One reason for this process is described as 'routinization', which may happen eventually to any radical new movement that is based on charismatic leaders advocating a philosophy of change from convention (James and Field 1992). It is unfortunate that the term routinization has a workaday, bureaucratic ring to it – this may lead to its being rejected by hospices as a negative act. But there are many positive aspects to routinization: gaining the respect of other professionals in 'mainstream' services, the ability to consolidate and not always having to break new ground, the ensuring of standards of practice and even its philosophy across the wide movement. Thus the charity Help the Hospices, which was set up to support independent hospices financially, has published guidelines on what constitutes a hospice and its staffing (Help the Hospices 1990). One of its unambiguous statements was on the need for hospice patients to have access at all times to a doctor, who should be experienced in palliative medicine. Does this amount to flagrant medicalization of hospice care, or is it reasonable for dying people to have the same medical rights as those who are not so seriously ill?

British hospices in the early 1990s can be divided into those with full-time consultant grade medical staff and those without. This is not an arbitrary classification: practically it differentiates those units which offer specialist treatments and those which cannot (Johnson *et al.* 1990). Is this technological medicalization brought in by the doctors, or conversely has the need that is being felt by many hospices to offer such services led to the employment of full-time qualified staff?

The emergence of specialities

At one time it might have been suggested that a doctor who wished to care for dying people in a hospice service required primarily a sense of kindly vocation, backed up by a broad medical background that was preferably based in primary (i.e. community as opposed to hospital) care. It is strange, then, for the establishment of 'palliative medicine' in 1987 to come from the Royal College of Physicians rather than the Royal College of General Practitioners, and for the accreditation programme to be seen increasingly as biased towards hospital doctors trained in internal medicine and specialities such as oncology. Moreover, the very necessity to train for care of the dying is revolutionary, when for years it was said that this was just a part of basic medical care.

Basic nursing training, too, is often said to incorporate all the skills needed for the nursing care of dying people. Why, then, has there been the establishment of two 'higher' qualifications of the English National Board for nurses who wish to practise palliative care? All those in the other disciplines, from social workers to paramedical therapists and chaplains, have also now formed their own specialist groups. Are these just for comradeship or the establishment of closed shops in employment? Perhaps the routinization of hospice care is leading to its demystification, and recognition as just another (rather special) speciality.

The move from 'terminal' to 'palliative' care

The terminology of terminal care has led to much unnecessary confusion. Until ten years ago, it was considered acceptable to refer to the care of dying people as 'terminal' care. With the emergence of specialities, this phrase seemed too blunt – and also too narrowly confined to the last days of life. Hospice professionals then took over a word that has been used in cancer treatment for several decades – 'palliation'. But whereas surgeons, radiotherapists and medical oncologists talk about palliative treatments in the sense of 'symptom-relieving and not life-prolonging therapy', hospice staff have sought to make the word synonymous with the broader concepts of hospice care itself (Saunders 1987) and it is in this sense that it is used in the title of the present volume.

By itself, this euphemistic sense of the term palliation could lead to some misunderstanding between professionals in discussing the aims of therapy. But the shift away from 'terminal' care also reflects a genuine desire to become involved with patients and families at an earlier stage in progressive, incurable and ultimately fatal diseases. Is palliative care therefore moving away from the original hospice concern with the care of dying people? It is not unreasonable for this to be so, as much of the distress of death is caused by poor communication and badly planned clinical care in the early stages of disease. So long as the inevitability of death is not denied, and the last few days and weeks are made comfortable, why should palliative care specialists not address the earlier, preventive issues?

Perhaps there are limits to how early this process of palliative care should begin. If hospice staff become involved with patients immediately after diagnosis of cancer or a similar fatal disease, what role is there for other specialists or indeed the family practitioner team? Too early deployment of hospice care may lead to unhealthy competition with other services, such as oncology, for scarce resources. Some would regard as an unpalatable consequence the displacing of genuinely terminal patients from hospice beds or home care teams, by patients with relatively early stage disease. It will be interesting to see how these issues will be resolved, as palliative care sets up its stall in the mainstream medical marketplace.

Distinctions between curative versus palliative treatments

The scope for confusion about therapeutic aims increases when palliative care is set against so-called curative treatment, for conditions such as cancer. Palliative care has been frequently said to start 'when cure is no longer possible'. This definition is quite erroneous, as it falsely implies that all (or even most) cancers start off as curable, and on failing to respond to treatment become ripe for palliative (hospice) care. Another cliché of early hospice literature was the distinction between 'cure *vs* care'. This could be offensive to the large numbers of practitioners (doctors, nurses, radiographers, etc.) who are engaged in anti-cancer treatments, as it implies that they do not 'care'. It could be argued in return that oncology has the much greater intellectual challenge, as it seeks to combine cure *and* care, while hospice care can exempt itself from providing the former. However, the continuation of this dogmatic 'them-and-us' confrontation benefits neither camp.

The relevance of this debate in an essay on medicalization is that, in this society, once again we must note that at present only doctors are empowered to make the important decisions about curability or need for palliation. This may be appropriate soon after diagnosis when complex and rapid choices need to be weighed up – and offered to the patient for final consent. When the stage of illness enters the palliative or hospice care domain, it would be quite unacceptable for the decision making to be seen as largely or entirely a medical matter, with other disciplines or indeed the patient having little say. Towards the end of life, the patient and family need to have increasing power of autonomy, guided by the professionals. The trend towards publishing algorithmic flow charts for the management of symptoms (Regnard and Ahmedzai 1990) in terminal disease is therefore useful to provide decision aids for the clinicians, but may insidiously be undermining the holistic, team-based and basically intuitive approach that characterized the earlier non-specialists.

Unhealthy obsessions of palliative care

Understandably, the earliest challenges for the new hospices in the 1970s and 1980s were the control of pain, and the distress of dying from cancer. The former was previously badly managed in hospitals and by general practitioners, and the latter had emerged, after the post-war removal of infective scourges such as tuberculosis and rheumatic fever, as the disease most dreaded. But has the continuing focus on these topics become an obsession, and has medicalization played a part in this?

Regarding pain, one of the most influential teachings was Saunders' brilliant concept of 'total pain', i.e. encompassing the psychosocial dimensions of distress as well as the physical (see also Chapter 9, this volume). However, the ease with which the term 'pain' has been applied to all sorts of suffering may have paradoxically led to its further medicalization, as simultaneously we were being taught that pain is a patho-physiological process that, once analysed and understood, can be treated with the judicious use of morphine and other medications. This mechanistic view of suffering was far from Saunders' point, but hospices have been indelibly branded with the concept of pain control in the minds of the public (a fact that is frequently used as a marketing strategy for fund-raising).

Is the connection with cancer still tenable for hospices? There is no doubt that, of all diseases, the various forms of malignancy (haematological diseases such as leukaemia and myeloma must be included as well as the solid cancers) are most readily associated with a certain poor prognosis. I have already referred to the nonsensical argument of 'cure *vs* care' for cancer. The apparent ease with which the point of entering a terminal phase can be identified in cancer patients (at least in retrospect), adds to its appeal for hospice staff (Seale 1991). Ironically, the new developments in palliative treatments such as bisphosphonates for hypercalcaemia, which relieve symptoms but can also extend life, will prove to be a challenge to hospice staff who prefer to have their patients' prognosis cut and dried.

Is the emphasis on cancer a true reflection of the public's concern, or yet another aspect of the domination of the medical and nursing professions' view? The answer is not known, as no research has been done into what illnesses really frighten the public. But the apparently arrogant assumption of hospices that the large majority of people who actually die of non-malignant causes such as cardiac, respiratory or cerebral degenerative diseases are not frightened, or do not suffer as much as cancer patients, deserves to be challenged by direct evidence. Proof that hospices need to review their traditional viewpoint is the ready support by the public (and the initial disapproval by cancer hospices) for children's hospices which take predominantly non-malignant cases. The remarkable popularity of new hospice-type services for AIDS patients is another reminder that not only cancer patients deserve special attention when they are dying (see Chapter 5, this volume).

The new focus on evaluation and audit

The recent radical changes in the funding of our health system have been linked to ways of proving the value of services, including the care of the dying, through the use of quality assurance and audit, discussed in detail in Chapter 2. Unfortunately, these management tools are rapidly becoming seen as ends in themselves, and this adds to the view by many staff in non-management posts that evaluation and audit are bureaucratic impositions. Audit itself incurs a significant cost in terms of staff time and data collection exercises, and in hospices where a significant proportion of the funding is voluntarily given by the public, there may be profound objections to using this precious public money to meet professional or government agendas. Yet it may be argued that precisely because charity money is used so heavily in hospices, accountability and evidence of good practice have to be obtained.

Doctors are usually ignorant of, and traditionally mistrustful of, qualitative methodologies for assessing subjective symptoms and feelings. They are used to recording and evaluating measurable problems. These attitudes are to some extent shared by nurses and paramedical staff working in care of dying people. Yet there is still little experience of valid ways of either numerically or qualitatively measuring the distress of dying (Ahmedzai 1991). With this background of prejudices, it is possible for the current first attempts at audit of palliative and terminal care to be seen as either too difficult, or too superficial. In caring organizations, the slogan 'value for money' seems to ignore the human – often voluntarily given – contribution.

Audit demands the identification of objective markers of a service's structure or process, or of the outcome of its work. In auditing the care of dying people, the medical model is attractive as it readily yields discrete problems and causes which may be monitored. This does not preclude the development of piecemeal multi-system pseudo-holistic audit, as described earlier in this essay. But how much easier it is to audit pain, waiting times for admission or the completeness of case-notes in a thousand patients, than say, the 'dignity' of a single death?

In practice, hospice teams are developing ways of combining medical and nursing perspectives into a hybrid, humane and more truly holistic form of 'clinical' or 'team' audit (Trent Hospice Audit Group 1992). If this collaboration is developed rigorously and disseminated as well as the control of pain or the use of syringe drivers, it is exciting to contemplate that this may become the next pioneering message to emerge from the hospice movement into mainstream health care.

References

Ahmedzai, S. (1991) Quality of life in research in the European palliative care setting. In *Effect of Cancer on Quality of Life*. Boca Raton: CRC Press.

Help the Hospices (1990) *A Guide to Good Standards and Practice*. London: Help the Hospices.

James, N. and Field, D. (1992) The routinization of hospice: charisma and bureaucratization, *Social Science Medicine*, 34(12), 1363–75.

Johnson, I.S. and Patterson, S. (1992) Drugs used in combination in the syringe driver – a survey of hospice practice, *Palliative Medicine*, 6, 125–30.

Johnson, I.S., Rogers, C., Biswas, B. and Ahmedzai, S. (1990) What do hospices do? A survey of hospices in the United Kingdom and Republic of Ireland, *British Medical Journal*, 300, 791–3.

Regnard, C. and Ahmedzai, S. (1990) Dyspnoea in advanced cancer – a flow diagram, *Palliative Medicine*, 4, 311–15.

Saunders, C. (1987) What's in a name? *Palliative Medicine*, 1, 57–61.

Seale, C. (1991) Death from cancer and death from other causes: the relevance of the hospice approach. *Palliative Medicine*, 5, 12–19.

Trent Hospice Audit Group (1992) *Palliative Care Core Standards*. Derby: Derbyshire Royal Infirmary.

9

Issues in Pain Management

RICHARD ATKINSON and GRAHAM DAVIES

Within the practice of medicine, much of our time is spent assessing the pain status of the patient. But what is pain? It is more than just a feeling of discomfort; in addition to the complex anatomical and physiological component, it envelops emotional, social, psychological and behavioural factors, often meaning that the severity of the disease causing that pain is not truly related to the intensity of the pain described.

Pain may be divided into acute pain, which is that which follows daily life incidents, causing varying degrees of discomfort and which, by the healing process of the body, gradually resolves over a matter of days, weeks or months. At the other end of the spectrum is chronic pain, which is a longer-term development of many additive factors, some quite difficult to define, but producing an all-embracing feature of life for the patient and, often, the family. Cancer pain has features of both acute and chronic pain and while one would classify it normally under the chronic heading, there are of course those patients who, sadly, do not survive six months and therefore are not strictly within the chronic pain category. Palliative care, therefore, embraces the concepts of both acute and chronic pain management. While there may be dependence on certain drugs for symptom control, addiction does not present a problem and should not deter carers from appropriate regimes and their adjustment.

This chapter is designed to help the reader, first, to understand the varied problems within the concept of pain while keeping in mind the psychosocial aspects. Second, the problems of delivering good pain management globally and locally are addressed. Third, we examine issues in relation to education and the future development of services.

Pain as a phenomenon

While approximately 20 per cent of the population will die of cancer-related illness, it is a sad reflection of our management of symptoms that the greatest fear is that of pain. Although this fear is particularly related to cancer, other terminal illnesses such as peripheral vascular disease, degenerative states, the arthritic diseases and metabolic disease, have significant and often seemingly uncontrollable pain problems. Pain, therefore, must be regarded as only one of many of the presenting symptoms at this latter stage of illness. Indeed, of those entering a hospice for terminal care, only about 60–70 per cent will have pain as their predominating symptom.

Pain must be evaluated in its presenting form, both as a physical and an emotional problem. The International Association for the Study of Pain (IASP) definition is 'an unpleasant sensory and emotional experience associated with actual or potential tissue damage or described in terms of such damage' (IASP 1986).

The extent of the overall picture is important to understand (Fig. 9.1). Pain may be a feature at the presentation of cancer or appear at a later date following initial treatment. Further investigations and tests, or even therapeutic modalities such as surgery and radiotherapy take place but still, in some, pain is a persisting factor. During this period, many of the accompanying psychosocial factors come into play as additive components. In the face of a life-threatening illness, work may no longer be possible; sleep is interrupted; concerns and worries about the future progression of symptoms and the cancer occur. Family life may also be disrupted by the illness, its treatment or mechanical restrictions. Hobbies, activities and socializing are also affected, while future aspirations in work, promotion and social status can be eroded. These collectively become the psychological and social magnifying factors of the underlying physical continuing entity of pain, and in its various aspects it begins to rule the life of the individual.

The management of pain in terminal illness must therefore concentrate on bringing patients to an understanding concerning limitations of the illness. As confidence is gained by symptom control, there is acceptance of some ongoing discomfort. Patients develop the ability to cope with the problem rather than pain ruling their existence. Modalities and management at this stage must concentrate not only on relieving that aspect of the physical suffering that is within our capability, but also involve the psychological and social coping strategies that are necessary support. Thus patients and carers can work together, so that goal setting and pacing become learned aspects of living.

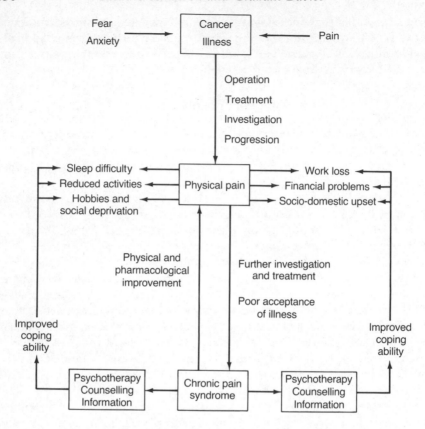

Fig. 9.1. Development and management of chronic pain syndrome.

To examine an example of such a situation, a patient with debilitating terminal cancer pain may not be able to pursue the hoped for holiday with relatives in Australia, but on the other hand can set sights on the more realistic goal of a short break in this country with appropriate input from care services. Likewise, a full day's work may not be possible, but pacing oneself for a few hours two or three times a week, negotiated with a sympathetic employer, may satisfy the cravings of a patient who has previously been very busy and active, and serve as good occupational therapy, even in the final stages of life.

Measurements of pain

Pain thresholds

Pain can be measured at two different levels. First, there is the pain perception threshold which is said to be reached when the quality of the experience produced by applying a stimulus changes and pain is felt for the first time.

This threshold is relatively fixed for a given environmental condition and varies little from person to person. It may be increased by pain relief measures, such as analgesic drugs, but is only minimally affected by placebo. Secondly, severe pain threshold occurs when on increasing the stimulus, the pain becomes unbearable. It is, therefore, a measure of the patient's reaction to pain and is a far more variable factor.

The interval between these thresholds is a measure of the individual's tolerance of pain and, therefore, is a measure of ability to withstand pain. The chief factors affecting the level of tolerance are:

- ethnic and social influences (Sternbach and Tersky 1965; Melzack 1977);
- the environment (Bond and Pilowsky 1966);
- significance of the wounds of the patient (Beecher 1956); and
- personality (Bond 1979).

It is appropriate to examine more thoroughly one of these factors.

Personality is dependent upon a blend of intellectual and emotional qualities reflected in our behaviour, and is unique to each individual. In people of normal intelligence, intellect plays a far less important role in the experience of pain, and consequently there is considerable interest for those studying the psychological aspects of pain. Personality may be examined clinically by dividing individuals into groups. From these we can demonstrate the common characteristics of emotion known as personality traits. Those traits which are important in our understanding of pain are:

1. *Anxiety*: pain will be greater for patients with a tendency to become anxious. Conversely, pain may produce anxiety, thus lowering the patient's tolerance and heightening the pain perceived.
2. *Depression*: chronic pain especially brings feelings of secondary depression which decrease our tolerance to pain and our ability to cope with it. This is particularly noticeable in those with a pre-existing depressive personality.
3. *Hysterical traits*: these will produce exaggerated symptoms and lead to poor tolerance.
4. *Hypochondriacal traits*: low-grade aches and pains are common among such people. They generally require little other than reassurance to reduce their symptoms, although they may also show marked reliance on repetitive visits to health professionals.
5. *Obsessional traits*: those who have obsessive personalities and a high degree of fitness over and above that which is required to live a normal healthy life, will be more aware of trivial aches and pains and attach greater significance to them than is considered 'normal'.

It is therefore evident that, for the most critical analysis of data obtained concerning pain measurement, one must always be aware of the different psychological variables that may affect the validity of any of the results.

Much work has been conducted to try to quantify the salient features a patient's personality which will in some way alter his or her tolerance and response to treatment. For this reason, such questionnaires as the Cornell Medical Index, the Eysenk Inventory, the Minnesota Multiphasic Personality Inventory and the Whitely Index of Hypochondriasis were developed. Results obtained using these have shown that the way patients describe and react to pain is dependent on a number of personality factors. These include past conditioning, the degree of neuroticism, extroversion and introversion. Such factors all, therefore, affect the way patients communicate pain.

When treating a patient in pain, it becomes apparent that we must decide how much emphasis should be placed on trying to define and treat the aetiology and how much should be placed on the treatment of the patient's reaction to it. Personality, therefore, not only governs the extent to which we feel pain, but also the amount of pain relief gained from any one form of treatment. In this context, three types of symbolism can be associated with pain.

1. Pain as evidence of physical damage.
2. Pain as a problem of communication.
3. Pain as a means of manipulating others.

In any attempted measure of pain relief following treatment, it is necessary to take into account just how much patients want to lose the 'sick role' or how much they depend upon it.

Patient understanding and belief about illness behaviour or the 'sick role' develop through the assimilation of new information, with pre-existing meanings and reaction patterns held by them. As a consequence of underlying pain and perception of a stimulus built upon pre-existing cognitions, patients develop a pattern of behaviour unique for each individual. The assessment of cognitive behavioural factors in chronic pain patients is therefore becoming recognized as an important component in a comprehensive pain evaluation. Pain clinic work in recent years suggests some patients are able to tolerate or reduce their pain by developing coping strategies. Examples of such cognitive strategies include relaxation and distraction techniques. Behavioural coping strategies involve activities such as walking, goal setting, exercising or talking to individuals and groups.

One interesting area of current research for behavioural scientists is centred on how the individual's 'locus of control' relates to his or her ability to adjust and cope with the pain problem (Crisson and Keefe 1988). Individuals who have an internal locus of control believe that a positive cause–effect relationship exists between their own behaviour and outcomes they experience. People having an external locus of control, on the other hand, perceive a lack of a relationship between activities and consequent outcomes. These individuals thus perceive the outcome as controlled by sources external to themselves; good examples are the power of others, chance factors and fate or luck. Work with cancer patients and chronic non-malignant pain groups suggests that those patients who have an internal locus of control experience less psychological distress and are more likely to develop appropriate coping strategies. In contrast, those who have an external locus of control would appear to have a greater chance of being depressed, and therefore rely more on passive pain coping strategies, viewing these strategies as ineffective.

Taking into account the psychological variables which influence the way in which patients respond to pain and the relief that can be obtained from treatment, it is possible now to move forward. Next we examine how it is possible to gain a specific measurement of pain for use diagnostically and therapeutically, particularly in a clinical trial situation.

Any assessment may be divided into subjective assessment (i.e. carried out by individual patients and excluding observer bias) and objective assessment (i.e. carried out by a nurse or doctor, and based on the patient's appearance or comments). However, where an observer is involved, bias may be a factor in view of their own beliefs about the level of pain to be expected in any given illness.

Descriptive aspects of pain

Pain, by its very nature, is a subjective symptom presenting problems of understanding and communication. Investigatively, our purely physical way of compartmentalizing a problem is an unsatisfactory reflection of our narrow way of interpreting illness. Investigations are invoked to give us a positive result to correlate with the patient's description. The presence of such positive factors provides us with an objective result to confirm the subjective symptom. Frequently, however, there seems to be a wide discrepancy between perceived pain in comparison with positive investigations.

Descriptions, therefore, must be based on models that the patients can understand and investigators, equally, can interpret. This allows a clearer perception of the problem.

Description among children

A particular problem in younger age groups is the inability to conceptualize severity, so it is important to devise a way which is descriptive to the younger mind, but understandable to the older one. Of special use under such circumstances is the series of faces ranging from sad and grimacing to smiling and happy, since degrees of pain will fall within those ranges in the mind of a child. Alternatively, building blocks of different colours may indicate pain and suffering where black and red are unhappy or painful colours and lighter colours are happier, pain-free representations.

Adult descriptions

Subjective descriptions vary widely but need to cover chronicity (how much of the time patients have pain), quality (those features that are most persistent) and severity (the intensity of pain). It is important to bear in mind that a person in the latter part of a cancer-related illness who has pain does not just have the pain of that illness but may have pre-existing conditions. These require definition, description and, if possible, an order of severity and importance to the patient. A pain at a distant site to that which they perceive as their origin of illness may have significance to some patients and no significance to others. Therefore, it is necessary to establish an understanding of the patient's various discomforts.

Pain itself may be nociceptive, neurogenic or psychogenic. Nociceptive pain has a dull, aching, constant quality that we are so used to in everyday discomfort, while contrastingly neurogenic pain has a sharper burning quality, often with shooting or lancinating components and is more likely to be indicative of nerve damage or involvement. Psychogenic pain, on the other hand, is rarely a pure feature of cancer pain but may be an indication of deeper concerns and worries which require to be evaluated. A patient's descriptions will, of course, indicate which of these exist, but in the real world cancer tends to produce a mixture of such pains.

Methods of rating pain

In palliative care, the following are simple, reliable and practical methods that can be applied in the varying environments (i.e. the hospice, hospital or home) in which care may be given.

Verbal rating scale

Patients are asked to choose from a list of words – such as mild, moderate, severe or unbearable – which word best describes the pain that is being experienced. This provides us with coarse ratings, since the limitations of language and occasionally a lack of understanding or communication, mean such words give only a rough estimate. The relative size of the differences between descriptive words in such a rating scale is unknown, and will vary with the patient's own interpretation, although the assumption is usually made, when attaching scores to such ratings, that the differences are similar.

In favour of this method, however, is that it rates highly on a scale of patient preference. On this basis, new ways of utilizing a language tool have been devised to allow for patient compatibility and also sensitivity in critical analysis. One such test is the McGill Pain Questionnaire (MPQ), in which a number of words have been brought together in groups which describe not only the pain intensity but also the patient experience (Melzack 1975). Melzack and Torgerson (1971) state that describing pain solely in terms of intensity is like specifying the visual world only in terms of light. They regard pattern, texture and colour as other dimensions of visual experience. Other versions of the MPQ have been described using a British population for the compilation of word tables (Reading *et al.* 1982), and are therefore probably more suited than the original MPQ for use in this country.

Numeric association

Patients are asked to rate their pain on a numerical rating scale, usually 0–10, the lower number being equivalent to only a mild pain and the higher numbers to more intense or excruciating discomfort. One disadvantage to the use of this method is that patients find it difficult to convert a sensory experience into a numerical factor. Like the simple verbal rating scale, it also fails to reflect adequately the complexity of pain felt, being only a crude assessment and showing no continuous variation.

The linear visual analogue

This consists of a straight line, with only the extremes of pain experience marked on it:

No pain at all _____ Worst pain imaginable

Patients place a mark at right angles to the line where they feel their pain lies. This allows patients more freedom of choice, hence a continuing variation of measurement, and is therefore a more sensitive test (Huskisson 1974). The distance, measured in millimetres from the left-hand side of the line, is referred to as the pain score.

The linear visual analogue has been acknowledged as the best paper and pencil instrument for the assessment of clinical pain intensity. It has been suggested that this one measure condenses many qualities of pain experience into a single measure (Gracely 1979).

Analgesic quantity

This is a measure of the quantity of a given analgesic required to achieve pain relief. It provides a good estimate of pain intensity if the patient has been instructed in self-medication of the dosage regime. However, it provides less accurate information at higher doses, since patients may experience drug side-effects and so maintain a lower dosage regimen than is appropriate to their pain relief.

In summary, therefore, to find an absolute measure for pain is difficult, since the pain experience is not solely related to the degree of perceived trauma or disease causing it.

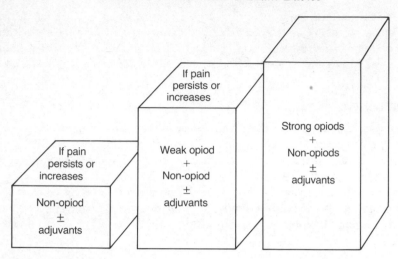

Fig. 9.2. The analgesic ladder for cancer pain management (from World Health Organization 1986).

Analgesics and their applications

The plethora of analgesics of different strengths and compounds may have contributed over the years to a poorer rather than a better quality of analgesia. Too much choice at the level of moderate analgesia, where it is appropriate to introduce weak opiods, has produced a tendency to prescribe alternatives at this level rather than progress to the use of a stronger analgesic. The World Health Organization (WHO) has tried to rationalize the situation and in doing so to take its message to many of the countries that have fewer drugs and, indeed, only minimal availability of opiates (WHO 1986). It seems appropriate, therefore, that the WHO analgesic ladder (Fig. 9.2) should just have three steps – mild, moderate and strong – such that in countries where there are restrictions, the availability of three analgesics in adequate quantities and appropriate usage will go much of the way to improving pain management in terminal cancer.

In Western society, we have many more drugs available to us and it is important to rationalize analgesic usage, moving upwards from step to step (rather than sideways) when illness progression requires increased analgesia. It may also be appropriate to apply the analgesic ladder to some other compounds, such as the non-steroidal anti-inflammatory agents, and in this way create an ascending order of strengths in appropriate concomitant disease usage. It is not however necessary always to be at the same level on the two ladders. In some instances, it may be necessary to use a moderate analgesic with a weaker anti-inflammatory agent or vice versa.

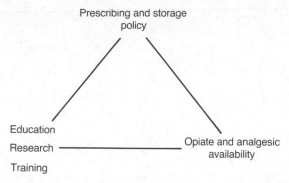

Fig. 9.3. Combined problems of opiate delivery.

Problems

While it is good practice to promote the logical progression to strong analgesia, there are underlying problems in achieving this (Fig. 9.3). Opiates are still unavailable in some countries of the world, and there are some in which they are available but there are considerable restrictions on the formulation of the drug which can be prescribed. The policies adopted in some countries are also a restricting factor, with constraints on total dosage prescribable or constraints on which medical specialist may prescribe, further reducing the availability of the strong analgesic. In some countries, the training, education and research programmes available to health professionals working in the field of palliative care may also be a restricting factor.

Therefore, it is essential to endeavour in any programme of management to pay equal attention to these three aspects, thus producing the highest quality of analgesic delivery.

Historical aspects

Modern pain management still centres on two of our oldest drugs – aspirin and morphine. These have been available for centuries in some form, but had they been produced as a modern addition to our pharmacopoeia and, as such, subjected to all the rigour of modern testing in clinical trials, it is unlikely that they would have ever reached patients. Although excellent therapeutically, aspirin causes considerable side-effects such as allergy, gastritis and intestinal bleeding as well as having a low safety margin in overdosage. Morphine, with its potential for respiratory depression, severe sedation and nausea, would also have difficulties in passing trials. However, much of the medicine practised in terminal care in the latter part of the nineteenth century and the first decades of this century centred on the use of these two drugs and little else. It is only in the last three to four decades that there has been access to many other drugs, both as entities in themselves or as combinations.

New drugs

Is there an alternative to morphine as a strong analgesic? Little has emerged as a viable option, and instead we need to use our best available drug more effectively. There is, however, a need for some medications of similar activity, and interest has centred on the group of partial agonists and their place on the analgesic ladder. Of these, buprenorphine has high affinity for the μ receptor (the receptor to which morphine binds to produce its pain-killing effect) and may appropriately be used at the start of step 3 where strong analgesics are indicated. Concerns about antagonism and a reduced pain-killing effect when used with the pure agonists (drugs which have a pure morphine effect and no antagonism in their action) are probably ill-founded as shown recently by Atkinson *et al.* (1990). Following regular full dosage of coproxamol or dihydrocodiene at step 2 on the analgesic ladder, buprenorphine has proved effective as the next stage. It was demonstrated that antagonism to morphine analgesia did not occur when progression was required.

In recent years, much research and clinical work has centred on the epidural and spinal use of opiate drugs. This more direct route is used to deliver smaller doses to the receptors of the nervous system when unpleasant systemic side-effects are experienced when using larger doses orally or parentally. However, only a small percentage of patients need to use this route. Hogan *et al.* (1991) have shown that morphine on its own is rarely sufficient, but when delivered with local anaesthetics it offers a viable alternative route.

Transdermal systems (the absorption of drugs through the skin from adhesive patches) offer a useful alternative for some strong analgesic drugs. Fentanyl, a short-acting synthetic opiate, has been extensively used in this form. Non-steroidal anti-inflammatory preparations have proved to be important concomitant drugs in combination with opiates, since their action in reducing the inflammatory response in bony pain and skeletal discomfort in cancer is complementary.

Despite all of the improvements, there are still some patients whose pain is only partially relieved by opiate administration. For these patients, therefore, it has been necessary to look to the co-analgesic drugs and accompanying therapies. Such groups include the tricyclic anti-depressants, some of the anti-epileptic drugs for their de-afferentation effect (the potential to reduce unpleasant neuralgic firing of the nerves), and beta blockers and alpha-2-agonists have also shown promise in this field. Local anaesthetic peripheral nerve blocks and trigger point injections also have an important part to play in helping to control this very difficult type of pain. It is therefore in this area that further research should be undertaken to improve pain management in terminal illness.

Non-drug remedies

For those cancer patients who suffer persistently from partial or severe pain, there remains a wide variety of non-pharmacological techniques which, if used appropriately, can help overcome or at least reduce the pain (Table 9.1).

Psychological methods

As we have seen, an individual's pain experience is influenced by psychological, social and spiritual factors as well as the underlying physical cause. In a cancer patient, this may be a fear of dying, leaving behind loved ones, or unfinished work. Such factors and many like them can add to or produce anxiety and depression which then lead to an exacerbation of the pain and suffering.

Table 9.1. Non-analgesic methods of pain control

Psychological methods
- communication with the patient
- cognitive–behavioural psychotherapy
- hypnotherapy
- relaxation
- art therapy

Regional blockade
- peripheral nerve block
- sympathetic block
- epidural
- intrathecal
- trigger point injections
- spinal opiates

Electrical
- transcutaneous nerve stimulation
- acupuncture

Inhalation
- Entonox

Radiotherapy

Chemotherapy

Surgery

Many of the psychological remedies are clouded in mystique. The simplest and most important is communication (see Chapter 4, this volume). The need of the professional carer to take time to listen and talk to the patient and relatives in an honest and sympathetic manner is paramount.

Cognitive–behavioural psychotherapy

Cognitive–behavioural psychotherapy involves using a three-systems analysis model. This allows both the therapist and the patient the opportunity to assess and treat pain under the headings of physical, behavioural and cognitive. By using this model, a patient can see how pain may take control of his or her life. During therapy, patients learn to relate the three systems to daily life. They learn to recognize the cycle between how they feel and think. This then affects what they do. Although a formal approach to this model may be inappropriate for many cancer patients, the principles involved serve as a useful reminder of how the mind and body interrelate (Fishman 1990).

Hypnotherapy

This requires the skills of a trained clinical hypnotherapist. Ten per cent of the population are somnambulistic such that they are able to derive maximum benefit from hypnotherapy, and as a result can do such things as anaesthetize a painful part of the body. However, for many patients, hypnotherapy is confined to relaxation or combating phobias and the side-effects of drugs.

Regional blockade

In the 1950s and 1960s, regional blockade was seen as the panacea for pain control. Clinicians are now more selective in its use. Whereas previously it was thought that noxious impulses were conveyed along precise anatomical pathways, neuroscience has provided us with evidence about the plasticity of the central nervous system, thus explaining why interrupting a single nerve, plexus or spinal pathway may fail to provide any analgesia at all, or only for a short period of time.

While local anaesthetic blocks last for only a short time, they can be useful diagnostic aids. The effect of a local anaesthetic block can be prolonged by infusing it down a catheter. Surprisingly in the case of some sympathetic blocks and trigger point injections, the therapeutic effect can last for several weeks. However, for 'permanent' blocks, neurolytic agents or neurosurgical techniques are used. The duration of block can last for several days to six months or longer. Because of the risk of side-effects and to ensure the continuing confidence of the cancer patient, case selection is vital.

Regional blocks can be extremely useful, but care should be again taken in case selection and this technique should only be performed by clinicians skilled in their use and in an environment where there are radiological and resuscitation facilities (Table 9.2).

Table 9.2. Pain-relieving procedures and where to perform them

	Home	Hospice	Hospital
Peripheral nerve			
Single shot	+	+	+
Infusion	−	+	+
Neurolytic	−	+	+
Radiofrequency[a]	−	−	+
Cryoanalgesia[a]	−	−	+
Trigger point injections	+	+	+
Sympathetic block			
Stellate gangleon	−	+	+
Lumbar sympathetic[a]	−	−	+
Coeliac plexus[a]	−	−	+
Presacral plexus[a]	−	−	+
Spinal block			
Intrathecal			
local anaesthesia	−	+	+
opiates	−	+	+
neurolyses[a]	−	−	+
Epidural			
local anaesthesia	−	+	+
opiates	−	+	+
neurolyses[a]	−	−	+
Neurosurgical			
Cordotomy (ablation)[a]	−	−	+
Pituitary ablation[a]	−	−	+

[a]X-ray facilities required; +, recommended; −, not recommended.
Source: The table appears by kind permission of Dr P.A.J. Hardy.

Electrical

The gate theory of pain explains how additional stimulation arriving at the spinal cord level can prevent noxious impulses travelling to higher centres. Transcutaneous nerve simulators are 'pocket-sized' devices which transmit impulses in the frequency range 10–100 Hz. The impulses are conveyed to the painful site by rubber electrodes, which can be worn throughout the day. The machines are relatively cheap, robust and portable. While they should not be used with patients who have cardiac pacemakers, the side-effects are few, skin allergies being an occasional problem. These stimulators are particularly useful for the treatment of neuromas, neuralgias, including post-herpetic neuralgia, phantom limb pain, and myofascial pain and osteoarthritis.

Acupuncture has gained in popularity in recent years. The discovery of endorphins has given credence to its validity as a treatment for pain. However, despite its proven value for the treatment of non-malignant pain, its use in cancer pain would appear to be limited. Acupuncture has, however, had some success in the management of intractable nausea and vomiting.

Inhalation

Entonox, a gaseous mixture of 50% O_2 and 50% N_2O, is available in portable cylinders. It is equipotent to moderate doses of pethidine and can be self-administered using a mask and one-way demand valve. Because of its physical properties, maximum analgesia is achieved after several deep breaths. Entonox is particularly useful during painful procedures such as changes of dressings, bed-baths, mobilization and physiotherapy, but should be avoided in severe bowel obstruction which affects some cancer patients.

Radiotherapy

Palliative radiotherapy is often used as first-line treatment for pain from bony metastases and myeloma, and its use should also be considered for fungating tumours, superior vena caval obstruction and spinal cord compression. Modified doses may minimize the incidence of side-effects.

Chemotherapy

Chemotherapy also has a palliative role and should be considered if pain is an unremitting symptom. It may be particularly valuable in the case of ascites, pelvic tumours, cerebral tumours and superior vena caval obstruction.

Surgery

Palliative surgery for the relief of pain should be considered if patients are fit enough to withstand invasive procedures. Defunctioning colostomy, fixation of pathological fractures and spinal decompression are such examples.

Success in pain management

It is a sad inevitability of terminal illness that all patients will die eventually, irrespective of how well their symptoms are managed. In this context, quality of care is a measure of patient, relative and carer satisfaction. Success in management outcome is a balance between symptom control, psychological and spiritual support, and an understanding of the disease state. It is hoped that good outcome, and therefore success, should be the result of treatment carried out in a special centre such as a hospice or continuing care unit, but true success lies in emulating such outcomes in other areas where care of the dying patient takes place alongside other care.

Care core standards are an important indicator of the multidisciplinary quality of care in palliative medicine. The Trent Hospice Audit Group (1992) has produced six standards which can be measured clinically through outcome and process audit:

- collaboration with other agencies;
- symptom control;
- patient/carer information;
- emotional support;
- bereavement care and support; and
- specialist education for staff.

When examining symptom control, it is possible to evaluate care to see that symptoms have been controlled to an acceptable level, while ensuring that a multidisciplinary team approach involving patient and carer has been used. Process audit from documentation will show whether a care plan was reviewed, whether the patient was involved in formulating that plan of care, and that it has been adequately documented.

Specialist services

The Macmillan nursing movement has done much to improve the understanding of the public and health professionals of the success that can be achieved with detailed terminal care management. A survey carried out by our own unit has shown the good understanding that these nurses have of palliative care symptom control and their relationship with the primary care team and other health professionals. Their unique position as counsellors with specialist knowledge of carer and family is also invaluable.

Further success in the last two decades has been demonstrated with the emergence of the hospice movement, providing highly specialized expertise for in-patient and home care, albeit for a relatively small percentage of patients. However, the expertise in looking after this small cohort of patients in specialized units provides a forum through which other professionals may rotate, and in which some may work for a varying period of their career. This enables them to take this expertise back into the working environment of other specialities. It may be reasonable to argue that we really do not need more in-patient hospices on which to centre this expertise, but that those which are already established should be used widely as a resource in the management of pain and other symptoms, thus improving terminal cancer care.

Education and development

In an ideal world, knowledge should be disseminated by comprehensive undergraduate programmes in medicine, nursing and the allied professions, but an enquiry of three medical schools in the Trent Region suggests that the overcrowded curriculum can only give an outline of the theory of pain management. Much, therefore, must still be left to the enterprise and personal initiative of graduates who eventually face the difficult problems of pain management in terminal illness in the clinical situation but with little training.

Medical undergraduate curriculum

The International Association for the Study of Pain has produced a comprehensive suggested curriculum which, if used appropriately, would enable students to maintain an overview of pain. It considers nine headings that should be used as the basis for discussion for curriculum committees:

1. Introduction and overview.
2. Definition of pain.
3. Ethical issues.
4. Basic sciences.
5. Clinical sciences.
6. The clinical presentation of pain.
7. Management, including general principles, pharmacology, physical and psychological techniques.
8. Pain in special context.
9. The evaluation of methods for treating pain.

Educational aspects

Pain management as a postgraduate subject draws interested professionals to courses as it is an emotive symptom whether acute, chronic or terminal in nature. Good pain management represents good care to patients and relatives. Budgetary constraints present the major drawback to comprehensive teaching programmes, but there is much value in one- and two-day release courses, especially if workshops and clinical presentations are included. Nurse specialists in pain management or tutors within nursing schools who have a particular interest in pain management are able to present an interesting and varied programme covering the different aspects outlined.

Specialist education

The availability of specialist education has lagged behind interest in palliative care, and it is only now that more attention is being paid to the multidisciplinary aspects of training rather than a narrow look from one discipline. The English National Board nursing courses are validated and comprehensive, offering a specialist training to nurses in this area of work.

Medical education has run along two parallel lines in recent years, with the Royal College of Physicians and the Royal College of Anaesthetists taking the lead. The College of Anaesthetists now require the teaching and training of pain management as part of higher specialist training modules at senior registrar level. All accredited anaesthetists therefore have at least a working knowledge of pain management under the guidance of the College and the input of the Pain Society of Great Britain and Ireland. Those who pursue this interest further than the basic module become appropriate candidates for consultant posts with a special interest in pain management. Such pain clinics will then develop links to local palliative care services.

On the other hand, the training of doctors in the career grades for palliative medicine has been undertaken by the Royal College of Physicians and their more comprehensive training progamme is aimed at full-time appointments in palliative medicine, usually leading to the appointment of hospice medical director or consultant physician with specialist interest in palliative medicine. It is hoped by such improved training programmes that cooperation between specialities will lead to improved treatment for patients.

We have examined the present and future status of pain management that can be achieved in the hospital, hospice and home environments. While a patient's basic treatment in any setting must be aimed at providing the best care, an effective use of resources will allow professionals to work together to enable a high proportion of terminally ill patients to die in their own homes. Hospitals, by the very nature of their acute involvement, will continue to be where most cancer sufferers die. It is to be hoped that the resources offered by hospices and their associated services will help to improve standards of management in such settings, especially where training has been given. Inevitably, the needy few with difficult symptoms and social problems will benefit from the care associated with death in a hospice.

References

Atkinson, R.E., Schofield, P. and Mellor, P. (1990) The efficacy in sequential use of buprenophine and morphine in advanced cancer pain. In D. Doyle (ed.) *Opiods in the Treatment of Cancer Pain*, pp. 81–7. London: R.S.M. Services.

Beecher, H. K. (1956) Relationship and the significance of a wound to the pain experienced, *Journal of the American Medical Association*, 161, 1609–13.

Bond, M.R. (1979) *Pain: Its Nature, Analysis and Treatment*. Edinburgh: Churchill Livingstone

Bond, M.R. and Pilowsky, I. (1966) Subject to the assessment of pain and relationship to the administration of analgesics in patients with advanced cancer, *Journal of Psychosomatic Research*, 10, 203–208.

Crisson, J.E. and Keefe, F.J. (1988) The relationship of locus of control to pain coping strategies and psychological distress in chronic pain patients, *Pain*, 35, 147–54.

Fishman, B. (1990) Cognitive-behavioural approaches. In K.M. Foley and J.J. Bonica (eds) *Advances in Pain Research and Therapy*, Vol. 16. Second International Conference on Cancer Pain. Raven Press.

Gracely, R.H. (1979) Psychophysical assessment of human pains, *Advances in Pain Research and Therapy*, 3, 805–823.

Hogan, Q., Haddox, J.D., Abram, S. *et al.* (1991) Epidural opiates and local anaesthetics for the management of cancer pain, *Pain*, 46, 271–80.

Huskisson, E.C. (1974) The measurement of pain, *Lancet*, 2, 1127–31.

International Association for the Study of Pain (1986) Classification of Chronic Pain Taxonomy, *Pain*, 3, S217 (suppl.).

Melzack, R. (1975) The McGill pain questionnaire: major properties and scoring methods, *Pain*, 1, 227–99.

Melzack, R. (1977) *The Puzzle of Pain*. Harmondsworth: Penguin.

Melzack, R. and Torgerson, W.S. (1971) The language of pain, *Anaesthesiology*, 34, 50–59.

Reading, A.E., Everit, B.S. and Sledmear, C.M. (1982) The McGill pain questionnaire: a replication of its construction, *British Journal of Psychology*, 21, 339–49.

Sternbach, R.A. and Tursky, B. (1965) Ethnic differences among housewives in psychophysical and skin potential responses to electric shock, *Journal of Psychophysiology*, 1, 241–6.

Trent Hospice Audit Group (1992) *Palliative Care Standards – A Multidisciplinary Approach*. Derby: Derbyshire Royal Infirmary.

World Health Organization (1986) *Cancer Pain Relief*, 2nd edn. Geneva: WHO.

10

Whither the Hospices?

DAVID CLARK

As we go through the 1990s, it becomes increasingly apparent that the hospice movement is experiencing a range of tensions and difficulties, mainly associated with its 'successful' expansion in the last few decades, and raising questions about overall future direction and orientation. While some might regard these tensions as sufficient to break up the 'movement' as previously understood, others interpret them as inevitable, indeed predictable and healthy features of the evolution of hospice care. In this chapter, I shall seek to identify the key issues which the hospices currently face, examine some aspects of the recent debate about their role and conclude with an analysis of strengths, weaknesses, opportunities and threats facing the hospice movement as a whole.

Hospices have expanded rapidly since the late 1960s, when the first, St Christopher's, was opened in London. By early 1992, in the UK and the Republic of Ireland, there were 178 in-patient units (113 of these independent charities) 186 day hospice services (many attached to hospices), 360 home care teams (community, hospital and hospice based) and 160 hospital support teams or support nurses (Hospice Information Service 1992: iii). As we saw in Chapter 1, this expansion has involved a shift in emphasis to the importance of domiciliary care, linked also to developments in day care for terminally ill people and the provision of specialist support services in general hospitals. A cornerstone of expansion has therefore been diversification and the wider promotion of hospice standards and ideals into other care settings. If we include each of these broad areas of development under the canopy of 'the hospice movement' (and some would challenge such an inclusion), then it is clearly facing a number of interrelated issues which will affect its future.

These issues encompass a range of factors linking both policy and practice and the value systems which underpin them. They alert us to the importance of understanding hospice care in its historical, sociological and cultural contexts. Five interrelated areas can be identified and I set them out here in general terms.

Issues facing the hospices

Structural

Hospice care, though often counter-posed to the mainstream of provision, does not exist in isolation from it. The place of hospice within overall patterns of health care delivery is therefore crucial. In the context of recent changes stemming from the National Health Service (NHS) and Community Care Act 1991, this raises the question of how hospice care is seen within the totality of purchasing and providing for health needs. Whereas in the past the position of independent hospices outside the NHS may have offered a high level of autonomy in both clinical practice and overall direction, increasingly the care which is given in hospices, if it is linked to NHS service agreements, will be subject to external scrutiny. In other words, contracts will be tied to audit and quality assurance.

Contracts will also be an ultimate solution to the problems of unplanned proliferation of hospices, in the last analysis denying funding to those developments which do not fit within district and regional strategic frameworks (Clark 1991). District health authority–hospice relations, increasingly seen within the language of 'partnership', do not always run smoothly. Recent case studies of new hospice developments show a mixed picture. In some districts, the existence of a voluntary hospice project has been a *sine qua non* for the development of palliative care services. The vision and foresight to be found within voluntary groups can act as the champion of new service developments. It can lead to a wider understanding of terminal care within the community and promote local support. At the same time, local enthusiasts, who sometimes appear more expert on palliative care services than the district officers with whom they are liaising, can hamper their own case. There is evidence of significant clashes between hospices and health authorities in a context where each group has differing priorities and where 'visionary, and 'bureaucratic' systems may come into collision (Clark 1993).

This can be exarcerbated by lengthening time-scales for the completion of hospice projects. From the initial conception, an in-patient hospice can now take ten years to become operational; a day unit may take five years. Early contact and agreement between a district health authority and a hospice voluntary group may be insufficient to sustain relations through this period. A high level of co-operation and trust will be essential, along with a sense of what might be termed structured flexibility. Over time-scales such as these, significant changes can take place in policy and legislation. Some recent hospice projects, for example, have straddled the introduction of major changes in the NHS. Similarly, models of care are also altering. With these points in mind, there may be a danger that some new hospices have a vision of, and system of care more appropriate to, the understandings of the 1970s than the 1990s. The need to more actively promote strategies for community care of dying people is an obvious example in this context.

The case is illustrated in a recent survey of 43 new hospices, conducted by the author, which showed that 79 per cent of the groups had aspirations for some form of in-patient care (including respite). Ninety per cent were planning day care, but only seven of these (16 per cent of the total) planned day care only. These findings can be looked at in two ways. On the one hand, they confirm the enormously increased interest in day care which has developed in recent years and show that this is seen as an essential component of new hospice services in most cases. Alternatively, this commitment to day care does not appear to have produced much by way of diminution in the desire to also provide in-patient services, which remain the goal of nearly four-fifths of all new hospice projects; this gives little indication of any significant change in approaches to hospice care in the period since the mid-1980s. Although hospice is often described as a 'philosophy and not a place', the continuing emphasis on traditional forms of in-patient care and on the 'bricks and mortar' of provision is striking.

A further factor shaping the types of services provided by hospices stems from the requirement that district health authorities conduct systematic assessments of needs for their local populations. As these needs assessments are conducted for palliative care, they will be used to inform subsequent purchasing strategies. In the future, therefore, detailed appraisal of local need, rather than the clammerings of local demand, will serve as the key guide to provision. As Stevens and Gabbay, (1991: 21) put it: 'Any useful assessment of need will require not only an analysis of the relationship between need, demand and supply for the many conditions under consideration, but an attempt to see how the three can be made more congruent'.

There are more general aspects to this, what we might refer to as the overall 'positioning' of the hospice services in relation to other providers of palliative care. For example, it is conceivable that NHS trust hospitals may wish to offer specialist services, such as the provision of in-patient units for terminally ill patients and that these might be seen as market competitors to the independent hospices. Similarly, fund-holding general practitioners may make demands for hospice provision, to which hospital providers seek to respond; there could be an important role here for community hospitals specializing in the rehabilitation or palliative care of patients from 'high-technology' settings and providing a quieter environment nearer to home, while also being served by 'outreach' from specialist teams. Squeezed in between these, however, may come the NHS hospices, denied the flexibility and funding advantages of the voluntary sector, but regarded as a marginal speciality within the provider groups that assimilate them.

Financial

Finance for the independent hospices has typically come from two sources, charitable giving and the NHS. In general, the capital costs of the UK's independent hospices have been the product of local fund-raising efforts rather than investment on the part of district health authorities. Subsequent revenue costs for operational services have been met from some combination of NHS and charitable monies. Since the early 1990s, a special allocation of Department of Health monies has been available to independent hospices. This figure has increased more than five-fold, from £8 million in 1990 to £43 million in 1993 (Department of Health 1990, 1993). Its allocation, via the regional health authorities, has caused a good deal of controversy within the hospice world: local competition for available funds, lack of clarity about criteria for eligibility, allegations of under-spending by regions. It has been suggested that by allocating monies specifically to the independent sector, the government has implicitly penalized those districts which had the vision to plan and implement their own NHS-funded palliative care policies. There have also been suggestions that the allocation of specialist funds may have fuelled the very problem of proliferation which ministers have been seeking to contain. Yet this uncharacteristic level of government support for the voluntary sector forms part of an overall commitment wherein purchasing authorities are to continue to work towards a position in which the value of their contribution to the revenue costs of independent hospice services matches that from voluntary giving. The allocation has been seen as money designed to prepare the hospices for the 'new world' of service agreements and to this extent there are doubts about the period for which it will remain ring-fenced. Thereafter, market forces will increasingly come into play. Coupled with the difficulties of fund-raising in protracted periods of economic recession, the financial outlook for the hospices could become considerably more straitened.

Organizational

Recent observers of the hospice movement on both sides of the Atlantic have commented on a complex nexus of interlocking trends in its development. Hospices are seen to be undergoing changes which 'routinize' (James and Field 1992) their earlier mission and which incorporate their work into the dominant health care system (Abel 1986) in a process characterized by 'institutional isomorphism' (Paradis and Cummings 1986). In general terms, hospices are becoming more like one another and less distinguishable from other care settings. At one level, this was always the intention, as in Cicely Saunders' much quoted phrase about hospices 'moving out of the NHS so that attitudes and knowledge could move back in'. However, a range of problems can also flow from these processes. With the decline of charismatic leadership and the succession to more formal patterns of authority can come new hierarchies, professional tensions, divisions of labour and threats to the 'teamwork' ethos of the hospice. It is a particular paradox that a movement which places the multi-professional team so centrally in its philosophy, should in recent years have spawned a range of mono-professional groupings, representing the interests and concerns of individual groups of hospice doctors, nurse managers, chairpersons, social workers, administrators and chaplains. Such tendencies have implications for the organizational culture of the hospices, which may appear less the 'anti-institutions' of the 1960s and 1970s and more the corporate health care providers of the 1990s, preoccupied with concerns about financial viability, market niche and professional status. Where, for example, is the role of volunteers to develop in such a context? And to what extent can a holistic approach to care delivery be maintained when there may be pressures to cut costs in order to compete?

Clinical

Such questions spill over into the clinical area. They manifest themselves in the growing debate, vividly highlighted in the essays here by Ahmedzai and Biswas (Chapter 8), about 'active' and 'passive' palliative care and concerns about the 're-medicalization' of hospice. The increasing involvement of career specialists at the consultant level is only one of several factors which may serve to promote the physical rather then the pyschosocial aspects of hospice care along with the reassertion of biomedicine and medical dominance. A recent survey of hospices in the UK and Republic of Ireland showed, for example, that units with a full-time consultant or medical director were more likely to choose a 'technical' description of their unit than those without. They also had a higher throughput and were more likely to refer patients for palliative surgery and organ donation. These differences seem set to increase with the appointment of more trained consultants in palliative medicine (Johnson *et al.* 1990).

There is also the issue of precisely who is cared for in the hospices. A national survey of 639 adults who died in 1987 contained only 44 (7 per cent) who had received hospice services, of whom only 2 were not suffering from cancer (Seale 1991: 13). To what extent can the hospices both increase their level of activity and move away from the emphasis on malignancy in order to care for significant numbers of people dying from other conditions? Should these be a requirement for further expansion, or is the present situation acceptable in terms of what is achievable? A further issue in this context is that of children's hospices, a number of which have become operational in recent years. Again, these appear to have captured the public imagination, but to what extent do they represent a viable strategy for responding to children and young people with life-threatening diseases, whose needs include domiciliary and respite care and a high level of co-ordination of available services?

Ethical and philosophical

Clinical issues of this kind overlap into broader questions of equity. One recent writer describes an 'underclass' of dying people resulting from the concentration of resources on those with cancer (Harris 1990). Some elderly people fall into this category. As O'Neil (1989) comments, within each district general hospital there are elderly patients dying with multiple physical and pathological problems who are not usually considered when planning services for terminal care. There is indeed some evidence to suggest that cancer patients in hospices, especially younger ones, have a special social status which is in marked contrast to patients in long-stay hospital wards or nursing homes (Seale 1989). Another group which appears to be excluded from the 'holistic' care of the hospices is made up of people from the black and ethnic minorities. Indeed, there are general questions about the extent to which the hospice model is taking account of a range of social differences relating to gender, age, sexuality, family circumstances, religion and ethnicity. The debate about whether hospices would care for people with AIDS, referred to in Chapter 5, is a case in point. Indeed, Carlisle (1992) has suggested that doctors are falsely confirming evidence of cancer in people with AIDS in order to get community nursing support from charities such as Macmillan and Marie Curie. Too often hospices appear as white, middle-class, Christian institutions serving a carefully selected group of patients, which the 'odour of goodness' (Smith 1984) surrounding them cannot fail to disguise.

The argument about hospices

If, as the proverb suggests, it is wrong to speak ill of the dead, it is perhaps even more unforgivable to speak critically about those who make a particular commitment to care for dying people. As Griffin (1991) acknowledges, the application of a calculative approach to the care of those with terminal illness is frequently considered to be in bad taste. The hospice movement grew out of a sense of dissatisfaction with a bureaucratic system of care which was poor on pain and symptom control and which ignored the complex interrelationships between physical, material, emotional and spiritual issues in the care of dying people. By championing holism and the reform of the dominant system, it attracted massive popular support and colonized a new field of moral concern. Professional scepticism was never far away, however, and more recently – fuelled no doubt by some of the issues already mentioned – this has hardened into abrasive condemnation, at least through the pen of one medical critic (Douglas 1991, 1992). Hospices are therefore no longer beyond the bounds of critical debate.

Colin Douglas's main objections, though flippantly expressed, are worth taking seriously. He makes three key points:

- Why should care at the end of an illness be separate from all that has gone before and why should collective dying be a good thing?
- Why should only a minority of a minority (those who die from malignancies) be singled out for special treatment?
- Why should a large and general need be left to the 'scanty and scandalously choosy efforts of a patchwork of local charities'? (Douglas 1992: 579)

His answer to these questions is simple. The hospice movement has drawn attention to earlier inadequacies in the care of dying patients, it has served as a base for the development of nursing skills and service innovations such as home care, and it has acted as a first home for the emergent medical speciality of palliative care. It must now wither away in favour of NHS palliative care support units offering 'consultations, home care services, and a few beds for the most difficult cases' (Douglas 1992: 579). The situation is of course not quite so straightforward, but Douglas's objections are nevertheless at the heart of current and future dilemmas for hospice care in the UK.

His critics reply that palliative cancer care requires special skills which work best in small units where morale can be kept high, that the NHS cannot hope to meet the needs of everyone and that the social base of the hospice movement is wider than he claims (Tulloch 1992: 718). They point out that home care teams working from hospices have done a great deal to ensure continuity of care for patients and families and that precisely because they attract significant donations, hospices provide a cost-effective service to health care purchasers (Jeffrey 1992: 718). They also argue that the task of disseminating hospice skills in pain and symptom control is still far from complete (Reid 1992: 718) and that patients in general hospitals are frequently denied the opportunity to die with dignity (Jankowski 1992: 718). To all of these must be added Douglas's well-known and widespread error of equating 'hospice' with a building, rather than a programme of cure and array of skills deliverable in a wide range of settings.

At the same time, others, such as Partridge, have put forward a sustained argument, similar to Douglas's, for the location of in-patient palliative care on the site of a district general hospital, easing the provision of diagnostic services, medical cover, therapeutic and social work support, and achieving economies of scale. Such an approach is believed to have major educational benefits in promoting hospice skills and standards in the mainstream context, where they can have the widest influence. It also seeks to offer continuity of care, by providing a focus for patients discharged from acute wards and an opportunity for them to be introduced to the domiciliary services. Partridge (1989, 1992) also argues that units of this kind will attract donations and additional funds which can be used for service improvements.

It is clear from these debates that hospices exist in a dialectical relationship with the NHS. As hospice practices have become better understood and disseminated through education programmes, they have had an impact upon attitudes and policies in the mainstream. Indeed, there is some evidence to show that hospice standards are being achieved in general hospitals (Field 1984). But the reformist isolation of the early hospices has proved necessarily fragile and unviable. The hospices have had to accept as a price of their success some degree of re-assimilation into the mainstream of provision. This would appear a plausible argument up to 1991. Since that date, new legislation for health and social services has begun to redefine the mainstream itself. We are now moving into an increasingly mixed economy of care, with a variety of providers in the marketplace. This may well prove a fertile environment in which the more innovative hospices can adapt and flourish. Inevitably, these are likely to be in the more affluent areas where costs of care can be subsidized and underwritten by large pools of volunteers and effective fund-raising. In poorer areas, the reverse will hold true. An inverse law of hospice care is thus likely to develop, where provision is in indirect ratio to need.

Strengths, weaknesses, opportunities and threats

Taking all of this into account, I conclude with a brief analysis of the hospice movement's current strengths, weaknesses, opportunities and threats (SWOT), drawing my evidence for the comments from an established group involved in palliative care.[1] SWOT analysis frequently highlights paradoxes and contradictions: weaknesses may appear as hidden strengths or threats may also be regarded as opportunities. In this case, the items covered represent several of the issues raised in the literature and reveal both an awareness of potential problems as well as a capacity for critical self-reflection.

Strengths

One clear area of strength relates to the resources available to hospices. People and skills are major components of these. The hospice movement appears to enjoy a high level of public support, manifesting itself in donations of cash as well as in the work done by volunteers. Staff are seen as highly committed to their work and contribute to a pool of expertise and source of knowledge which is a resource for others, assisting the dissemination of good practice into other settings. The work is now recognized as a speciality and has a reputation for high-quality holistic care, giving attention to the physical, emotional, material and spiritual.

These strengths are heightened by the settings in which care is delivered. Small units allow a clear focus for activity and have a sense of independence, with more relaxed norms about how services are delivered. People are felt to have time for what they do and there is a strong emphasis on the patient-centred approach.

Finally, these attributes are underpinned by the financial benefits which result from charitable status: beds can be provided at half price and this in turn is contributing to increasing demand. Independent units can also be clear about the costs of their services, something which is perceived to be far more difficult within the NHS.

Weaknesses

A number of intrinsic weaknesses can be identified. The hospice movement is for some characterized by insularity and elitism. It can appear 'holier than thou' in ways which are antagonistic to other health professionals and it can be subject to 'management by personality'. Contrary to the strength of popular support, some of those working in hospices may feel that what they do is not well understood by the public.

In addition to these are several extrinsic weaknesses. These include the insecurities which stem from a reliance on the vagaries of charitable giving and a sense of being vulnerable to the whims of health authorities and individuals within them. Paradoxically, the success of the hospices might itself be a weakness, creating new problems in its wake.

Opportunities

Several opportunities are currently in evidence. The hospices have now created a reputation for reliability and new government monies are available in recognition of this. Community support for the work of hospices is an important platform for development. Even the competition created by a deregulated health service market can be construed as an opportunity. There is further work to do in responding to the needs of people suffering from non-malignant conditions, such as multiple sclerosis or motor neurone disease. And there are opportunities to do more education in the health professions.

Threats

A number of the perceived threats, like the strengths, centre around resource questions. In general terms, the creation of the internal market within the NHS is the major area of concern. There are potential threats from the NHS trusts, which might not only provide rival services, but also make a further impact on the charitable giving sector. This is further exacerbated by

David Clark

problems of economic recession which are likely to impact upon charities. Increasing demand is likely to lead to further competition for resources. There are also potential threats from general practitioner fund holders as well as uncertainties about the policies to be adopted by future purchasers of services. There are fears about increasing bureaucratization, both from within (e.g. the National Hospice Council) and without (district health authorities).

A more insidious threat is that of creeping medicalization, which may mark a move away from patient-centred care. There are also anxieties about being linked particularly to the care of those with cancer.

Conclusions

The fate of the hospices is clearly tied up with the broader future for palliative care. Independence and autonomy will not be readily given up, yet, paradoxically, the apparent freedoms of a market structure for care provision may mean less, rather than more, manoeuvrability than in the past. The hospices of the 1990s will have to take their place in a more competitive environment than previously and at the same time submit to higher levels of service specification from purchasing authorities. If they can retain high levels of charitable giving and voluntary input, they clearly stand an excellent chance of survival where costs are an important determinant of viability. It is unlikely though that growth will continue at the rates of the 1970s and 1980s. It is now very important that we guard against a viewpoint which sees the hospices as the sole repository of good practice in terminal care. Learning and skills have been disseminated from the hospices into wider settings and there are indications of palliative care being taken far more seriously in general hospitals and in the community. It is this triad of services that should be the focus of attention and which has been highlighted in the recent report of the Standing Medical Advisory and Standing Nursing and Midwifery Advisory Committee Joint Working Party on Palliative Care (SMAC/SNMAC 1992). The Wilkes report when it appeared in 1980 saw no reason why hospices should go on proliferating, preferring instead to 'encourage the dissemination of the principles of terminal care throughout the health service to develop an integrated system of care with the emphasis on co-ordination between the primary care sector, the hospital sector and the hospice movement' (Wilkes 1980: 10). Well over a decade later and despite some significant changes in government health policy, there seems to be little justification for challenging this assertion.

Note

1 Some of the areas covered in the SWOT analysis resulted from a brainstorming session involving members of the Trent Hospice Group, which took place at the Trent Palliative Care Centre, Sheffield, on 4 April 1992. The group consisted of hospice

trustees, volunteers, nursing, medical and other staff, as well as others variously involved in aspects of hospice care. I am grateful to members of the group for their participation in the exercise.

References

Abel, E.K. (1986) The hospice movement: institutionalising innovation, *International Journal of Health Services*, 16(1), 71–85.
Carlisle, J. (1992) Terminal care limited for AIDS, *Nursing Times*, 88(15), 7.
Clark, D. (1991) Contradictions in the development of new hospices: a case study, *Social Science and Medicine*, 33(9), 995–1004.
Clark, D. (1993) *Partners in Care? Hospices and Health Authorities*. Aldershot: Ashgate.
Department of Health (1990) *Press Release*, 15 March.
Department of Health (1993) *Press Release*, 27 January.
Douglas, C. (1991) A doctor writes, *Observer Magazine*, 9 May, p. 74.
Douglas, C. (1992) For all the saints, *British Medical Journal*, 304, 579.
Field, D. (1984) We didn't want him to die on his own: nurses' accounts of nursing dying patients, *Journal of Advanced Nursing*, 9, 59–70.
Griffin, J. (1991) *Dying with Dignity*. London: Office of Health Economics.
Harris, L. (1990) The disadvantaged dying, *Nursing Times*, 86(22), 26–9.
Hospice Information Service (1992) *1992 Directory of Hospice Services*. London: St Christopher's Hospice.
James, N. and Field, D. (1992) The routinisation of hospice: charisma and bureaucratisation, *Social Science and Medicine*, 34(12), 1363–75.
Jankowski, S. (1992) Letter, *British Medical Journal*, 304, 718.
Jeffrey, D. (1992) Letter, *British Medical Journal*, 304, 718.
Johnson, I.S., Rogers, C., Biswas, B. and Ahmedzai, S. (1990) What do hospices do? A survey of hospices in the United Kingdom and Republic of Ireland, *British Medical Journal*, 300, 791–3.
O'Neil, P. (1989) Services for the dying, *Nursing Times*, 85(9), 36–7.
Paradis, L. and Cummings, S.B. (1986) The evolution of hospice in America: toward organizational homogeneity, *Journal of Health and Social Behaviour*, 27, 370–86.
Partridge, M.R. (1989) NHS provision for terminal care: one district's deliberations, *Journal of Management in Medicine*, 3, 362–71.
Partridge, M.R. (1992) Letter, *British Medical Journal*, 304, 718.
Reid, W. (1992) Letter, *British Medical Journal*, 304, 718.
Seale, C.F. (1989) What happens in hospices? A review of research evidence, *Social Science and Medicine*, 28(6), 551–9.
Seale, C. (1991) Death from cancer and death from other causes: the relevance of the hospice approach, *Palliative Medicine*, 5, 12–19.
SMAC/SNMAC (1992) *The Principles and Provision of Palliative Care*. London.
Smith, A. (1984) Problems of hospices, *British Medical Journal*, 228, 1178–9.
Stevens, A. and Gabbay, J. (1991) Needs assessment needs assessment . . . *Health Trends*, 23, 20–23.
Tulloch, D.E. (1992) Letter, *British Medical Journal*, 304, 718.
Wilkes, E. (1980) *Report of the Working Group on Terminal Care*. London: DHSS.

Index

KING ALFRED'S COLLEGE LIBRARY